Our Europe, Not Theirs

In this great European crisis, any progressive proposal to change course, to reassert European solidarity, strengthen the efficiency of its actions internationally, and to boost growth, jobs and competitiveness, is welcome. That this proposal comes from British sources at a time when the actions of the UK government threaten British membership of the Union may seem almost paradoxical. But the Labour MEPs and officials, and Julian Priestley, who edited this book, have a deep understanding of European issues which adds to the interest of their ideas.

Jacques Delors, former president of the European Commission

This book by Labour MEPs and officials is a timely and useful contribution to the debate, not just to the one raging in the UK, but also among European progressives. It postulates a radical alternative view very different from that of the conservatives, while supporting firmly Britain's place at the heart of Europe.

Martin Schulz, President of the European Parliament

European democracy is facing its most significant historical challenge since its reconstruction following World War II – an existential crisis that, to paraphrase Antonio Gramsci, consists in the fact that 'the old is dying and the new is not yet born'. To save and relaunch Europe we need a quantum leap. We must pave the way for a progressive Europe – and Julian and Glyn's book is an essential piece of this strategy for change. It also shows how much the European socialists owe intellectually to the British left.

Gianni Pittella, Leader of the Socialist Group in the European Parliament

This book recognises the crucial importance of change in Europe. Julian Priestley and his colleagues put forward a radical socialist alternative to the ruinous policies of austerity that the conservatives have used their strength in Brussels to impose. This book is a useful antidote to the negative voices we usually hear from the other side of the channel.

Harlem Désir, leader of the French Socialist party

Our Europe, Not Theirs

Edited by

Julian Priestley and Glyn Ford

Second edition

Lawrence & Wishart, London 2016

Lawrence and Wishart Limited
99a Wallis Road
London
E9 5LN

Cover: Andrew Corbett
Typesetting: Etype
Printed by ImprintDigital, Devon

ISBN 9781 910448 793

British Library Cataloguing in Publication Data.
A catalogue record for this book is available from the British Library

Contents

Notes on contributors

The authors have known each other for a long time, and share the same commitment to a progressive Britain pursuing its aims through a strong European Union, while also recognising the need for EU change and reform. The reforms sought are very different from those supported by the British government.

To the extent that there are still in any meaningful sense 'wings' in the Labour Party, or more widely on the left, the authors come from different traditions. Some of the policy conclusions in the chapters reflect that diversity in approach. There is certainly a difference in style between the more measured tone in many of the chapters, and the polemical tirade preferred by the two editors. None of us would agree on every single idea put forward, but all believe that Labour must now urgently flesh out a European agenda which is radically different from the one being followed by the current conservative majority in Brussels and in most national capitals including London.

THE AUTHORS

David Martin has been a Labour MEP since 1984 and is Scotland's senior representative. He has served as leader of the Labour delegation, and was vice-president of the Parliament and latterly its senior vice-president for a total of fifteen years. He authored the European Parliament reports on the Maastricht and Amsterdam treaties. He currently sits on the international trade committee where his focus is on aid for trade, and global access to medicine and human rights.

Linda McAvan MEP leads for the Socialist and Democratic Group on environment and climate change issues. She has represented her home region, Yorkshire and the Humber, since 1998.

Derek Reed is deputy Secretary General of the Social Democratic Group in the European Parliament, and was formerly head of research for a British trade union; he was a Labour parliamentary candidate in 1983.

Patrick Costello has been an EU official since 1996, currently in the European External Action Service, previously with the Commission and the Parliament. He served in the private offices of EP President Josep Borrell, Commission vice-president Margot Wallstrom, External relations Commissioner Chris Patten and leader of the Socialist Group, Enrique Baron Crespo.

Glyn Ford is a former Labour MEP, deputy leader of the Socialist Group, and EPLP leader. He is a member of the Steering Committee of Unite Against Fascism, and is the elected representative of South West Labour Party members on the Labour Party's National Policy Forum. His book *Fascist Europe* was published by Pluto Press.

Nick Costello has been a European Commission official since 1990. He currently works on social policy. He has worked in the private office of Commission Vice-President Pandolfi and on development policy, with postings in Nigeria and China. He was co-author with Seumas Milne and Jonathan Michie of *Beyond the Casino Economy*.

Julian Priestley is a former Secretary General of the European Parliament, and prior to that of the Socialist Group in the EP. He was head of office to EP President Dr Klaus Hänsch. He was Labour's candidate in three general elections. He now writes, speaks and advises on European politics and is the author of two books (one with Stephen Clark) on the European Parliament. He was knighted in 2008.

CONTRIBUTORS TO CHAPTERS

Stewart Lansley is visiting fellow at the Townsend Centre for International Poverty research at Bristol University. He is the author of *The Costs of Inequality: Why economic equality is essential for recovery*, Gibson Square 2011.

Andrew Watt is head of department at the Micro-economic Policy Institute (IMK) in the Hans-Böckler Foundation.

Chris Poles is a policy adviser in the Social Democratic Group in the European parliament.

Anand Menon is Professor of European Politics and Foreign Affairs at King's College, London.

OTHER ACKNOWLEDGMENTS

The authors would also like to thank many others who contributed to the work of this book, including Sally Davison and the team from Lawrence and Wishart, for their confidence in us, and their advice and suggestions; to Alison Birkett for her encouragement, suggestions and editing skills; to Maria Laura De Angelis and Stephanie Ghislain in Glyn Ford's office; to Jenni Dunsmore, parliamentary assistant to David Martin, for her extensive work in helping to research and draft the chapter on trade; to Belinda Pyke for casting her critical eye over some of the texts; to David O'Leary for his suggestions about the use of social media to spread the word; to Valerie Bryce in the private office of the President of the European Parliament, Martin Schulz; to Ute Guder, deputy Secretary General at Notre Europe/the Jacques Delors Institute; and to Jean Schons for saving the text on a number of occasions.

But no blame should be attached to these kind friends for the mistakes, infelicities or indeed the political judgments in the book, which are exclusively the responsibility of the authors and among them principally the two editors.

Introduction to the Second Edition: The Left's New Challenge on Europe

A PROMISE UNFULFILLED

In 2013, we wrote *Our Europe, Not Theirs*, with the aim of pointing out that in key policy areas – the economy, social and environmental policy, foreign and trade questions, and immigration and home affairs – the left and the right had competing visions of the future of the EU, and that these policy differences should be the focus of the then upcoming European Parliament elections in 2014. We believed that it would be a mistake to concentrate exclusively on national themes, as this would confuse voters, and would also mean opting out from the debate about Europe's future, leaving the goalposts unguarded as we faced the right-wing, xenophobic, populist onslaught.

We also argued more specifically that Labour should engage politically and more intensively with its socialist and social-democratic partners in the EU; commit to strong, progressive anti-austerity policies; and campaign together with its partners on an alternative programme for Europe and its institutions in 2014. This implied seeking to change the leadership of the Commission, which was for the first time to be decided through the elections. We argued that Labour should back a European socialist candidate to succeed the outgoing conservative President of the Commission, Jose Manuel Barroso – whose ten-year tenure had been marked by a consistently supine attitude to the diktats of the large member states, a simpering obsequiousness to right-wing economic nostrums and the atrophying of the Commission's right to initiate new policies in the common interest.

We contended that Labour should resist siren calls for holding a referendum on EU membership, on the grounds that it was likely to disrupt the business of a future Labour government; to undermine the confidence so necessary to sustain growth; and to cut us off from our European partners, who would simply not understand how a Labour Party espousing a strong Europe-wide alternative could run the risk of the UK leaving the EU. We also pointed out the tactical folly of entering into a eurosceptic bidding war with UKIP and with the Tories, which Labour 'me-tooism' could never win.

Since our book was published, torrents of water have flown under these particular bridges.

In the 2014 European Parliament elections, the centre-left gained some ground on the centre-right, which suffered heavily in the polls, in Southern Europe and elsewhere. The centre-left campaigned on a stronger platform than had been the case in earlier elections, and most of the parties openly promoted the candidature of the German social democrat, Martin Schulz, to succeed Barroso. Overall, the number of voters supporting social democrats and socialists slightly exceeded votes for the Christian democrats, but this was not translated into EP seats. Because of the structural over-representation of small countries, the Christian Democrats had a thirty-seat edge, and so it was the Luxembourg Christian democrat, Jean-Claude Juncker, a veteran of EU politics, whose name was put forward to have first crack at forming a majority – by all five European political parties which had contested the EP elections with their own 'lead candidates'. After much gnashing of teeth in national capitals, including in Berlin, 26 out of 28 member countries went along with this, leaving David Cameron on his own in what one would hope even he might regard as the embarrassingly uncongenial company of Viktor Orban – the hard right semi-authoritarian Hungarian prime minister – in opposing Juncker becoming President of the Commission.

CHANGE IN THE EU INSTITUTIONS

The arithmetic from the elections made it absolutely clear that there was not even a paper majority for a left alternative. Even combining Socialist, Green, radical left and Liberal votes would not constitute anything near a working majority. But – and this was the constitutional novelty – to get an EP majority for himself and his team of Commissioners, Juncker had to negotiate a programme with the progressive groups in the Parliament.

The outcome of these negotiations was a five-year work plan for the Commission which took on board several key socialist planks, including an investment fund of 315 billion euros to kickstart job creation; a stronger social dimension; more transparency in trade negotiations and with more conditions attached; and a thoroughgoing review of the EU budget in 2016 to switch more resources to social and infrastructure investment, along with a serious push against tax avoidance and fiscal dumping (made all the more pressing by Juncker's own rather delicate position as a former prime minister of Luxembourg for eighteen years).

So the new way of appointing the Commission did affect outcomes, even if the centre right remains in charge. The balance in the composition of the Commission has not greatly changed, but two of the big-hitters among the Commission vice-presidents are from the Progressive Alliance of Socialists and Democrats (formerly Party of European Socialists) – Federica Mogherini, the effective external policy vice-president, and Frans Timmermans, the former Dutch Labour Party leader, and this means that, by accident or design, the left has a more visible presence on the new Executive. Perhaps the biggest tilt has come from the change of President. Juncker is at the centre of the centre: his party – the Luxembourg Christian Democrats – are more social-democratic on economic and social issues than some that are formally within the socialist family.

And some of the promises in Juncker's programme are being delivered, not least the investment fund, which has already started operations, even if the size of the fund and scope of its operations do not match the scale of the economic and social challenge facing the Union. And this is a Commission which takes responsibility: over Greece Juncker and his team went out on a limb, seeking – by no means always successfully – to soften the impact of some of the austerity conditions attached to the bail-out, much to the annoyance of the German government, which seemed to object to this 'interference'. Most importantly, the Commission was the first to realise that a European response was required to cope with, or at least alleviate, the humanitarian catastrophe in the war zones that was leading to the exodus from Syria and elsewhere, and it insisted on burden sharing by European governments so that the costs of solidarity would be spread more fairly. Hence the refugee quotas proposed by the Commission in May 2015. These were at first dismissed by governments but they were then forced to take on even larger quotas in the autumn. Hence, too, Juncker's initiative for the EU to assume real responsibilities for managing Europe's common external border, a task which was proving increasingly overwhelming for smaller and sometimes poorer member states. And the Commission has now committed itself to bring forward proposals for a common policy on legal migration, without which these external borders of the Union cannot be effectively managed, or the free movement within those borders sustained.

The EU executive is of course by no means socialist in either its composition or in intent. Many believe that its espousal of the 'better law-making' agenda could in time lead to watering down some of the key social, environmental and consumer protections enshrined in European law. Here a progressive coalition in the European Parliament will be vital in blocking any unravelling of citizens' rights.

But the broader message is that the Commission is back. The Juncker Commission, showing an institutional confidence enhanced by the new legitimacy conferred by its parliamentary majority and the involvement of voters for the first time in the election of its president, doesn't wait to be asked before doing things. It has become again, for the first time since Jacques Delors left office, a political executive.

It is fair to underline three further points about the 2014 election. First, the new 'presidentialising' of the elections did not lead to an increase in voter turn-out, although its decline was just about halted. It is worth adding that some gains in turn-out in countries participating fully in the 'European campaign' were wiped out by chronic collapses in some East and Central European countries. For example just 13 per cent of those eligible voted in Slovakia. This appears to tell us more about what Slovakians and voters from other abstentionist states think about their political class than their stance on European issues.

Second, the elections saw substantial gains by populist parties: in France, where the Front National of Marine Le Pen topped the poll, but also in Scandinavia, and in large parts of Eastern Europe. The gains registered for a right 'without complexes' (code words for borderline fascist and xenophobic) were at the expense of both the centre-left and the centre-right. The driving force appears to be immigration at a time of austerity (of course much broader than the 'free movement' of EU citizens from one country to another but the far right manages to meld the two issues together). The steady rise of the hard right started before the great refugee crisis that was so mismanaged by national governments, and which put huge strains on public services in many EU regions. All these right-wing populists have two things in common: their detestation of 'Brussels' and the simplicity of their demands, 'we want our country back'. And the reluctance and timidity of the left in confronting that message helps explain why it has suffered so greatly and lost large tracts of its traditional support.

Third, since the elections, the centre right's domination of the EU has been further challenged. At the time of writing, for the first time in fifteen years heads of government from the parties that make up the Progressive Alliance of Socialists and Democrats (PASD) have caught up numerically their European People's Party counterparts, and actually have more votes to cast in meetings of the Council of Ministers. The picture is patchy, and the outcomes diverse, but in Stockholm and Lisbon broad progressive coalitions have formed governments which seem to show that reports of the inevitable demise of the European left may be premature.

Which brings us neatly to the situation in the UK. Labour came second in the European elections in May 2014, just one seat ahead of the Tories and several paces back from UKIP. So much for the springboard for victory in the 2015 election. The least that can be said of the campaign is that ignoring European policies, and indeed pretending that the Commission presidency was somehow not at stake, did not prove to be stunningly successful. For an account of the Feydeau farce of Labour's failure to engage with the campaign for Martin Schulz as the PASD candidate for Commission President, see Peñalver and Priestley, *The Making of a European President*, published by Palgrave in 2015. It is not our contention in the book that building the campaign around Schulz would have transformed Labour's performance, but we do argue that support for a common European platform – as a progressive alternative to the right's agenda of austerity and the chipping away of social and environmental standards – would have made the campaign more coherent; and for many Labour supporters the reluctance to put this up front undermined the sense of the elections. Any idea that the outcome of the EP vote could have an effect on the UK cost of living was seen as symptomatic of a reluctance to engage with voters' concerns; it was as if electors wanting to see one film had found themselves by accident watching a Japanese language movie (without subtitles) showing on the screen next door. It also needs to be added that Labour's travel ban on Schulz and the absence of a pan-European element to the campaign did little to consolidate the continent-wide progressive cooperation which is a prerequisite to any credible alternative to a resurgent far right.

To its credit, despite all the temptations Labour refused to wrap itself in populist vestments in the 2015 national election, and rejected an in/out referendum on the EU. The reasons for its defeat are complex, with very significant regional variations, and are largely outside the scope of this book, as is the election of the new leadership of the party, which is, to put it mildly, in an effervescent moment of change. The most credible hypothesis which has thus far been advanced is that Labour's economic programme failed to convince voters in the South East; that traditional Labour votes in the North were lost mostly to UKIP which addressed popular concerns about immigration; and that the party was outflanked to the left in its Scottish heartland.

What is relevant here is that the disappointingly dismal outcome cannot be attributed to the party's support for continued membership of the EU, or to its failure to back a referendum. The question of 'Europe' remains stubbornly low amongst factors affecting voters' behaviour. What is also manifest is that Labour at no stage in its campaign sought to give ballast and credibility to its economic and social goals with a wider European strategy of growth and jobs, or to give voice to the seething hostility of voters here and on the continent to the politics of austerity, inequality and unbridled capitalism. For example, when hundreds of business leaders were corralled into supporting the Tories' economic plans, the moment would have been appropriate for Labour to start talking about European alternatives: a Europe-wide attack on corporate tax evasion; a Europe-wide transactions tax; and a Europe-wide strategy of investment; it could also have pointed to the need to sustain European standards in the negotiations on the Transatlantic trade and investment pact, and to ensure that the advantages of free movement of labour were not undermined by the unreformed agency and temporary workers Directives, which enabled employers to by-pass minimum social standards and force down pay levels.

The moment came and passed, and with it the credibility of Labour's riposte to the sustained attacks from the Tories, the media and business. Those who shied away from bringing in this European dimension gave us instead the 'Ed stone', and the rest is history.

POLITICAL UPHEAVAL AT HOME AND ELSEWHERE

The election of Jeremy Corbyn, which ranks as the political surprise of 2015, can be seen at one level as the rejection by party members and activists of the failures of nerve which contributed to the defeat in the 2015 election, and more broadly the turning of the page on the 'old' politics of the Blair/Brown New Labour project. The vehemence of opposition to greater military involvement in the conflict with Islamist extremists certainly has its roots in the bitter legacy of the Iraq war. Much has been, and will be, written about the Corbyn phenomenon and the unfolding of this domestic drama. In a European context, its interest lies in the parallels and differences with the radicalisation of parts of the left elsewhere in the EU. The particularity in the UK is that the upheavals have occurred within the established principal party of the left, not to 'the left of the left', beyond the party: it is almost as if in Spain, PSOE had morphed into Podemos, or as if in Greece, Syriza had risen out of the grave of PASOK. A closer analogy is perhaps with Portugal where the traditional Socialist Party is now the lynchpin of a broader left coalition: imagine if the SPD in Germany were to leave the comfort zone of its grand coalition with the conservative CDU/CSU and form an alliance with the Linken and the Greens, or if the French socialists with their backs to the wall were to renew the Popular Front with other left forces.

Progressives in Britain should be mindful of the changes taking place at different speeds and in various ways in other EU member states when we start to consider the referendum.

A TORY REFERENDUM

Once the Tories won an overall majority, however slender, a referendum became inevitable, and the Labour party then took the not unreasonable position of abandoning its opposition to the vote. Attempts to extend the suffrage to 16 and 17 year olds (on the not unreasonable grounds that the question to be decided will be one which future generations will have to live with) have been defeated by the Tories, who are also seeking to gerrymander the electoral roll. You can make a case for excluding ex-patriates (although the Tories propose extending the vote to all of them for national elections), and you can argue that this matter is primarily for British people and not for those who because of EU membership now reside and pay taxes in the UK. To exclude both categories looks like sharp practice. The question to be posed at the referendum marks a new departure in the way it is framed: for the first time the voters will not be asked a 'yes' or 'no' question. Instead they will have to mark their crosses against 'leave' or 'remain'. Each time, the playing field becomes a little less even. But these matters have now been resolved, and a referendum on Brexit will take place before the end of 2017, in accordance with the commitment made by Cameron in his Bloomberg speech in January 2013 – and very probably considerably earlier.

KNOW THE ENEMY

Before discussing the stance the left might take during the referendum, it is worth reflecting on Tory attitudes to the Europe question. The prime minister and the bulk of Tory high command never wanted a referendum, and have no wish to have as their lasting legacy the UK's withdrawal from the EU, for almost exactly the same reasons that led Labour to oppose an in/out vote. David Cameron has two characteristics which together form a dangerous combination – an overconfidence borne of his sense of entitlement, and a consistent cravenness when called on to confront his backwoodsmen and women. So, where Labour held firm, he crumpled in 2013 and accepted holding a referendum. Hints from Cameron that he might lead the campaign to leave the UK if he does not succeed in renegotiations of the terms of membership will be seen for what they are – sixth form bluffing born of an overgrown schoolboy mentality.

Were Britain to vote to leave the EU, the business of government (and indeed the EU) would be disrupted by the legal and economic complexities of extrication, a scenario envisaged by the Treaty but never thus far applied (Greenland's withdrawal forty years ago providing only the scantiest of precedents). If we are now in a flirtation with what even the Tory leadership know to be a disaster, it is because of the external threat of UKIP, and for reasons of internal party management. The Tory rank and file is massively anti-European because the EU is held responsible for all the changes to our society which the average Tory activist detests. The shire Tories are just as much tempted by the simplicities of 'we want our country back' as the saloon bar nationalists and xenophobes in UKIP. 'Europe' has changed the face of our cities; 'no one on the bus or the train speaks English any more'; we are 'swamped' by migrants; we've lost control of our borders; the England so cherished by John Major of old maids on bicycles riding past pubs serving warm beer while cricket is being played on the village green has gone, seemingly for good – and it is all the fault of the EU. Such people have long ceased trusting the metropolitan elite running their party, twittering on about global warming or the cultural richness of diversity, ring-fencing aid to the third world and bringing in gay marriage. Large numbers of Tory activists are deeply suspicious of their current leadership.

There is also another strand of Tory euroscepticism. In 1975 the 'yes to Europe' side could count on the support of the whole of the business community and the financial services sector (less almighty than today), and the near unanimity of the media (with the perennial exception of the *Express*). Today the business community is less united on the pro-European side, some of the larger hedge funds are bankrolling the Leave campaign, and the press is for the most part implacably opposed to the EU (in this it has been consistent for a long time, as it has been rubbishing Europe day-in and day-out for the past thirty years). Why this change of heart?

Three factors seem to be at play here.

Part of the business community fell out of love with the single market when it became clear that there were social, environmental and consumer dimensions built in to the structure of the European regulatory framework. What the political authorities sought was a balance between economic efficiency and solidarity, to prevent or circumscribe the risks of social dumping. For businesses, this became 'heavy regulatory burdens', forgetful of the fact that however complicated it sometimes might seem, one regulatory framework is always going to be simpler than twenty-eight if you are doing business in the wider European market.

The second factor has been that until the credit crunch induced by the reckless irresponsibility of the financial sector, financial services had largely escaped European regulation. As late as 2008/2009 the line taken by liberal ayatollahs like Barroso and Charlie McCreevy (the Irish free marketeer Commissioner who was responsible for internal market questions) was that regulating financial markets was a matter for member states. This line of reasoning – long criticised by the European left, but often supported by Labour governments still looking for the chimera of 'light touch' or 'smart' regulation – was exposed when the banking crisis took the world to the brink of ruin at the end of the first decade of the century. Since then some twenty or so EU laws have been put into place to provide a European framework for banks and the financial services, building in elementary safeguards, and, in a touch of lèse-majesté, even limiting those banking bonuses which positively encouraged reckless behaviour that was potentially catastrophic in its effects, but never on its perpetrators. It is therefore a matter of no surprise that some leading players in the financial community want out of this system, and prefer to have any legal constraints on their activities imposed by a British Tory government, which they largely finance, and is therefore more likely to listen to what might be charitably described as 'their concerns'.

The third factor is quite simply one of press freedom. For years, long before the UK hacking scandal, a very broad centre and centre-left coalition in the European Parliament has been highlighting the dangers of media monopolies and the need to safeguard pluralism. This is a Europe-wide problem requiring European solutions. The media in Spain and in Italy and elsewhere is increasingly concentrated, under the control of a handful of plutocrats who have an agenda which has political power in its sights, and which values providing objective accurate information to its readers not at all. As the increasingly strident right-wing British media regains its balance after the Leveson Inquiry into hacking and other malpractices, many of its press barons have come back to the Brexit as the preferred option because, basically, they find it easier to impose their writ on Westminster and Whitehall than on those European institutions which are just a little bit more complicated.

These elements help to explain the tangle in which David Cameron now finds himself, but they are also useful pointers for those on the left deciding what attitude to take in the forthcoming referendum. At the very least, finding oneself on the same side of an argument as Murdoch, the Barclay brothers, Paul Dacre and the bulk of Tory activists looking for a one-way ticket back to the England of the 1950s should give pause for thought.

THE MYSTERY OF CAMERON'S TERMS

The European negotiating tactics of our prime minister have been slow-moving and sideways, in the manner of a doped-up crab. Confronted with the contradictions of his position he has been coy about committing himself to precisely what changes would be required in the EU to enable him to recommend staying in. It has already been decreed that the Tory Party machine will abstain from any collective role in the campaign, so divisive is the European issue. It was only when the cry 'but what do you want?' became so insistent and so public, not least from his negotiating partners, that in the late autumn of 2015 Cameron laid down not exactly conditions but four main headings where he needed progress. This was brilliantly summarised in a cartoon by Matt in the Tory Party house journal, the *Daily Telegraph*, set in an eatery where the two diners were saying, 'This is an EU themed restaurant. We don't tell them what we want, and they don't give it to us.'

There are four basic British demands, which, wisely, the prime minister declined to flesh out. These are: that the United Kingdom insists on clarification that 'ever closer Union' – mentioned as an objective of the EU – does not oblige member states to take any particular cause of action; that the EU should encourage greater competitiveness, the single market should be strengthened and there should be no discrimination against member states not participating in the euro; that the role of national parliaments in decision-making should be strengthened; and that non-UK nationals from other member states should not be entitled to welfare benefits at work for the first few years of their residency in the UK, in order to discourage the scourge of 'welfare tourism', an urban myth exploited daily by the Murdoch press, the *Daily Mail* and the *Telegraph*.

The first reaction from one prominent anti-European Tory, Bernard Jenkin, was, 'Is that it?' Indeed one can only imagine the reaction of our EU partners, wrestling with climate change negotiations, terrorism and the humanitarian refugee crisis, as the UK prime minister chunters on about a clause of the Treaty (which is merely declaratory), the single market (which is a shared objective of all member states and the Commission), and giving national parliaments a greater say (when they have almost invariably declined to use their current rights under existing treaties). Only the last demand about in-work benefits presents a major difficulty in the ersatz negotiations underway in Brussels.

A comment or two on these 'demands' is relevant to the argument on the left.

Firstly, it is important to note what is not included in them: contrary to earlier expectations, the proposals do not seem to imply any general roll-back of the frontiers of European protection enshrined in current legislation. This is for the simple reason that each amendment to existing EU legislation would have to get majority support in the Council and Parliament, and the latter is judged unlikely to countenance any watering down of social and environmental standards. (As already noted, there is currently a general push to simplify EU law, and progressive lawmakers will have to be vigilant that this process does not unravel what has been achieved, for example in the area of workplace rights. But this problem is distinct from the Brexit argument.)

Three of the demands can relatively easily be met by clarifications or a declaration of intent. Thus, for example, the phrase in the Treaty about 'ever closer union' as an EU objective is not a legal basis for 'mission creep'. This can be further clarified without changing the Treaties. Its practical effect is nugatory. But it's a chip which can be easily cashed in. Similarly, there is not much of a problem with an assertion of a commitment to the single market and not to discriminate against non-members of the euro.

On the issue of national parliaments having a greater say, the current situation is that a minority of national parliaments can hold up EU legislation (though not veto it) by issuing what is called a 'yellow card' if it thinks proposals made by the Commission go beyond the competences of the EU, as defined by the Treaty. In nearly ten years of practice, this right has seldom been exercised (twice, to be precise, and in one of these cases the Commission withdrew its proposal, though for other reasons). The real role of national parliaments for most member states is to control what their ministers get up to in Brussels. In Finland, for example, at the end of each week ministers, including the prime minister, meet with leading MPs to go over the EU's agenda for the following week and to get a mandate on each major issue coming up. This detailed scrutiny works well in Scandinavia, but Westminster and some other parliaments have shied away from this intensity of parliamentary oversight. Yet if the government were truly interested in boosting the role of national parliaments, its best course would be to reform the way that Westminster works.

The aim for the Brexit negotiations would appear to be the ability to turn the yellow cards into red ones: if a significant minority of national parliaments were to oppose a Commission proposal then the proposal would be withdrawn, not just reconsidered. To formalise this right would require Treaty change – which everyone, including the UK, recognises could not happen within the referendum timetable. There is nothing, however, to stop the Commission off its own bat from saying that it would not proceed with proposals if a 'blocking minority' of Parliaments declared their opposition. After all, if those parliaments are strongly opposed to a measure, it is a fairly reliable indication that that the proposal would not get the required votes in Council in any case.

The demand for discriminatory measures on in-work rights is more problematic: the UK's usual allies in East and Central Europe are understandably opposed to this, and progressives in the Parliament are almost by definition against any breach of the principle of 'equal pay for equal work', preferring to attack the root cause of such breaches, in particular the incentives to employers to use agency or temporary workers from other member states, thereby by-passing EU law and national minimum wages and standards. This is the one area where no easy 'formula of words' could do the trick. It is also the one which will arouse the greatest media interest given the press obsession with 'foreigners coming over here and taking our jobs'. A cynical fix might be based on forging some kind of agreement on this, knowing that, some way down the track, when the first case becomes before the European Court of Justice, it will be struck down because of its clearly discriminatory nature. But another solution could be little more than some kind of understanding to come back to the matter in a future Treaty change – because it is highly improbable that any legislative change introducing such discrimination could get approval by the European Parliament.

This saga of Cameron's shopping list should conclude with two points: first, the outcome of the pre-Brexit referendum negotiations will have little or no impact on the poll itself. There are not millions of voters out there waiting with baited breath to see if national parliament yellow cards turn red, or if the phrase 'ever closer union' is qualified by some clarifying declaration by all the governments making the obvious point that the phrase in itself has no practical value. These negotiations will not change the way the UK votes, unless, either the government is seen as having been rebuffed and humiliated in the talks, or, paradoxically, if the outcome is seen to be a threat to the positive things that progressives like about the EU. For the moment neither eventuality seems probable. But if Cameron repeats the mistakes he made over the nomination of Juncker as Commission president, and boxes himself in by sticking with demands which are politically impossible and legally dubious, he could be forced into a public recognition of his defeat. But the left needs constantly to bear in mind that Cameron is battling not for Britain but to save his own skin. The issues are stake are not on the agenda because the voters insist on them, but because they are judged to be the minimum face-saving required for his continuation in office.

ARGUMENTS FOR LEAVING

So, for the referendum, how should progressives vote? There are some in the Labour Party, trade unions and other left organisations who have never felt at ease with 'the European project'. Those of us who believe that the argument has been settled, even after Jeremy Corbyn has come down firmly and unconditionally for staying in, may be deluding ourselves.

The 'leave lobby' on the left will make the following arguments.

Why give the Tories a free run on this? There is a serious chance that the Tory leadership will cut itself off from the rank-and-file, that the cabinet will split, that a majority of Tory MPs not on the government payroll may campaign against. Certainly the 2010 and 2015 in-takes have been strongly anti-European. If the government implodes, disavowed first by its party and then in the referendum outcome, why rescue it? There is a subtle variant on this theme. Labour can keep up the pressure on the government by saying that if during the negotiation of the terms of EU membership certain red lines are crossed then support for staying in on these terms cannot be guaranteed. This could significantly add to the tensions within the Tory Party, many of whose members and MPs are already dismayed at the modesty of the government's 'war aims'.

The solidarity which was supposed to be one of the founding principles of the EU is now almost a distant memory. The Greeks have been ground down by Brussels-imposed austerity. A frontier-less Europe has now been replaced by walls and barbed wire, humiliating refugees fleeing wars and devastation. Is this the Europe we want? The social-democratic, humanitarian, vision of a Jacques Delors has now been sullied in the mud, snow and ice at the borders of Balkan states and in the Calais camps.

The European Union is now descending into a shambles: a common currency which doesn't work; institutions people don't understand; the chain of democratic accountability broken; austerity throttling growth and bringing real hardship to millions; no common approaches to immigration, asylum and the external challenges faced. Europe's citizens are now challenging this Europe: the UK left should be leading the charge and getting out of this failed bureaucratic, quasi-state.

The populist extreme right is in the ascendant to such an extent that the Union's institutions are or will inevitably be pushed to the right. With Viktor Orban's Hungary, the coalition in Slovakia, the return of the populist right in Poland waiting to inflame tensions with Russia, and with seemingly embedded corruption in Romania and Bulgaria, how can even a modest social-democratic strategy bring progressive policies to fruition? And what if Le Pen continues her forward march in France (even her failure to win any of the thirteen separate regional elections in December 2015 should not mask the fact that her party poses a threat in every corner of the country), or if the Italian democrats are replaced by right-wing populists, or if those nationalistic and xenophobic voices in Denmark, Finland and Sweden become ever more dominant?

There is a new alternative left out there, but any chance of progress to a better, fairer Europe requires starting over again and abandoning this ship, which is in any case heading for the rocks.

This is the charge sheet and the arguments need to be confronted seriously because they are based on an analysis which is not without foundations even if the conclusion is wrong.

ARGUMENTS FOR STAYING IN

Taking the tactical advantage question first, and the alluring prospect of creating mayhem for the government, the first answer has also to be a tactical one. The risks for Tory unity are just as great if the pro-Europeans were to win the referendum as if they were to lose it. Cameron's betrayal will never be forgiven by the bulk of his party, so deeply rooted is their visceral loathing of Europe. The Conservative

Party has become increasingly ideological. As noted earlier, many Tories and their supporters in the City and in the press want to roll back the frontiers of the state. Their aim is not just smart regulation but preferably no regulation, and they see Europe as the principle obstacle to a totally different economic model.

Had the government proposed full opt-outs from the social, consumer and environmental protections through Treaty change then the idea of making Labour support conditional on the outcome of negotiations might have made some sense. But since the UK 'demands' are little more than a charade (with that one caveat on workplace discrimination), and since no significant Treaty change can possibly be agreed and ratified before the next UK elections, then anything coming out of the negotiations, even on this rather flimsy basis, could be reversed if there were to be a change of government in the UK at the 2020 election – just as Labour in 1997 reversed the Tory opt-out of the social chapter. The damage to the most positive aspects of the single market could be short-lived.

And the left should be wary of being seen to play tactical games. If the message goes out to supporters and voters that it is possible that we might not support staying in, it then becomes more difficult to bring people back on board when the vote comes – or it may give the impression that the question itself is not of such crucial importance.

The right is rampant almost everywhere in Europe. Its fifty shades of egregiousness are fuelled by contempt for politics as usual and the petty or not so petty corruptions, mendaciousness and political timidity of too many mainstream politicians. It is also bolstered by the fear of immigration, which is stoked by the media and too many political parties not normally on the far right, and draws sustenance from the deprivations of austerity and the injustices of inequality – to which the traditional parties of the left too often do not appear to have an answer. Combatting populist nationalism and xenophobia should be the left's priority here and elsewhere in Europe.

And this will be done not by retreating behind boundaries which are no more efficient a protection against the spread of evil doctrines than they are against climate change or terrorism. What the extreme right – which is unanimous everywhere about one thing, hatred of the EU, seen by them as statist, humanitarian in ambition, supportive of diversity and liberal to its core – lacks is some tipping point that will give it sufficient critical mass to lend credibility to its prejudices and poisonous propaganda. Does the British left want to serve this up on a plate? To combine with UKIP, the BNP, the English Defence League and the right wing of the Tory Party to support British withdrawal from the EU and provide a majority for Brexit? The referendum will take place in all probability several months before the next French presidential election. One can just imagine a triumphant Marine Le Pen telling French voters, 'The British people have shown it's possible. You can win your country back' – just before she creates the big upset and wins the power to start on the first of the mass expulsions of 'people of colour', the anti-Muslim discriminations, and the purging of French public service of left-wingers, marginals, deviants and dissenters. Le Pen has already likened the UK referendum on the EU to the liberating fall of the Berlin Wall. Meanwhile the German elections in the following autumn could easily see the strengthening not just of Alternative für Deutschland (which is like UKIP but for people who've read books) but other forces well to its right, reminiscent of something we thought had been eradicated seventy years ago. All deriving succour from the carelessness and lazy thinking of some on the left in the UK who imagine that somehow Brexit is just about Britain.

The continental radical left appears to be more aware of these dangers. That is why, despite having in many cases suffered the most from 'austerity imposed from Brussels', they stand fast by their European commitment. Neither Syriza nor Podemos nor the new Portuguese left coalition, nor other new leftist movements elsewhere, support the withdrawal of their countries from the EU nor indeed from the euro. Syriza has learned the hard way that creating a socialist nirvana in a cold climate is not an easy task. However they may feel about the humiliations meted out by Merkel's Germany and other member states, they have not succumbed to the temptation of taking a 'national road to socialism' – which in a globalised economy, with the hostility of the markets, the ratings agencies and the corporations whose power exceeds that of individual elected governments – is condemned to end in failure. The Tsipras-led government has always recognised that you have to try to work within the EU system in order to change it: it has never been tempted by the isolationist path. It is a mistake to imagine that there is an alternative structure for a Europe-wide progressive alliance in which to cooperate to build the new Jerusalem.

Of course none of this matters if the EU is finished anyway, as some commentators seem to believe: if, like the Roman Empire, the USSR, the Austro-Hungarian Empire, and the Third Reich, this Europe has now retreated to its bunker and is on the brink of collapse, a failed experiment which has now run its course and is about to be consigned to the dustbin of history. And it has to be conceded that even the most ardent Europhiles would be hard pressed to say that the last two years have been Europe's finest. But, to be precise, it should be noted that more often than not the failures have been not the failures of the EU institutions, but of national governments, which, almost without exception, have been behind the curve and gutless in tackling common problems. Nevertheless, whoever is to blame, there is a general sentiment that Europe is in a mess which is difficult to contradict.

Most of Europe languishes in deep recession, with living standards remaining at levels lower than those of ten years ago (almost a peacetime first). The crisis has severely aggravated economic and social inequalities. It is not an exaggeration to talk of a lost generation of young people, out of work or in work which is precarious, unrewarding and unfulfilling and which – again another first – has poorer prospects than those of the previous generation. The European Union response since the credit crisis has lurched from inaction to a draconian austerity that has exacerbated inequalities, before its more recent, and belated, conversion to a very watered-down Keynesianism. The design faults of the euro and the mandate for the European Central bank – whose main priority is to control inflation, which is practically inexistent in a stagnant economy and which can currently only intervene by the back door – can only be rectified by a very significant treaty change, which may have to come but not any day soon.

The refugee crisis has shown the countries of the EU in their worst light. Even Germany, which in statements from its chancellor appeared to open wide the door for refugees, did this without any prior consultation with those countries which separate it from the EU's external boundary. And the language from Berlin has now changed. Nearly all the other member states have reacted timidly, only accepting Juncker's quotas when global outrage exploded as the humanitarian crisis unfolded before our eyes. Since then some countries are reneging on their commitments, while others are subjecting the refugees to inhumane treatment even when they are clearly from war zones, in part because the EU has not made available sufficient resources to the some of the poorest member states to help them manage the exodus from the most blighted zones. The budgets for this were decided long before this crisis developed, and even some fancy footwork in moving funds between different priorities cannot disguise the fact that, on the one hand, the EU is underfunded to carry out all the tasks it has been given, and, on the other, no member states appear ready to countenance the substantial increase in resources necessary to meet these challenges at a time when the same EU is seeking to impose strict limitations on national spending. And the public administrations of quite a few member states appear incompetent to deal with a flux of refugees or migrants on this scale. This bodes ill for any future climate change refugee exodus from Africa, likely even after the rather more successful than hoped for COP 21 negotiations, and even if the agreement is effectively implemented.

The growth of a new and even deadlier form of terrorism, which the right tries to link with the refugee crisis, has brought a sluggish response from the EU. The sharing of information between member states about potential terrorist suspects is also poorly implemented. Effective transfrontier police cooperation remains a worthy aim far removed from reality, again in part because of the poor quality of policing, including in the host country of the EU institutions. There may be a case for a European equivalent of the Central Intelligence Agency, but many will view such an idea with horror given the difficulties of holding such agencies to account and the patchy record of the EU in reaching high standards of efficiency in many of its cooperative ventures. And there appears to be no appetite in national capitals for such an innovation. Instead there is a kneejerk reaction in some countries to close the internal frontiers – as if nothing had been learned about home-grown terrorism. And despite all the rhetoric about defeating the terrorist threat by holding fast to our attachment to civil liberties, bit by bit those liberties are being undermined by national governments who feel they have to show voters they are taking tough decisions. This then adds to the dangerous spiral towards a more authoritarian, less liberal, environment, and this, in turn, plays into the hands of the extreme right, which can sit back and say, 'We've been calling for this for years'.

The effectiveness of the EU's foreign policy is hampered by all key decisions having to be taken unanimously. Despite the obstacles, however, it now has a functioning external service, and is proving effective where its form of soft power makes it more likely to be trusted by partner countries than other world powers who ruthlessly pursue their purely national interests. But this relaxed approach reaches its limits at times of crisis. So, in the case of Ukraine, the EU, in its confused and contradictory reactions, ended up by making the worst of a bad job. An attempt to rush through a bilateral deal between the EU and Ukraine led the Ukrainians to think they had been given a blank cheque, and to start a ratcheting up of the crisis with Russia. The belligerence of some of the east and central European countries towards Moscow has further aggravated the situation, notwithstanding the fact that their belligerence is essentially rhetorical, and the sanctions a double-edged sword. Most importantly, all this has hindered cooperation with Russia, in quite frankly the much more important question of creating a global coalition to push for an end to the civil war in Syria and coordinated and efficient action against ISIL, there and in Iraq. In terms of the role of Assad in any future Syrian settlement, the different European powers at the table have been all over the shop. The common European position is, as too often, strong on ringing declarations of condemnation and of commiseration with victims, but toothless in action and decision.

This charge sheet is long and grave, and it has a cause. The EU has tasks given to it freely and democratically, but without the institutional means and resources to carry them out. The argument about it being undemocratic is threadbare: no decision of any significance can be taken without the agreement of a clear majority of democratically accountable member states and a clear majority of directly elected MEPs. The new procedures for electing the Commission require parliamentary backing for the executive, exactly in the way that national governments do. It is depressing to hear left-of-centre commentators borrowing from the right-wing media the stale accusations about an anti-democratic Europe where decisions are all made in secret by technocrats.

But there are some areas where the EU has to act unanimously. While this can be a sign of strength when the 28 agree, as over the Iran nuclear deal, which enabled the EU to play a lead role in the breakthrough in de-thawing relations with Teheran, it can hinder effective EU action elsewhere. In the long run, a union of 28 is too big to conduct a foreign policy in the interests of peaceful multilateralism if every single decision has be taken by all member states at the same time. The same applies to an economic and monetary policy which creates jobs and promotes equality, and a homeland policy which protects citizens while not depriving them of their basic rights. Yet the EU is now at the centre of a vicious circle: unable to act for its citizens, it is losing their trust, making it ever less likely that it can win public support and the necessary consent for reforms and changes to the EU treaties.

But to say that the EU has been performing poorly is one thing: to conclude that anything is solved by walking out and starting afresh is something else.

THE KEY QUESTIONS

For the left needs to remind itself of the great challenges to be faced in the next fifty years. They are easily restated: the threat to the planet from global warming, with economic and humanitarian consequences on an almost unimaginable scale; the linked question of handling in a humane fashion massive migratory flows that will dwarf the current exodus from the war zones; and upheavals and conflicts mostly concentrated in Europe's neighbourhood and the Middle East, which could easily degenerate into the most serious conflagrations since the second world war. Then there is the need find ways of striking a balance between combatting terrorism and preserving liberty; of harnessing the digital revolution so that it works for people and is not just synonymous with large-scale job destruction and the loss of the essential right of anonymity; of combatting inequality and unemployment and creating the millions of rewarding secure jobs our future generations require; of stimulating global trade without abandoning our social and environmental standards; and of shielding communities, people at work and consumers from the arrogance of unaccountable corporate power.

This is not some fictional speculation about a dystopian future: these are the challenges the world faces now and we are in the front line. Anyone calling themselves a progressive has to care about these issues.

In this context, fretting about how many national parliaments would be needed to block some Brussels directive or whether the words 'ever closer Union' need watering down seem almost laughably trivial. Is this what Britain has come to?

On the great challenges, the EU has at least passed the first hurdle. It has identified the problems. On climate change, for decades it has fought a sometimes lonely battle, led by progressives in the Parliament and the Commission, and it now seems to be on the brink of spearheading serious global action by the world community.

The experts can and will argue about the success of the Paris agreement in December 2015, but no-one can deny that progress almost unthinkable two years ago has been made, nor the key leadership role assumed by the EU in taking the whole of the world community along with it, in at least now unanimously recognising the problem, setting ambitious targets, putting in place a process for monitoring them and establishing funds to assist the poorer nations in transition.

Despite being hampered by the strict limits on its action, it is pushing for comprehensive but balanced responses to the challenges of refugee flows, immigration and security in the neighbourhood regions and on our streets.

The EP has consistently called for fiscal responsibility to proceed in parallel with job-creating investment. It has opened the debate on the full ramifications of the digital agenda. And if corporate power is now turning away from the European project, it is in no small part due to its standards of social, environmental and consumer protections, which, though far from ideal, are still the world standard.

So then the question to be answered by progressives is a simple one: in tackling these almost breath-taking challenges that will dominate public affairs in the next decades, would we be better off confronting them alone or through Europe? Is it seriously imagined by anyone on the left that action on climate change, on the different humanitarian crises, on the challenges to world peace, on the threats posed by corporate power, on creating a fairer economy, would somehow be faced more efficiently if Britain faced them alone?And, if not alone, with whom exactly? With the United States, with China, with Japan, or with a Commonwealth which now values so much the UK's presence in the EU? Is there an alternative for international action on offer which could pursue the left's goals more effectively?

We contend that separatism is rarely the answer in a globalised world. Not for Scotland, or Catalonia or Wales: and by the same token not for a narrow, insular Britain outside Europe – a Britain which would soon become a narrower, smaller, more insular England – pretending that our global prestige is so secure and entrenched that it can defy all the laws of economics, indeed of physics and geography, and create a prosperous secure socialist idyll on part of this small island. For we should be under no illusions: Brexit would be the prelude to the break-up of the UK, and, collaterally, could even cause substantial damage to the reconciliation of the communities in Northern Ireland.

Membership of the European Union is not a panacea for all the ills of the world. The left has had a decisive influence on some of its decisions but is certainly not in the driving seat. But do we really believe that in a Britain, or England, set on an isolationist course, turning its back on the key structure for cooperating with others, we would have a greater impact?

So the cause of staying in the EU is the progressive cause, and the case for the EU needs to be made by progressives, not least because it is a much more convincing and powerful case than the arguments that are being put forward by the ex-CEOs of FTSE 500 companies who threaten the terrors of the earth for business if we leave. The left needs to be a very prominent presence in the campaign for precisely this reason, but it behoves us to spell out more clearly its aims in Europe, and as an earnest to start a much more intense cooperation with other socialist and progressive allies in the Progressive Alliance of Socialists and Democrats (which is crying out for reform), and to point to the way to achieve an unstoppable force for real change in the EU. In turn this requires a convincing result for staying in the EU. A wafer-thin majority for staying in will not only impede the European debate from moving on; it would also hobble our influence and weaken the chances of building a different Europe.

This will not be a walk in the park, but whoever thought that the path to democratic socialism would be easy? But that path, we are now clear, goes through European integration. Leaving the European Union is for the left at least to take a fork in the road which leads to a dead end.

Julian Priestley, with Glyn Ford

1. How on earth did we get here?

Julian Priestley

A POTTED HISTORY OF BRITAIN AND EUROPE: A BIT OF AGONY AND PRECIOUS LITTLE ECSTASY

First, to help understand the present, here is a telegraphic political history of post-war Europe.

Although some visionaries on the British left even before World War Two supported a European federation, the European institutions that emerged after the war were mostly dreamed up, supported and run by the centre-right, principally the Christian Democrats. Opposition to the European Defence Community, and then to the European Community, particularly in Germany and France, tended to come from the centre-left. Their argument, taken over by the British Labour Party, was that this common market was not Europe. Rather, it was just a small part of the continent, a rich man's club, which would heighten cold-war tensions, undermine welfare standards, exploit workers, prevent radical governments from implementing socialist programmes, and turn its back on its responsibilities to third world countries freeing themselves laboriously from the imperialist yoke.

By the 1960s this left-of-centre opposition to European integration was becoming more muted. The German SPD made its peace with the project in 1959. The French left was split on the issue, but most socialists came to terms with French membership even while still in opposition. The Italian communists became enthusiastic Europeans as a way of making more palatable – or at least less alarming – to international opinion the idea of communist participation in a national government ('the historic compromise', which never quite happened) anchored in a stable (West) European framework. Clandestine socialist movements in Spain and Portugal were enthusiastic supporters of European integration as an inspirational example of freedom and democracy.

In Britain hostility on the left to Britain in Europe was more deep-seated and long lasting. It was a Tory government that had tried to take Britain into the common market in the early 1960s, and it was a Tory government which did the deed in 1973. Anti-EEC motivation on the left was diverse: commonwealth obligations; the threat to an alternative economic programme based on a command economy; and the cold war argument. Each carried sway. And, inevitably, the whole European issue became entwined in domestic struggles for the soul and indeed the leadership of the Labour Party. Even after 1975, when a Labour-inspired referendum on continued membership produced an unexpectedly resounding victory for staying in, support for ending membership – but this time without the encumbrance of a referendum commitment – remained the official position of the party for another full decade.

Labour's own historic compromise with the European project came about because the party leadership drew the conclusion from successive election defeats not simply that anti-Europeanism was not an election-winner, but that it made Labour seem unfit for office. And the political map of Europe was changing. The centre-right's stranglehold on political power was broken in Germany in 1966 and in France in 1981; and the entrance of new countries like Greece, Spain and Portugal meant that the old jibe about 'the rich man's club' was no longer pertinent. Within a couple of years of Labour dropping its policy of immediate withdrawal the other arguments – about the Cold War and being 'only part of Europe' – had also become redundant. Indeed the new democracies of East and Central Europe joined the queue of prospective members that was already headed by the impeccably social-democratic countries of northern Europe. The old caricature of the capitalist conspiracy was now unsustainable.

And Europe itself was changing. A customs union with only one integrated policy – agriculture, apparently designed to feather-bed large profitable farms in northern Europe – was now developing new activities and policies. Structural funds supported development in the poorer regions and constituted a resource transfer in their favour. Somewhat tentatively in the first instance, new policies to support training, research and international development were added.

Democratic participation was enhanced by direct elections to what had previously been a largely consultative ersatz 'parliament', but which now, fortified by its new legitimacy, had begun its long march towards legislative power and political control.

Most importantly, in taking the internal market forwards in the mid-1980s, a compromise had been struck between market liberalisation and maintaining high common social and environmental standards. The two men most responsible for this 'deal' were the ill-assorted pairing of Jacques Delors, the former French socialist minister who was president of the Commission, and the Lord Cockfield, a Thatcherite transfuge who as Commissioner for the Internal Market had gone native almost the moment he arrived in the Belgian capital. So as directives to liberalise the EU's domestic market were piling up – after Member States, including the UK, had accepted that in this area the veto had to be surrendered – new proposals were coming forward for higher health and safety standards in the workplace, greater equality, consumer rights and stricter environmental controls.

For Labour and the TUC these developments seemed to open up a second front against Thatcher's Britain. By 1989 a mild euro-enthusiasm had taken hold of the party, flushed as it was with a stunning electoral success in the European Parliament elections that year. The dramatic change was best illustrated by the openness of the Labour leadership to the idea of the single currency, which had by then moved to the top of the EC agenda. But just as one stately galleon – the British Labour Party – was changing course on Europe, so the other liner had started its own half-circle turn. The political assassination of Margaret Thatcher when she was outwitted at a European summit by the Italian prime minister, the late Giulio Andreotti, and then vented her spleen back home, started the political blood-feud which still resonates in today's Tory Party – and, conversely, has sustained Labour's generally milk-and-water Europeanism in the twenty years since her martyrdom.

This engagement of the left in Europe has had its high and low points. New Labour, untroubled ideologically by any putative interference by Brussels in jeopardising a socialist command economy, should have found itself very comfortable with a strengthened European commitment. And indeed Labour's landslide victory in 1997 was followed in quick order by the victory of the French socialists in parliamentary elections, the accession to power of Gerhard Schroeder – another third-way social democrat in Berlin – and the more transient triumph of Romano Prodi in Italy. This should have been the great socialist opportunity, with a fundamental change of direction in Europe being spearheaded by a centre-left that was in power simultaneously in the four most important capitals.

It did not happen. Labour, under pressure from the media and already riven by division at the top, baulked at the prospect of early entry into the euro. Further treaty negotiations saw a Labour government seeking opt-outs reminiscent of those sought by its predecessors. Labour bought the Treasury line, and in particular became uncomfortable with what was perceived as the heavy regulation streaming out of Brussels, which was seen as sapping British competitiveness. Compulsive triangulation meant that joint initiatives with conservative governments in Spain and, later, Italy, were preferred to more natural cooperation with social-democratic leaders in Paris and Berlin. And then, of course, Iraq changed everything and blew to smithereens social democratic unity, and wrecked the prospects for a natural leadership of the European left to which perhaps only Tony Blair could have aspired.

Possibly of even more significance was that Labour in power took counsel from its media advisers and swore an oath of silence about all things European. So, for the thirteen years of New Labour in power there was never a counter-strategy or any antidote to the steady flow of bile and poison against the EU from the media. At no stage did either of the New Labour prime ministers take on the press. Tony Blair did indeed label the press 'a feral beast' – but as he was leaving office. The case for Europe, which could only be argued effectively at the top, was left unmade. New initiatives – including the Lisbon strategy for competitiveness; stronger cooperation in justice and home affairs; defence cooperation with the French agreed at St Malo; the successful completion of the largest ever EU enlargement – all of which were witness to the efficiency of the British in their institutional dealings, were victories that were left unsung. On the other hand, the government went to the barricades to fight against the Working-Time Directive or protections for agency workers – or even the for the interests of the duty-free drinks outlets at airports.

Politically, the euro crisis has made a return to a 'heart of Europe' strategy through taking up the euro almost unthinkable. There are currently no leading voices making the salient arguments: that the importance of remaining in the EU in order to influence outcomes applies with just as much force to the question of adopting the euro; that countries such as Poland – arguably the most successful new economy in Europe – are queuing to join; or that more euro 'in' countries than 'outs' enjoy triple A status. The Labour Party attacks Britain's economic performance but has been slow to point out that it has been no better – and slightly worse than – the euroland average; that the so-called freedom to fix our exchange rate has actually led to temporary overvaluation of the pound, making our exports uncompetitive; and that a permanent aura of uncertainty about the pound's future value is generally harmful to business.

Worse, some in the party have felt obliged to 'apologise' publicly for having ever supported entry, as if they had bit-parts in some Soviet-era show-trial. The claim that 'at least he kept us out of the euro' is now the politically acceptable default defence for the Brown era.

Since leaving office the Labour leadership has resisted the temptation to play the anti-European card, and to cosy up to UKIP. But even the most positive reading of the latest chapters in the saga that is the party's relations with the EU would be hard-pressed to identify the outlines of a strong and distinctive European policy that Labour in power – this time in cooperation with socialists in other Member States – could pursue.

And in the rest of the EU, the political balance has also shifted.

THE RESILIENCE OF THE RIGHT

Twenty years ago few would have predicted the dominant position of the right in Europe today. Social democrats were the main force in eleven of the fifteen EU governments in the decade which straddled the millennium – and this included, for a short time, simultaneously holding office in all of the four largest Member States. Until 1999 the centre-right appeared demoralised and divided. The successors to the Gaullists and the emerging populist right in Italy sat outside the main centre-right grouping, the EPP (the European People's Party). The mainstream of moderate conservatism was 'Christian social' – centre-right on cultural issues, centre-left on economic and social policy, and federalist in ambition.

Between 1989 and 1999, the centre left had a clear relative majority in Parliament and Council; and this was reflected in the composition of the Commission – even if for the last five years of the period it was led by a very centrist Christian Democrat, Jacques Santer. But what did the left actually do from this position of relative strength?

Domestically, the record seems strong. In a period of more or less uninterrupted growth, public infrastructure and social investment generally contributed to the modernisation of the economies. But in terms of a more ambitious political programme, results were disappointing: redistribution, greater equality of outcomes, and challenging unaccountable corporate power were generally down-played, even in those Member States where the ideological stance of the governing party was more radical. Instead, 'light regulation', supply-side labour-market reforms and extreme latitude for the activities of the financial services sector were the lodestar.

As to European policy, the lease of life of 'big coalition' politics was extended, in part because of the need to construct 'qualified' majorities in both the Council and the Parliament. Within the Council, a higher degree of collaboration between leading left-of-centre governments did not materialise. Chancellor Gerhard Schroeder was what was then an exotic exception – a leading German politician who was eurosceptic and had campaigned against the single currency. Lionel Jospin was a far cry from the French socialist European traditions of Mollet, Mendès-France, Mitterrand and Delors. Tony Blair, who at one moment had seemed to be the European left's man of destiny, developed no close relationship with his German and French opposite numbers, and in government surrounded himself with border-line eurosceptics. The European policy initiatives, when they came, were just as likely to be launched with an Aznar or a Berlusconi, as with fellow social-democrat leaders.

The period of progressive hegemony left slim pickings: the Amsterdam treaty, which effectively anchored the social dimension into the development of the internal market; higher environmental standards; and some progressive public health and consumer protection measures. But at the same time there was the single currency, which gave primacy to the Central Bank – and specifically ruled out assistance to national economies in difficulty; and the Lisbon Agenda, whose modesty of social ambition was only matched by its nugatory results. All Europe's problems of competitiveness were to be solved by supply side measures, peer reviews and incitement. Significant extra public resources to beef up research, innovation and training were not part of the picture. And the EU would always take the lead in the

WTO to push globalisation, even without adequate safeguards against social and environmental dumping.

While the left did little to force home its political advantage, the right regrouped. After some initial resistance from the Benelux holders of the 'flame' of centrist Christian Democracy, the ever more dominant German CDU pushed its partners into accepting into the ranks of the European right a whole series of parties whose traditions were far distant from centrist founding fathers like Adenauer, Schumann and DeGasperi. So into the European People's Party fold came, successively, the post-Franquista Partido Popular from Spain, the Greek New Democracy, the French Gaullists and Silvio Berlusconi's Forza Italia. To make up the numbers and to add to the spoils, the British Tories were also brought into the parliamentary group (but not the wider party) – albeit on folding seats. This changed fundamentally the nature of the centre right in Europe: it became more economically liberal, less social, and to a degree less federalist. This reshuffling of the pack was in part the dress rehearsal for the 2004 and 2007 enlargements, a political opportunity that was seized on by Helmut Kohl and largely ignored by the socialists.

The new parliamentary democracies of east and central Europe were indeed happy hunting-grounds for the conservative and liberal politicians who now scoured the hedges and ditches searching for suitable partners – avoiding as far as possible those with too embarrassing a history, and placing their bets on those capable of achieving a sustainable level of public support. The left on the other hand was reduced to scraps from the table. In one or two countries, Poland and Hungary, the trend seemed reversible, with initial successes for reformed ex-communist parties; but in the main the EPP policy of mergers and acquisitions paid off handsomely. By 2009, the Socialists in the European Parliament could count on only a few dozen members from the ten countries that joined the EU in 2004.

Even allowing for some fragmentation, with the British Tories and the Czech conservatives stitching together a separate parliamentary group on the anti-federalist right, with a particularly hard-line social, economic and societal agenda, the EPP remained pivotal in all three institutions.

At European Council meetings, half the heads of government are now from the EPP. Add in the other right-wing formations, and you have more than 60 per cent. The Liberals take the count to 70 per cent. Socialist presidents or prime ministers do not even account for a quarter of participants; and some of these, like the Belgian Elio di Rupo, head coalitions in which the centre-right is in the majority.

In Parliament, the EPP is by some stretch the largest group. Socialists can muster a quarter of MEPs. The left fares a little better, because of other progressive groups like the Greens and the radical left, but in any vote where the EPP can win support from the liberals they do win it. And the record shows (courtesy of votewatch.eu) that on economic and social issues the centre right and the liberals have a firm grip on the outcome. While the liberals will on occasion side with the centre left – for example on environmental standards, press pluralism, and on some external questions – for core business the right carries nearly all before it. And when the centre right in Council is on the same side as the centre right in the Parliament, they win nearly 100 per cent of the votes.

For the Commission, the picture is still clearer. Even before the Lisbon treaty had consecrated the procedure, it made sense for the heads of government to choose someone likely to command support of a majority of MEPs. But since 2004, the right has enjoyed a de facto majority in both the Council and the Parliament. What changed in 2009 was that there was a large majority of non-socialist governments as well as a right-of-centre European Parliament majority, and these combined to ensure that the left in the European Commission is now in very much reduced circumstances. In the current Commission there is a clear majority of EPP commissioners, with a socialist or neo-socialist rump of six out of a total of twenty-seven – fewer than the liberals and trailing way behind the conservatives.

These statistics translate into power and the way that it is exercised. When, in the margins of a celebratory drink in Frankfurt, an informal working-group to pilot the euro into safer waters coalesced around Chancellor Merkel and then-President Sarkozy (a group that included IMF Director-General Christine Lagarde, President of the Central Bank Mario Draghi, President of the euro group Jean-Claude Junker, President of the Commission José-Manuel Barroso, President of the European Council Herman Van Rompuy, and Commissioner responsible for the euro Olli Rehn), there had been no deliberate attempt to sideline socialists: it was simply that there were no socialists in jobs that would necessitate their involvement in a directoire to run the economic and monetary union, so completely had they wiped themselves off the political map.

Of course there are socialists on the scene, but they are not central to determining the principal economic policies of the Union. If Baroness Ashton has a strategic position in the increasingly important area of the Union's external policy, her contribution has essentially been that of building from scratch a new 'diplomatic service' and trying to persuade a majority of conservative governments to accept a leading role for a common policy that some have been more reluctant to concede than others. And if Martin Schulz as President of the Parliament – and a trenchant critic of the prevailing orthodoxy in Council – has achieved a much greater degree of visibility than many of his predecessors, the Parliament's role on economic policy questions is essentially regulatory not prescriptive.

The right's hegemony in this area has huge political consequences. There is little doubt that whatever judgment may finally be made on the records of Socrates, Zapatero and Papandreou (respectively the outgoing socialist prime ministers of Portugal, Spain and Greece), the conditions imposed on them during bail-out negotiations by the right-wing Commission, the IMF and the ECB, with the immense and scarcely-concealed influence of the German Chancellor, were of such extreme severity that their political fates were all but sealed. Not surprisingly, their right-of-centre successors have found a little more sympathy and understanding from their political friends in Brussels and Berlin; conditions have marginally eased; the language is more upbeat; and the repayment deadlines have lengthened a little. In the case of Italy and Greece, though they stopped short of actually conferring the right of appointment directly on Angela Merkel and the board of Goldman Sachs, it would be stretching credulity to imagine that the change in national leaderships was organised against the will of the European conservative confraternity.

Nevertheless, the fate of millions of Europeans is more important than the survival of one group of politicians or another. The right can and should now be judged by its record – for indeed it does have a record.

A discussion of the origins of the multiple credit, debt and economic crises is beyond the remit of this chapter. If the sub-primes and other questionable credit activities triggered the near collapse of the world financial system, then it has to be recognised that governments of left and right in Europe managed to work together to stave off an immediate melt-down. Before the collapse, governments of all hues had fallen sway to a general neoliberal orthodoxy that somehow regulation was the enemy of competitiveness, and that regulators should be forbearing in their scrutiny of financial services for fear of stifling essential risk taking. And the European institutions were for the most part slow to react to the gathering storm. At least socialists in the Parliament had taken an early initiative to insist that the Commission bring forward regulations to control hedge funds and personal equity (and had forced the debate, which it won in the very week of the spectacular fall of Lehman Brothers); whereas, even at this late stage, the Commission was arguing that these matters were best left to national governments. This was the passing of the buck by a right-wing Commission that was ideologically driven, and led to the principal role in the crisis drifting to the European Council – the Commission thus bringing upon itself a setback to its own right of initiative from which it has scarcely recovered.

But if the European Council – with Gordon Brown and the French presidency working effectively together – did manage to get a common line for the G20, and make a major contribution to staving off an immediate global credit crisis, its reaction on sovereign debt and the ensuing economic crisis has been either too little too late or plain wrong. It has also been a slow-motion communications disaster.

When first Greece and then other Member States reached the brink of bankruptcy, the partner governments of the right all followed the same pattern: they ignored the problem for as long as possible; nor did they contradict the tabloid media portrayal of the debtor countries as feckless wastrels sponging off virtuous and hardworking German/Dutch/Finnish/Austrian workers; they expressed vague sentiments of optimism for the future and agreed small-scale bail-outs with huge punitive penalties. Then, when successively each bail-out proved insufficient, they agreed to any extension only with the maximum of reluctance and a further ratcheting-up of the conditions and tightening of the deadlines; and they repeated the mantra about the unconstitutionality of the ECB intervening (as if it was self-evident that the Bank had no responsibility to uphold the currency it is supposed to manage). They also allowed senior ministers in their own governments to speculate openly about countries leaving the euro; they refused any measures to recreate an economic future for countries now in the grip of unparalleled recession; and they carried on writing off the idea that social and infrastructure investment should balance the savage current expenditure cuts (dismissed as 'spending your way out of the crisis'). Finally, when the euro itself was on the edge, and when the Bank itself indicated it would intervene without limit, they started to talk about new Treaties and enshrining the principle that the Commission should get line-by-line control of national budgets of bail-out countries.

And in this vale of misery the European Council offered the spectacle of a score of crisis-dominated meetings, each of which was preceded with every high-wire metaphor known to every third-rate commentator. Conclusions were presented in the early hours for extra dramatic effect. A ripple of relief in the markets was invariably followed by the realisation that the outcome had solved nothing, at best securing some temporary relief, and that the major decisions would have to be taken the next month or the month after that. The insensitivity of the language used has sometimes beggared belief. Boasting that 'the crisis is over' is not only false; it shows how far-removed decision-makers are from the fears and concerns of the twenty million unemployed in Europe, the 50 per cent of Spanish and Greek youth who are jobless, and the growing numbers in dire poverty.

The apogee of incompetence (so far) was reached during the Cyprus bail-out discussions in early spring 2013. A plan to punish all deposit-holders in Cypriot banks was hatched up one weekend, and then had to be abandoned as fury spilled out onto the streets of Nicosia and the plan was rejected *unanimously* by the national parliament. The sound of blame-shifting and serial evasion was heard all over Brussels – as if, uniquely, a Troika which puts every dot and comma of all bailout plans under the microscope had simply not noticed that this plan had within it a time bomb which could reignite a general banking crisis. The deal was revised, forced through, and Cyprus now shares the bleak future of its Mediterranean neighbours. Remarks by the Dutch neoliberal new chair of the eurogroup, Jeroen Dijsselbloem, to the effect that the banking sector had to be cut down to size (presumably by similar methods) in Malta and Luxembourg, had to be withdrawn hastily to prevent a new banking crisis that could have brought down the whole financial house. It was an object-lesson of bad decisions, made poorly and presented lamentably.

But, as the following chapters demonstrate, it is the economic illiteracy of the decisions themselves that is the most damaging aspect of the right's suzerainty. As things stand now the chances are that Greece, Ireland, Portugal, Spain, Italy and Cyprus will all remain in the euro and will gradually return to some form of solvency. But because the only policy instruments that have been vigorously used are longstop support for banks, swingeing cutbacks in public expenditure and supply-side economic and labour-market reforms, a deep steep-sided slump for at least a decade is the prospect that conservative economics have dealt to the hundred million European citizens at this front line.

The long term effect will be 'more flexible labour markets', which, in the lexicon of the right, can be translated quite simply as meaning: it will be easier to fire people; people will work for less money; their jobs will be precarious; for many part-time workers, minimally decent working conditions will be junked; and wage costs will be screwed down. The downside to this – seemingly imperceptible in certain parts of the Commission, the ECB and the German Chancellery – will be a sustained fall in living standards and purchasing power; a return to extreme inequalities; many more European citizens living in dire poverty and a whittling away of welfare state protections; long-term mass youth unemployment; and a systematic brain drain. And what starts in Thessalonica, Valencia, Turin, Cork and Setubal will not stop there. The dramatic lowering of labour costs through a collapse in social standards is already infecting the European economic system, not least in the UK, as social dumping and delocations spread to even those Member States which currently consider themselves to be immune form such pressures.

It is also right-wing ideology that saps even the most modest of measures to act as a mild antidote to the crisis. A European industrial policy? It's not up to public institutions to substitute themselves for the market. More European resources for research, training and apprenticeships? National public expenditure is to be forced downwards to contain deficits, so we cannot allow the European budget to increase – even if that budget is by law always balanced, and even if allocated sums are unspent year on year. Indeed the EU is supposed to set an example, and actually cut overall spending, thereby depriving its already very limited budget of any potential catalytic effect to stimulate competitiveness and create jobs.

This policy is of course the antithesis of the founding principle of solidarity. To say that is not to defend the way that governments in parts of the Union have managed their economies over many of years.

But however harsh the judgment on them may be, no-one can pretend that at least some of their turpitudes were not very widely recognised beyond their frontiers; and that some supposedly virtuous Member States willingly turned a blind eye in the name of subsidiarity. And indeed banks and financial services from precisely these paragons were instrumental in miring those countries in the depths of financial ruin. But it is not necessary to play a blame-game to see that millions of young Europeans are now suffering, that their hopes are being extinguished, and that for the first time in thirty, forty, fifty years the prospects of many young Europeans are dramatically lower than they were for previous generations. And instead of extending a helping hand, this flint-hearted blinkered conservative Europe lectures them on the virtues of thrift and abstinence, while continuing to tolerate organised corporate and plutocratic tax evasion and avoidance on a heroic scale, along with all its vulgar and ostentatious displays of personal wealth in celebration of this new age of inequality.

So far, protests on the street, except in Greece, have been generally muted. And despite the demagoguery on the far right and the extreme left, most of these protests have not yet gone beyond certain bounds. Furthermore, even in the darkness of the worst slump in at least eighty years, the simplistic populist remedies still seem irrelevant to many of the worst affected: despite all the failings of the European institutions, most Europeans still realise that a return to national answers is not the recipe. They understand that the world has moved on; and that if Europe does not cooperate to protect its social and economic model then the salvation of that system will certainly not be found by skulking behind newly-erected national frontier posts. But if an obvious great and cruel injustice is committed, and not rectified, a historic resentment builds up which can at some point create a firestorm. Time is now running out fast: current social tensions may be leading to a political explosion which could threaten the whole edifice.

CAN THE LEFT WIN BACK?

The anger is out there and needs a constructive channel for its expression. Progressives now as a matter of urgency have to join together to look for ways of articulating that anger – through pitiless criticism of the right's stewardship of the EU during the crisis; and, even more importantly, through proposing an alternative that is achievable and credible.

Joining together requires a joint programme of the left for the European elections and for national elections before and after. There is, quite frankly, no point in a separate SPD, or British Labour, or French socialist programme for Europe. The French socialists won back power in France after a fine election campaign during which they said sensible things about Europe – a better balance between responsible finances and growth; reciprocity and fairness in trade. But in power they have found that they could not renegotiate the Fiscal Compact; and, as yet, the better balance with growth-friendly policies is proving elusive – as the prevailing European conservative orthodoxy weighs down their expansionist aspirations, and as their national support melts away in record time. In trade negotiations their influence will remain limited unless the political composition of the Commission, which leads on trade, is altered. The agreement of a group of Member States to move forward on the transactions tax shows that change in one member state can have an influence. But to tip the balance away from a blinkered programme of austerity to jobs, growth and fairness requires more than winning a few national elections. It will need a wave of electoral success nationally and in Europe as a whole.

So 'winning' for the left is no longer a simple case of the SPD getting back into government in Berlin, or Ed Miliband becoming UK prime minister in 2015. It means making the socialists the largest group in the European Parliament, and building around them a progressive coalition with Greens; pro-European forces on the radical left; progressive Liberals disenchanted by the betrayal of their convictions by conservative coalition partners; and those social Christian democrats who have remained faithful to their origins and are horrified at the rightward tilt of the moderate centre-right they once joined.

Is this too tall an order? There is no reason why the left cannot win on a wide front. Last year's victory of François Hollande in France was instructive on a number of fronts. First, incumbency in the current crisis is a heavy burden: the one upside of having so many right-wing governments is that there are many right-wing incumbents who could be kicked out. Second, it showed that a socialist campaign with a limited number of radical promises could be perceived as realistic but also as a break with the past. Third, the campaign talked about Europe but in a critical and constructive manner. When Sarkozy attempted to play the eurosceptic card over Schengen and intra-European trade, the socialists resisted the temptation to outflank him in the populist stakes and saw him off. Fourth the socialist campaign was professionally run, using old and new media intelligently, but also conducting an effective ground war. The margin achieved was substantial, though not huge; but of perhaps greater significance was the massive turnout. In other words, socialists cannot win by stealth. Campaigns for change must capture imaginations, enthuse, and offer hope and change.

The left has performed relatively well in recent elections in the Netherlands, and to an extent in Denmark and in regional elections in Germany, but it will be the strength of the performance throughout the Union which will determine whether power at the European level can be wrested from the conservatives. Europe-wide tracking of polling for the European elections in 2014 at the time of writing puts the socialists neck-and-neck with the EPP, and, despite the hazards of polling in 27 states, forecasts like these proved accurate in 2009. However, there are serious question marks over the centre-left's ability to perform in parts of East and Central Europe, and its capacity to stage a comeback in Spain and Greece. Moreover, holding office but lacking sufficient power to effect the changes it seeks – in part because of lack of European allies – is part of the reason why the French left will face a particular challenge in the European elections.

There will be some in the high command of socialist and Labour parties who will feel distinctly uncomfortable with the idea that European elections should take on a greater significance, or that they could in any way be politically decisive. Old habits die hard. But there are a number of reasons why the 2014 elections hold out the promise of being different from the past.

It is true that if you ask British voters to rate 'Europe' among other factors that determine how they vote, its ranking remains stubbornly low. This is in part because so much of the debate in the UK about membership so obviously misses the point. Whether or not the UK stays in Europe will be decided at the next national general election. The real argument at European elections should not be whether Europe but whither Europe. If we take the issues which really register with voters – jobs, public services, immigration – the link with Europe is now much clearer than before. It is austerity policies pursued in Brussels and imposed on Member States which stoke youth unemployment (though some governments, like our own, are also as avid in their austerity zeal). It is public expenditure cuts insisted upon by the troika of the Commission, the ECB and the IMF which oblige public authorities in Member States and the regions to cut welfare benefits, reduce school-building, and ration medical treatment. And, to be frank, concerns about immigration have been fuelled by unmanaged free movement within the EU at a time of recession; while the Union's failure to promote growth and higher living standards in its neighbourhood has added to strong migratory flows from the former Soviet republics and from the southern banks of the Mediterranean.

So more clearly than before, in 2014 there will be European themes for European elections. Already in 2009, parties which campaigned purely on national issues ('a referendum on the government') fared less well than those which talked about Europe (from UKIP, to the French Greens, to the German CDU). And since then, the crisis has brought home to electors that what Europe decides – or as often as not fails to decide – makes a difference to their daily lives.

But the elections will only become a meaningful democratic exercise if there is conflict and competition between parties. People will not be motivated by a simple parroting that the elections are important; and that Europe matters. They will need to know that the way they vote can change things, and that there is genuine difference between the parties.

Four conditions are required: greater public understanding of what Europe's institutions do and what they decide; programmes which differentiate; personal confrontation; and campaigning vitality.

It would be wishful thinking to imagine that governments, assisted by media, will suddenly embark on a belated public campaign to provide accurate, unbiased, unvarnished information to citizens about what the EU does and what is at stake in the EP elections. The institutions have raised their communication game but cannot compete with the tidal wave of biased and inaccurate reporting that is churned out by the media on a daily basis. But elections hard fought and concentrating on issues which people care about are themselves an exercise in public information.

The way in which Socialists in the past have drawn up their manifestos for European elections could have been tailor-made to repel voters. Programmes have been agreed behind closed doors with the lowest common denominator as the rule of thumb, and then ratified by a 'congress' of delegates – often hand-picked by national party leaderships – in a display of unanimity that would not have disgraced the Soviet-era congresses of the people.

The French socialists with their open primaries have taught us that the wider the involvement of members and sympathisers the more successful the outcome. In practical terms, and for the immediate challenges ahead, a number of measures could be implemented: national parties should foster debates in their ranks about what the socialists should be saying in 2014; delegates to European congresses should have the greater legitimacy that would be conferred if they were designated after democratic votes by parties in the regions; and there should be majority voting at a democratically convened congress, which would enable the party to make radical proposals rather than regurgitate platitudes.

National parties should accept the new rules of the game. We accept majority voting of governments in Council, why not in party congresses? There will be winners and losers, just as in national parties. But if we want the socialists to be saying something relevant on job-creation, trade, resources, investment and regulation, that means forsaking the pursuit of consensus-at-any-price.

A second hurdle to involvement in European elections has been the absence of 'personalisation' in the campaign (notwithstanding purist regret about the passing of a mythical age when issues alone counted and personalities mattered little). Until now the only 'personalities' who have got a look-in have been national leaders of parties talking about national themes. In some countries, MEPs or candidates from the parliament have been kept well away from the cameras for fear that their presence in the campaign might frighten the horses by giving it a European focus.

However, with the Lisbon Treaty, this situation is about to change – though whether this helps or hinders depends on the way that things is managed. The Treaty clearly states that the next president of the Commission should be proposed 'taking into account the results of the European elections'. The main European parties have rightly taken this as the cue to prepare to put forward their 'nominee' for the presidency before the elections. So, in all likelihood, in the first three months of next year, European socialists, the EPP, Liberals and others will have in the field the name of someone who will almost ineluctably lead the campaign, and who, in principle, will be appointed by the

Parliament as the successor to Barroso were his or her party to get most seats.

The mechanism is therefore available. But for this to make a difference the parties will need to use this opportunity with intelligence and energy.

First, the candidate should not 'emerge' from some smoke-free room in Brussels late at night with tired bureaucrats from national parties horse-trading over putative spoils. The successful socialist candidate should have the legitimacy that an election by a democratically elected Congress would confer. Over time a system of national or regional primaries, preferably open ones, would develop as a sign of democratic maturity and vitality, but it is probably too late to do this for 2014. However, at the very least, the candidates should have to come forward before the Congress, issue their platforms, take their argument to socialists in the Member States, and be elected by delegates.

Second, the candidate's platform has to be more than an embellished CV. It should, of course, chime with the manifesto that would be drawn up almost in parallel by the European socialists. But its value-added would lie in translating the principles of the party into a programme of action. And the nominee will have to take risks. To hide behind the collegiality of the body he or she aspires to lead, or the need to concoct compromises with governments and group leaders after elections, will no longer cut it. He or she must let delegates and the public know who they are, where they stand, and what will change with their election.

The third condition to make this personalisation work concerns the vigour and focus of the campaign. The nominees, once selected by the different European parties, will have to engage in debate by confronting each other not just in beltway conferences but in public meetings and media debates in regions throughout the Union. For some this would mean leaving their comfort zone; but for the most important executive office in the Union a little rough-and-tumble might seem a price worth paying. The media scrutiny to which they will be subjected will be testing, but it is the only way to get the arguments about Europe's future out there to a wider public.

For the socialists the choice is crucial. The standard-bearer must be politically free to lead the onslaught on the way the conservatives have mismanaged the crisis and forfeited their right for renewed authority.

He or she will have to argue for a new programme to relaunch Europe. As is advocated in subsequent chapters of this book, that programme must be policy-based; there is no refuge to be found in hiding behind new Treaties or institutional reform. The socialist programme for the 2014 EP elections, and the European planks of national manifestos, need to concentrate on what policies need changing, and what new actions are required. When public trust in the Union has been restored by its institutions being seen to be acting on behalf of Europe's citizens – rather than like some European branch of the IMF shoring up bankers and corporate power – that will be the time to open any debate on institutional reform.

Finally, armed with a programme approved democratically and with a standard-bearer to lead us, the socialists must campaign as if they meant it. In the UK, in particular, European elections have in the past not been second order. Rather, they have scarcely bothered the mainstream parties whose efforts have been routinely perfunctory. Of course resources have to be rationed carefully. It would be naïve to imagine that the efforts deployed at European elections could match the levels achieved for national contests. But there are reasons to expect that the 2014 elections will, for once, generate public interest and avoid seemingly inexorable decline in participation.

In the UK the contest will be watched with particular interest. It will be the last nationwide poll before the general election scheduled for nearly one year later. In Scotland it will be the last test before the independence referendum. The press will devote great attention to the UKIP/Tory battle if only because a strong showing for UKIP in 2014 will make a Tory overall majority in 2015 even more improbable.

But the election will also be looked at closely, here and throughout Europe, as being relevant to the Tory pledge of an in/out referendum before the end of 2017. Moreover, by this stage the Tories may have begun to come clean about which powers they would wish to see repatriated in the 'new settlement' that they will ultimately submit to the electorate.

This heightened interest in the European elections is both a danger and an opportunity for the left. The main risk is that the elections will revolve around the theme, 'Let the people decide', with Labour on the back foot for having rejected the long haul referendum. Some in the party would like to pre-empt this with a commitment to a referendum in the next parliament. But having castigated Cameron for his irresponsibility and pusillanimity in going for a referendum which puts in question investment decisions, trade and the very viability of the UK economy, a U-turn by the Labour leadership would give opportunism a bad name, and almost certainly be punished by the electorate.

Similarly, if the Tories start to issue catalogues of powers to be handed back to Member States, or just to Britain, the truly cardinal error for Labour would be to enter into a Dutch auction with its own list of competences to be restored to Whitehall, or with a separate renegotiation package. The robust attack by the TUC on the real agenda behind the Tory demands – the weakening of the already fragile social Europe, the unravelling of workplace rights and the dilution of environmental standards – is surely the best response to the Tory assault on the social dimension that is wrapped up in the Union Jack and accompanied by bogus pleas about democracy. That counter-attack by the unions will be blunted if Labour takes up the language of lighter regulation, protections for the City and repatriation of regional policy.

The aim of Labour from the beginning of the electoral cycle in 2014 right through to the national election in 2015 must be to shift the debate away from the 'smoke and mirrors' prestidigitations of the Tory 'renegotiation and referendum', and towards a discussion about the European reforms we seek.

And those reforms should above all be to policies not to process. In the end, people care a lot less about who decides and a lot more about what they decide. Most electors understand that today there are different levels of government. If they dislike having decisions taken in Brussels, it is their dislike of the decisions, or of a more widely perceived policy failure, that motivates them. The left cannot win the argument about a 'new settlement': the right has cornered that market. And any attempt by progressives to join in looks like almost infantile 'me-tooism.' But the left is perfectly placed to attack the decisions taken by the right in Europe because they mirror the decisions of the Tory-led coalition at home: austerity beyond reason, the stifling of growth, the unravelling of social protection, threat to the welfare state, and a failure to stand up to unaccountable corporate power.

So the attack lines are clear. What is now needed, as with Labour's domestic policy agenda, is to flesh out a credible policy programme which can put Europe as a whole back on the road to rising living standards and job creation. This would include measures to modernise infrastructure; reduce inequalities; combat home-grown and international tax evasion; harness innovation and new tools for industrial policy in the greening of our economies; tackle the corporate abuse that undermines consumer rights; use our international clout to sustain our welfare states and our ecological goals; and support democracy and economic development in the neighbourhood as well as in the wider world.

Taking these points together, the ambition of such a programme for the left could change the political weather. It could provide a unique chance for the European left to break out of a cycle of decline. But, more importantly, it could provide a glimmer of hope for millions of Europeans who will face the bleakest of futures if a new direction is not taken.

All the authors of this book are British and so the peculiar evolution of the UK's European debate is very much present in our reflections. But we are wholeheartedly convinced that the solution to the problems we face is to be found by accepting neither the miserable status quo of the current conservative European establishment, nor the crass irresponsibility of the new right-wing isolationists in the UK, but rather by working with socialists and other progressives on a new policy agenda, and cooperating at all levels to implement it. The following chapters are our modest contribution to fleshing out an agenda for reform and change for the European Union.

2. It's the politics, stupid: Towards a progressive European economic strategy

Derek Reed

The European Union is mired in a prolonged recession. And in the EU, just as in Britain, disastrous political choices have made matters worse. The budgetary austerity espoused by right-wing leaders has deepened and prolonged the recession, destroyed jobs and services, widened economic inequality and – particularly at EU level – has fuelled political distrust, populism and nationalism.

From the perspective of the British left, it is hard to overstate the importance of developing a credible alternative European economic strategy. In part, this is because the British and European economies are so closely intertwined: the EU takes more than half of all British exports, far outstripping any other market; integrated production chains dominate the British and European economies; while free movement of capital and labour, freedom of establishment and free access to the single European market are at the heart of many business models.

But the political economy of a European approach is, if anything, more crucial than the economics. There can be no progressive economic alternative without a radical shift in tax and regulatory regimes – especially, but not only, in the financial sector. And it's hard to see Britain achieving anything like this on its own, in a world of open borders and global financial markets. The price of tax and regulatory choices that look beyond short-term business and financial interests would be just too high, with capital simply shifting to more profit-friendly locations.

The EU, by contrast, with a population of over 500 million, is the world's biggest economy, accounting for 20 per cent of global GDP and over 20 per cent of world exports and imports. That degree of economic muscle gives the EU potentially much greater power to rewrite its rulebook than the government of any single middle-sized country. What is lacking is political will – a function, of course, of political control, and of the left's failure to contest sufficiently vigorously the European political terrain (not to mention its having bought into a great deal of the right's neoliberal doctrines for much of the period); this has left the right in power for a decade.

That has to change, if we want to deliver a genuine economic alternative to Osborne-weary Britain, because it is hard even to imagine a scenario in which the UK successfully implements a strategy for growth – never mind the radical restructuring needed to reshape our economic model – without parallel action at European level. For good or ill, the only available left turn takes us straight through Brussels.

The problems of the UK and EU economies are also linked, however, in another, more fundamental way. To think clearly about Europe's economic problems, forget for a moment about the EU. The headlines may be hogged by Eurozone crises, the role of the European Central Bank, tensions between North and South – or between Britain and the rest. But go deeper, and the inventory of Europe's most urgent economic ills – mass unemployment, heavy budget deficits, prolonged recession – looks horribly familiar from our side of the Channel. Different institutional and political contexts mean that the consequences play out differently in Britain, and, in particular, countries in the Eurozone. But they are the same problems, with the same origins, and to a great extent they call for the same solutions.

We argue in the next section that the origins of the financial crash of 2008 – and therefore of our current woes – lie in the sweeping structural changes that have marked the last thirty years in industrialised economies. While different in degree, these changes are broadly the same throughout Europe. To a remarkable extent, they are political or ideological in origin.

Following the collapse of post-war welfare capitalism, amid the turmoil of the 1970s, a new, more right-wing received wisdom emerged, which emphasised the power of markets, the limitations of government and the inefficiencies of regulation. In macro-economic policy, the old objective of full employment took second place to a new preoccupation, the conquest of inflation. And there was a narrowing of political vision, as the idea took hold as never before that all policy objectives, all projects of social advancement, must be subordinated to perceived economic imperatives, the first of which was competitiveness.

We show below how the thirty-year ascendancy of free-market financial capitalism has made our economies more fragile, undermined economic stability and precipitated the financial meltdown from whose after-effects we are still suffering. Since the underlying problems are structural, it follows that a progressive vision for European economic policy cannot just be about economic recovery. It is a conservative ambition to restore the European economy as it was in 2007, even if the economic illiteracy of conservative governments is making that an ever more remote prospect. The left's ambition must be both recovery and transformation.

A radical European economic strategy therefore needs three interconnected elements: a co-ordinated recovery strategy; reform of economic governance; and structural change. After a brief detour into economic history, this chapter sets out proposals on the first two points, while chapter three shows how a progressive strategy of structural change can reshape the economy in the interests of the citizen.

THIRTY YEARS OF TINA: THE ECONOMIC CONSEQUENCES OF THE RIGHT

In the last thirty years, a growing number of countries across the European Union have become wedded to an increasingly market-led economic strategy. Governments have cut back on regulation, weakened the role of trade unions and given more power to finance. They have argued that by steering a greater share of national output towards profits and allowing higher rewards at the top, and placing a greater emphasis on markets, investment is boosted, bringing greater prosperity for all.

It is a theory – for theory it is – that emerged in the post-war teachings of a small group of pro-market thinkers. They argued that the more equal, 'managed capitalism' of the post-war era had been a serious drag on prosperity. As the Austrian-American economist Ludwig von Mises, a leading prophet of the superiority of markets, put it in 1955: 'Inequality of wealth and incomes is the cause of the masses' well-being, not the cause of anybody's distress'. Eventually this idea was embraced across much of the political spectrum. In 1975, a highly influential book, *Equality and Efficiency: The Big Tradeoff*, by the late American economist Arthur Okun, argued that you could have greater equality or more prosperity but not both. The same idea was later essentially endorsed by the American Democratic Party and the leadership of New Labour in the UK.

This theory was first put to the test from the early 1980s in the UK and the US, with both countries deregulating their economies and allowing the concentration of income and wealth to return to levels last seen previously in the inter-war years. Eventually, similar, if weaker, versions of this model were applied across most of Europe, and indeed much of the rich world. In search of greater efficiency, a growing number of countries became economic laboratories in which the fruits of growth became increasingly colonised by a small business, financial and corporate elite.

This experiment in 'unequal market capitalism' has left a majority of European workforces with a shrinking share of their national outputs, while boosting the share going in profits to big business. In the last twenty-five years, the share of wages in GDP across the Euro area has shrunk by 10 percentage points, from around 70 per cent to 60 per cent. This is a trend – mirrored across the OECD club of rich nations – that has been fuelled by policies aimed at weakening labour's bargaining power, and by giving financial institutions more prominence in national economies.

The shift from wages to profits has been associated with a growing concentration of incomes at the top, with the gap between rich and poor widening in three-quarters of OECD nations. Inequality has risen in countries that have traditionally been more equal, including Finland, Sweden and the Netherlands. In the UK, the share of income taken by the top 1 per cent has almost trebled since the mid-1970s – from just under 5 per cent then to almost 15 per cent by 2010. In Germany, personal income distribution was stable until the mid-1990s. Thereafter, the lower end of the distribution lost ground, and since the millennium real wages have more generally stagnated while inequality has grown sharply. As a result of these trends, countries like Germany, the UK, Ireland and Spain have seen big rises in numbers of low-paid employees.

The architects of the free market strategy made big claims for this political and economic revolution – that it would boost investment, enterprise and growth – but they have been proved badly wrong. While inequality has surged, the promised pay-off of wider economic progress has failed to materialise. On all measures of economic success bar inflation, the post-1980 era of rising inequality has a much poorer record than the egalitarian post-war decades.

Unemployment over two decades

Let's look for example at how labour market liberalisation affected unemployment in Europe over the last twenty years, as shown in Figure 1. In the early 1990s unemployment was in double digits. This was portrayed as evidence of 'eurosclerosis' and used to justify the liberalization of labour markets and welfare states – a prime cause of the fall in the wage share discussed above. In the next few years there was, it is true, some slow improvement in the unemployment rate. This was claimed as a success for liberal reforms – although in fact it was mostly due to the ending of restrictive macroeconomic policies following the collapse of the European Exchange Rate Mechanism.

Since 2000, and above all since 2007, labour market developments show how untenable the neoliberal view of labour markets is. During the 2000s, pre-crisis, while neoliberal reforms were grinding on, the unemployment rate first jumped when the new economy bubble burst in 2001, and then fell as recovery set in – with very little by way of overall improvement. And the dramatic leap in unemployment since 2007 – up more than four percentage points – just does not fit with the view that supply-side rigidities are the primary cause of unemployment. Unemployment in Europe now, after twenty years of neoliberal 'structural' reforms, is substantially higher than in the bad old euroscleroțic days of 1993. Not that this has prevented a renewed attack on labour market and welfare-state institutions. The ill-advised response of the EU's conservative-led institutions to the crisis has been: more of the medicine that has not cured – and very probably has harmed – the patient. Under neoliberal hegemony, economic policy in Europe has been on the wrong track for a long time, and it shows.

Figure 1: EU unemployment, 1993-2013

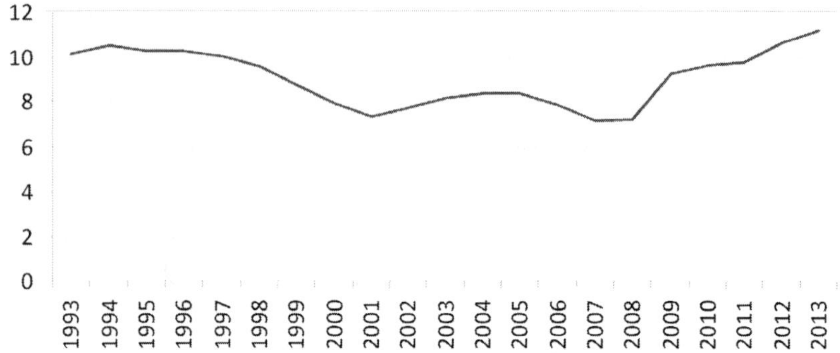

Note: Figure is based on old EU15 to get the required time series

Market reforms – instability instead of growth

Since 1980, the rich world in general has grown more slowly and delivered higher levels of unemployment than it did in the post-war era. In the UK, for example, contrary to the theory, the boost to the profit share since 1980 – shown in Figure 2 – has been associated with a decline in the level of investment. Growth and productivity rates have been about a third lower since 1980, while unemployment has averaged more than three times higher.

Figure 2: Rising profit share and falling investment, UK, 1948-2010

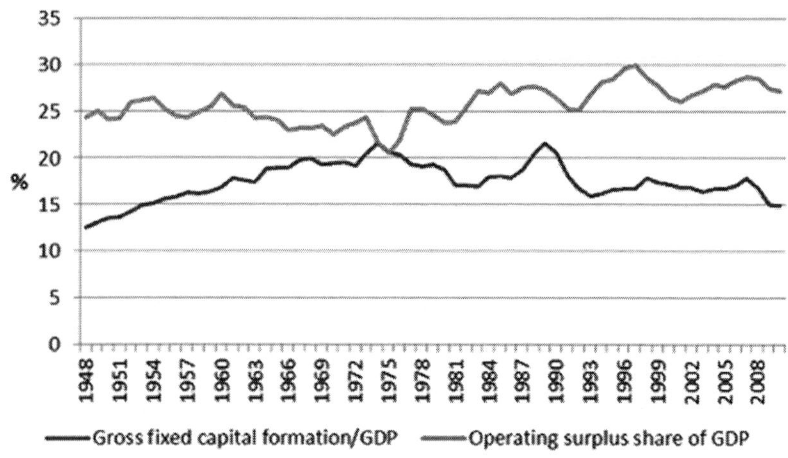

The historical evidence is that the 'efficiency/equality trade-off theory' has failed to stand up to real world application. The more market-led, high-inequality model has not only failed to deliver higher investment and faster growth, it has also been associated with greater instability. The apparent surge in growth and decline in volatility in the US and the UK (the 'great moderation') from the mid-to-late 1990s was largely an illusion created by bubble economics, while the post-1980s has seen longer and deeper recessions than the 1950s and 1960s. It is now widely accepted that excessive inequality played a critical role in both the 2008 crash and the persistence of the current slump. The Great Depression of the 1930s and the Great Crash of 2008 were both preceded by sharp rises in inequality. In contrast, the most sustained period of economic success and stability – from 1950 to the early 1970s – was one in which inequality fell and the proceeds of growth were more evenly shared between wages and profits and across earnings groups.

In Europe as elsewhere, far from triggering a sustained investment boom and delivering more robust economies, the main outcome of the post-1980 experiment in market capitalism has been more polarisation between rich and poor *and* greater fragility and turbulence.

There are two key mechanisms that link growing inequality to economic crisis. First, reducing the relative incomes of large sections of the workforce stifles purchasing power and prevents economic output being sold. The political solution to this problem of weakened consumer power in the neoliberal period has been to pump economies full of private debt. In many EU countries, including the UK, Spain, Ireland and Portugal, but also Finland, the Netherlands and many of the newer, eastern European Member States, levels of personal debt soared sharply in the decade to 2008.[1] None of this prevented recession: it just delayed it. The same factors were at work in the 1920s. The 1929 Crash was preceded by a sharp rise in inequality with the resulting demand gap filled by an explosion in private debt.[2]

Secondly, the swollen corporate and personal wealth surpluses that were the flipside of these shrinking wage shares have been used in ways which have greatly damaged the real productive economy. Instead of boosting investment, these surpluses have led to a giant mountain of footloose global capital that has ended up fuelling commodity speculation, financial engineering and hostile corporate raids – activity geared to transferring existing rather than creating new wealth. By contributing to the creation of asset bubbles, the same process greatly amplified the risk of financial crisis. Again there are striking parallels with the 1920s, when swelling surpluses were poured into real estate and the stock market, creating the bubbles that triggered the 1929 crash.

Having helped trigger the 2008 crash, the income divide is now helping to prolong the crisis. Across Europe, real wages have been falling, contributing to the lack of demand that is preventing recovery. In the UK, wage-earners today have around £100 billion less in their pockets (roughly equivalent to the size of the nation's health budget) than they would if the cake was shared as it was in the late 1970s. In Germany's bigger economy the shortfall stands at £230 billion. In contrast, the winners from the great upward redistribution – big business and the top 1 per cent – are sitting on growing corporate surpluses and soaring private fortunes that are mostly sitting idle – 'dead money', as the Bank of England Governor Mark Carney has called it. This imbalance is a central explanation of the economic paralysis that is crippling the European, and much of the global, economy.

The importance of inequality to the policy agenda

Today, global leaders are finally beginning to acknowledge the cost of the market-led revolution – and that the enrichment of the few is not the way to build robust economies. 'Inequality', according to President Obama, 'is the defining issue of our time'. In January 2013, head of IMF Christine Lagarde went further: 'Excessive inequality is corrosive to growth; it is corrosive to society ... the economics profession and the policy community have downplayed inequality for too long.' But although the economic divide has become an increasingly hot political issue, little real action has been taken to tackle it. The dominant market model that drove us over the cliff has survived the second deepest recession of the last hundred years largely intact. At the same time, the best evidence is that the billionaire class has got richer through the crisis while most of the rest of us have got poorer.

In contrast, the economic crisis of the 1930s was to prove a decisive political and economic turning point – one that eventually gave rise to a very different model of political economy. The current crisis provides a similar political opportunity to fashion a progressive alternative that recognises that economic health and social justice go hand in hand. At the heart of a new model of capitalism should be a commitment to the reversal of the declining wage shares and widening pay gaps of the last thirty years, with a set of measures that deliver a bigger share of the economic cake to workforces and especially to those on low and middle earnings.

This would require a new social contract that would ensure a better balance in bargaining power between labour and capital; using profits in a much more productive way; pro-active industrial policies aimed at boosting productivity and ensuring that output gains filter down to real wage and employment gains; and a much tougher cap on unjust rewards at the top and a transformation of boardroom culture. Markets need to become the servants of society – with, for example, finance subordinated to the needs of the real economy.

This in turn requires a fundamental shift in our approach to political governance. There needs to be wider recognition that we have been backing the wrong theory on the impact of inequality. A model of capitalism that fails to share the proceeds of growth more proportionately is not sustainable. The traditional case against the growing income gap, based on social justice and fairness, needs to be extended to embrace the evidence about the damaging economic impact of more polarised economies.

The pursuit of more equal societies needs to be elevated to become a primary goal of domestic and global economic policy. In the UK since the 1980s, under governments of all political colours, the role and impact of inequality have played at best a marginal role in decision-making. In the EU, the idea that reducing inequality should be a main object of policy has never been seriously entertained, and yet it will be an essential element in reducing the instability of the European economy. In the section on governance, below, we shall see how the EU's 'European Semester' process could be redirected towards more progressive ends. The case for such a re-orientation can be seen from the failures of the neoliberal economics promoted over the last three decades.

The econometric model on which the European Commission bases its forecasting and policy decisions makes no provision for the impact of changes in income distribution on vital outcomes like private investment, consumption, living standards, overall demand in the economy and key asset prices. But distributional issues ought to be a key issue in strategic economic thinking. These determine the course of average living standards and have a major impact on economic stability and durability. Yet they slip through the net of current policy-making machinery not just in the EU, but also at the level of global institutions like the OECD and the IMF. All need to translate their new found concern with growing inequality into actively promoting the case for greater equality. The sustained force with which the EU encouraged countries to back market reforms has helped fuel the rising tide of inequality of the last three decades. It can play an equally powerful role in helping to undo some of that damage.

Economic policy, at European and Member State level, needs to target a wider set of economic indicators than inflation, productivity, growth and unemployment. New indicators should include pay ratios, wage share, concentration of income amongst the top 1 per cent and the pattern of effective tax rates. To date, analysis of these data sets and their implications has mostly been left to independent researchers.

Each indicator should be given a target that is compatible with economic stability. The wage share target could be set at the average of the two post-war decades, a level that brought equilibrium and sustained stability. Effective tax rates should rise by income decile. At the moment, they are often higher amongst lower than amongst higher income households.

The new indicators should be the basis for setting policy targets, backed by effective policy instruments for reaching them. These need to be designed to restrict the level of economic inequality to within the limits that prevent instability. They would range from tax and industrial policy to the role of collective bargaining and corporate governance. When the targets are breached – as they clearly are at the moment – then policy needs to be adjusted accordingly. In the last section of this chapter, we consider how European economic governance can contribute to this change.

The New Bourbons: the thinking that gave us the Great Depression is alive and well (and living in London, Brussels and Berlin)[3]

You need not look very far to see what you need to know about the Second Great Depression in Europe. Namely that it was an entirely avoidable policy disaster and that the policy failure had two main causes: the dominance of policy-making by the political right and neoliberal economic thinking; and the lack of a coherent and effective European-level regime for managing the intertwined European, and especially Eurozone, economy. A simple but devastating story can be told with the help of four pictures. The unemployment data bear sad testimony to the destructive power of another tenet of neoliberal-inspired European thinking: fiscal austerity.

Figure 3: EU Unemployment since 2008

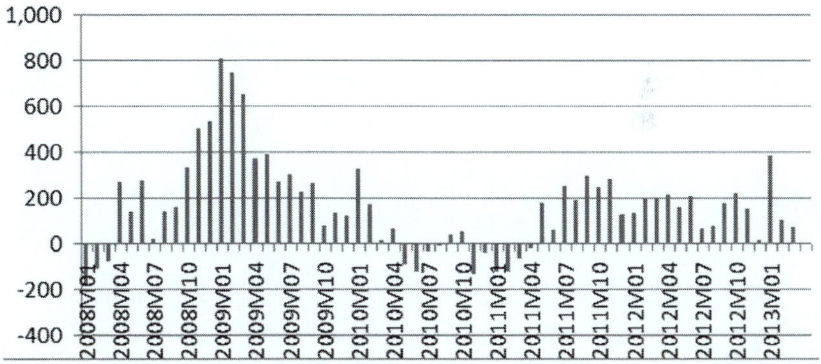

Figure 3 shows monthly changes in EU unemployment since 2008. The massive job losses – peaking at 800,000 a month – in the early part of the crisis are not news; nor is it that, five years on, unemployment is continuing to rise.

What is surprising is this: the economic and labour market situation in the EU was improving strongly from the spring of 2010 to early 2011. For a year from May 2010, unemployment fell by almost 700,000, reaching a rate of more than 100,000 a month around the turn of the year. From May 2011, the inexorable rise in unemployment resumed, adding almost 4 million workers to the dole queues. But that year of growth and job creation gives the lie to the claims that rising unemployment is an inevitable result of the crisis. The real question is clearly why the 2010-2011 recovery was aborted. The answer is simple: from the start of 2011, Europe switched from stimulus to austerity. Country after country tightened its fiscal belt, urged on by the European Commission, while premature interest rate hikes by the European Central Bank added fuel to the fire.

Let us consider the initially similar but then very different fates of Europe and America since the crisis.

Figure 4: Employment in the USA & EU since 2007

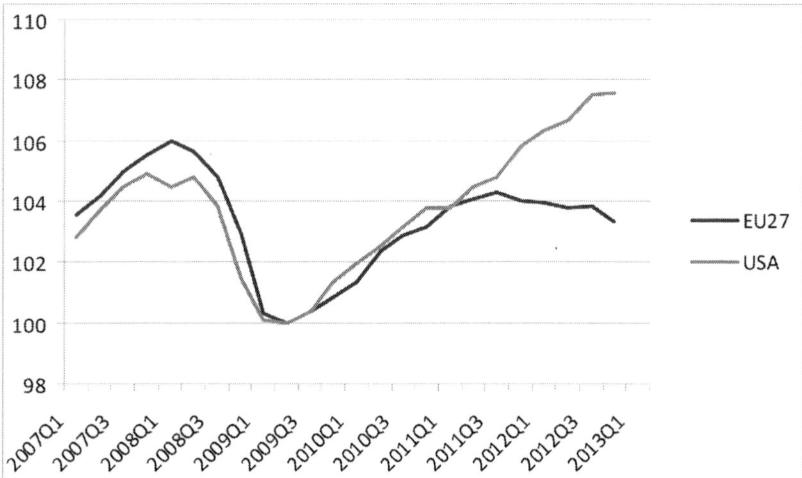

Both economies hit bottom in the second quarter of 2009.[4] It can be seen that the American and European recoveries were uncannily similar under the influence of expansionary policies. Until the middle of 2011 that is. Since then the US has continued the process of slow but steady recovery. Unemployment has edged down as inexorably as it has risen in Europe. In Europe, recovery was aborted and the gap between the world's two largest economic areas has widened every quarter since then. Partly this reflected the institutional problems related to the architecture of the euro area, of course, but in no small measure the widening gap reflected the shift to austerity and monetary tightening in the EU, only cautiously and belatedly reversed. In contrast, in the US monetary policy was pulling out all the stops to stimulate recovery and bring down unemployment, while austerity measures were successfully averted by the US administration until the start of 2013.

Europe's lamentable decision to scupper its own recovery reflects a total incapacity of European policymakers to take Keynesian economics seriously, and a fanciful belief that fiscal rigour would, via imagined 'confidence effects', have only a limited short-run dampening impact on growth, and in the medium run would have a positive impact.

The extent of the failure by EU policy-makers to understand how the European economy works can be seen by looking at their forecasts for estimated growth for European countries in the context of their forecasts for reductions in those countries' budget deficits. Analyses reveal a strong correlation between the two:[5] wherever they expected a big deficit reduction, their growth estimates were systematically too optimistic. Put simply, EU policy-makers have systematically underestimated the negative impact of fiscal consolidation on output.[6]

The second major failure by EU policymakers was allowing interest rates paid by governments, firms and private households to rise dramatically in the euro area crisis countries. Conservatives argued that this was just retribution by the markets for governments that had allowed their deficits and debts to get out of control. This is incorrect. As can be seen from Figure 5, governments with high debt-to-GDP ratios do tend to face somewhat higher interest rates (the many dots around the red trend line). However, in 2011 the rates demanded of countries such as Greece, Ireland and Portugal were crippling, and bore no relationship to their public debt burden.

Instead these penal rates were a 'fear premium', to compensate investors for the risk of a break-up of the euro area and/or the imposition of a haircut. They thus constituted an indicator of the failure of EU policy to get a grip on the crisis at an early stage. Countries such as Japan, the USA and the UK had higher debt burdens than most euro area countries but very low interest rates, because investors had confidence that their respective central banks stood behind their governments and default was not an option. That is why interest-rate spreads in Europe declined sharply, although not enough, when the ECB finally made clear, in the summer and autumn of 2012, that it stood ready to buy unlimited quantities of sovereign bonds to defend the euro. Too little, too late, and following long months of unnecessary pain and crisis.

Figure 5: the fear premium on Greek and Irish debt

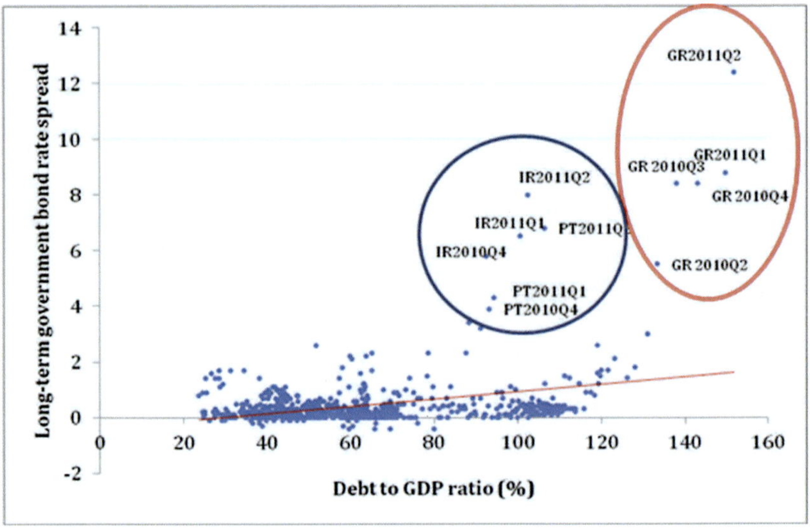

Source: P. De Gauwe and Y. Ji, 'Mispricing of sovereign risk and multiple equilibria in the Eurozone', *VOX* 23, January 2012.

Figure 6: Labour cost movements in Eurozone countries, 1999 to 2014

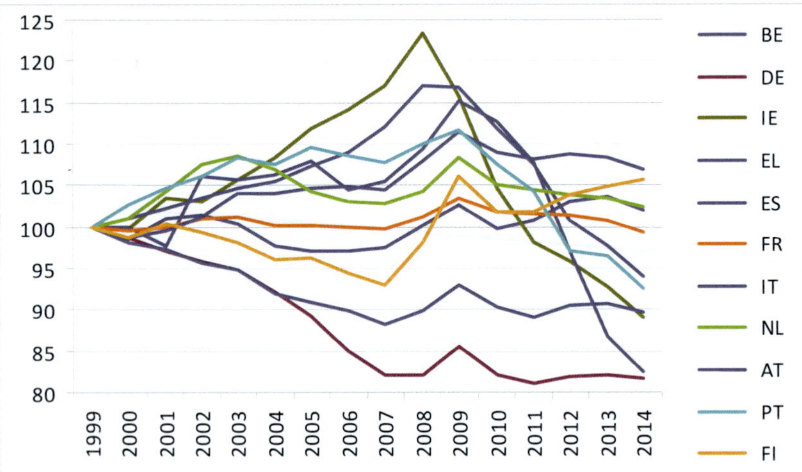

For each country, unit labour costs (the total wages costs to produce one unit of GDP) are set at 100. The lines then plot the increase in (nominal) wage costs making allowance both for productivity gains, and (at 1.9 per cent a year) for the rate of inflation targeted by the ECB.[7]

The third and final major EU policy failure was to have allowed competitive imbalances to build up within the euro area and then to seek the rapid resolution of this long-term problem asymmetrically, by squeezing wages in the deficit countries.

The imbalances arose because, in accordance with their economic ideology, the architects and guardians of EMU were convinced that problems of competitiveness within EMU would be solved by the market. If a country's prices and wages got too high or too low, it would lose or gain competitiveness. This would rebalance demand and bring its price and wage movements back into line. Figure 6 shows that this did not work out as intended.

Before the crisis, labour costs in countries such as Ireland, Spain, Greece and Portugal increased consistently faster than the ECB's inflation target. Less attention is typically accorded the systematic undershooting of that same benchmark by, in particular, Germany and Austria. The widening competitiveness differential was not checked by market forces. Instead, they drove the imbalances further apart because – with common interest rates set by the ECB – high inflation in the booming peripheral economies meant they had lower *real* interest rates than the then struggling German economy. These widening competitive imbalances were unsustainable, of course: the high-inflation countries moved into trade deficits, while Germany posted ever growing surpluses.

The global financial and economic crisis then triggered a sharp correction, but what is striking is the profoundly asymmetric nature of that correction. The full burden of adjustment is being borne by the deficit countries. Spectacular downward adjustments have occurred in Ireland, Spain, Greece and other countries, as recession and austerity drive down wages and prices.

The economic and human cost, in terms of loss of output and falling living standards, has been immense. Far preferable would have been a strategy in which measured fiscal consolidation and steps to regain competitiveness in the periphery were offset by demand-expansion and faster wage and price increases in Germany. The European Commission, for its part, reinforced the pressure for the burden of adjustment to fall on the deficit countries by inventing and then gerrymandering the so-called Macroeconomic Imbalance Procedure, which wrote asymmetrical rules on policy correction into EU law.[8]

Overview: derailed by bad economics

The EU's curse has been that for years now economic policymaking in Brussels and in the leading European countries has been in thrall to erroneous theories of unemployment, competitiveness and growth.

During the crisis, the liberal-conservative parties which held power in key countries and in the European Council and Commission, aided by the ECB which shared the same ideological mindset, deployed the wrong policies – in particular pro-cyclical austerity and asymmetric adjustment.[9] They failed to deploy the policies of coordinated expansion and balanced adjustment needed to underpin confidence in Eurozone stability and ensure a balanced economic recovery.

The policies of austerity are now intellectually discredited in their own terms, not least by their own long-time allies. IMF studies have shown that the 'fiscal multiplier' is far higher than had been assumed, so that cuts in public spending have produced much larger falls in private consumption and in economic activity than expected, undermining the official aim of reducing the deficit. And the Harvard study most-cited by the likes of Economics Commissioner Rehn, supposedly showing that public debt above 90 per cent of GDP is bad for growth, has been shown to be invalidated by elementary errors of calculation.

But we should not expect this to lead to a change in policy, until we first achieve a shift in the political balance of the European Parliament and Commission, because one of the right's real motivations continues to be to roll back public provision and leave everything to the market.

The architecture of the euro area does need reform, as its critics have long claimed: it is at least in part based on flawed and discredited ideas. But the disastrous outcomes of recent years have been in no small measure simply due to the implementation of perverse policies that were at the discretion of elected governments. Thus, while architectural reform is certainly needed, the most urgent consideration is to achieve a left majority in the European Parliament and Commission and to replace current governments by those willing and able to implement the policies – already permissible under current treaties – that are needed to get the European economy swiftly back on its feet.

A NEW GOVERNANCE, TO SERVE A WIDER ECONOMIC VISION

While British politicians and pundits tend to obsess about 'reform of the EU', most of what's wrong with EU economic policy is just that – policy. Just as the cure for Britain's Osborne-led recession is to change the government and change the policies, so the same is largely true at European level. Contrary to the mind-set of many Brits, politics doesn't stop at the water's edge. Winning elections and changing the policies is what European politics – just like national and local politics – is all about.

So any discussion about reforming EU governance needs to come with a health warning: the right and the Europhobes will be only too happy with a debate focused on EU reform, because if EU reform is the answer, it rather implies that the EU is the problem. Yet the simple truth is that right-wing majorities give you right-wing policies, and that's what we currently have in all three EU institutions – Parliament, Commission and Council of Ministers. And for a future left majority at EU level, the shortcomings of the decision-making structures are unlikely to be their biggest challenge.

Nevertheless, while the EU's big problem is right-wing policies, rather than the rules of economic governance, there's also plenty of room for improvement in the latter.

Fighting the wrong war – how Maastricht got mugged by reality

We must never allow the conservatives to forget that Europe's recession, and the Eurozone crisis in particular, are aftershocks of the 2008 global financial crisis – a failure of light-touch regulation and blind faith in market forces. But the Eurozone was especially vulnerable to the financial storms because of deep economic and policy imbalances in EMU. And both the Eurozone's difficulties and the wider European recession have been prolonged and exacerbated by mismanagement by the Commission and Council – reflecting partly their misdiagnosis of the problem, but also inadequate governance, with poor public accountability and a weak democratic mandate, which prevented decisive action.

A credible reform of EMU has to tackle the twin problems of imbalance and weak and undemocratic governance. And the sharpest lesson of the Eurozone crisis is that monetary union without economic and social union is unstable, socially regressive, vulnerable to external shocks and incompatible with the goals and values of the Union.

The authors of the Maastricht Treaty did not foresee the problems of chronic trade imbalances, divergent inflation rates and widening gaps in productivity and competitiveness that have bedevilled the Eurozone since its launch. As we have seen, market forces were expected to take care of all that, but in practice these persistent imbalances – particularly between Germany and the so-called PIIGS (Portugal, Italy, Ireland, Greece, and Spain) – led directly to the Eurozone crisis. Monetary union allowed cheap money to flood into less-performing economies, creating over-extended banking systems and, particularly in Spain and Ireland, massive house price bubbles.

These distortions made the PIIGS especially vulnerable to the loss of investor confidence following the 2008 global financial crash. To prevent the collapse of their domestic banking systems, governments were obliged to take over massive debts from their fragile banks. Now laden with debt and mired in recession, they were seen to have poor prospects of eliminating their budget deficits. To make matters worse, the hesitant and disunited response of Eurozone leaders encouraged fears both of a Eurozone break-up and of a partial default or restructuring of the debt of the crisis countries. So investors took fright, the sovereign debt of the PIIGS was judged a bad credit risk, and interest rates soared to ruinous levels – leading to the now familiar saga of EU bailouts and rescues.

A progressive reform of European economic governance needs to tackle the structural weaknesses that led to the 2008 financial crash and the Eurozone debt crisis; and to ensure a quick and effective response to asymmetric shocks and wider economic fluctuations. Counter-cyclical policy should be able both to nip inflation in the bud and to promote a rapid recovery from an economic downturn. Far from helping recovery, the deflationary bias in the EU's current fiscal rules has prolonged it.

Equally important, reform has to strengthen democratic control, accountability and transparency. In some respects – such as the troikas, the European Stability Mechanism, and the European Central Bank itself – we should perhaps be thinking in terms of establishing democratic control, since there's almost none there to strengthen.

European economic governance has three pillars – monetary policy, economic coordination and what may be called EU fiscal policy in its own right – meaning the EU's own revenues and expenditures and those it can leverage through, for instance, the European Investment Bank. Let us look at them in turn.

1. Monetary policy – servant of European values, not of financial markets

The task of dragging Europe out of recession has been made doubly difficult by the response of financial markets. (Ironically, the same financial markets which plunged us into recession in the first place now sit in judgement on our efforts to get out.) In the three years to July 2012 the interest rates on borrowing by the Spanish government, for instance, rose from under 4 per cent to almost 8 per cent. The cost of interest payments in 2013 will represent almost 40 per cent of Spain's budget deficit, accounting for a bigger share of government spending than education. The experience in other 'peripheral' EU economies has been similar, and in Greece far worse.

This massive transfer from public funds to financial markets could have been avoided by coherent and determined EU intervention. If the ECB had been ready – like a normal central bank – to act as a lender of last resort, making it clear that it was ready to buy Eurozone sovereign debt whenever interest rates threatened to exceed a given ceiling, investor confidence could have been maintained and interest rates stabilised. Comparison with Britain is instructive. While interest rates soared on the debt of the PIIGS, rates in Britain – equally plagued by recession and a massive budget deficit – stayed at historic lows. The difference is the Bank of England. Investors in UK bonds know they'll always get their money back because in the last resort, if the government can't balance the books, the Bank will print the money.

Similarly, the ECB should be the lender of last resort for Eurozone governments, but its statutes have a 'no bailout clause' that, it was argued, prohibited that role.[10] Yet when finally, in September 2012, after three years of uncertainty and deepening crisis, ECB Chairman Mario Draghi hinted that the ECB was ready – Treaty notwithstanding – to intervene, this effectively ended the market panic and started a return of interest rates on the sovereign debt of the PIIGs closer to normality. As many commentators have pointed out, the same action taken in 2009 or 2010 when Greece first ran into trouble would have prevented the contagion from spreading to other Eurozone countries.

Although the ECB, since September 2012, is often hailed as one of the few effective elements in EU economic governance, its tardy response cost the EU and the world economy dear. This, and the stark evidence in recent years of the Bank's economic and political power, raises questions about its lack of democratic accountability, to which we return below.

The European Union could and should also have moved quickly to break the vicious circle whereby governments already in fiscal difficulties had to take on the debts of fragile domestic banks. It has already been agreed in principle by the European Council and the Parliament that the European Stability Mechanism should do this by providing recapitalisation direct to troubled Eurozone banks.[11] But at German insistence it will not start to provide funding directly to banks until current proposals for Banking Union are completed, moving responsibility for banking supervision from national to European level.[12] The ESM, and the conditions it places on its lending to banks and governments, must be subject to Parliamentary control at European level and in the recipient country.

In the longer term, the vulnerability of national budgets to financial market pressure should be reduced, and the cost of public borrowing lowered, by the adoption of Eurobonds: a European agency, backed ideally by all EU Member States, would handle the borrowing of Member States. A well-developed economic literature shows that Eurobonds could deliver both greater stability and substantial cost savings to European taxpayers, especially in the less developed economies but also, to a lesser degree, even – through its scale of operations – to triple-A rated governments like Germany, Netherlands and (until last February, when the markets woke up to the failure of Osbornomics) the UK.

Some of these proposals could be implemented simply by policy changes, either in the ECB or in the Council of Ministers, while others need Treaty changes. This chapter has argued, of course, that changes in economic policy are properly the domain of the normal political battle, rather than 'EU reform'. The ECB, however, is in principle insulated from politics by the Treaty clause which guarantees its independence of all political authority. This central bank independence is for Germany in particular a fundamental and cherished principle, for reasons grounded in German history. But the Eurozone crisis has seen the ECB playing an increasingly powerful role, and it has had to make some highly political choices – with, for instance, substantial distributional consequences. This growing political power is currently exercised with very limited political accountability.

Many models of central bank accountability are available around the world, some of which offer a greater degree of democratic control while stopping short of the old UK model (pre-Gordon Brown) of full political control. Progressives should be insisting that any future round of EU Treaty change looks closely at finding a better balance. At the same time the mission of the ECB should be revisited – the ECB needs a wider mandate, encompassing not only price stability but also the promotion of full employment and supervision of the financial sector. Its duty to 'do what it takes' to defend the currency and prevent speculators hounding out Eurozone Member States going through economic difficulties should go without saying, but sadly needs also to be spelled out

2. Economic coordination – underpowered and misdirected

From coordinating austerity to coordinating growth

Under right-wing leadership, the European Commission and Council have become cheerleaders for pan-European austerity. In response to the crisis they have produced one tightening of Europe's fiscal rules after another, sometimes in intergovernmental agreements, sometimes through legislation. Where legislation has been needed, the outcome has generally been noticeably more nuanced, and with more gestures towards a space for growth and investment, in order to win support from the European Parliament – where social democratic influence is markedly stronger than in the other institutions.

Nevertheless, the Commission and Council have used tightening of fiscal rules in order to force governments to cut spending and raise taxes in the teeth of a recession. A social-democrat-led Europe should revise these rules – through the normal legislative process, no need for 'reform of the EU' – to allow and encourage governments to follow anti-cyclical economic policies.

In particular, the rules should give explicit recognition to the 'golden rule' observed by Gordon Brown when he was Chancellor – a policy that social democrats have championed in the European Parliament since 1995. In EU terms, what that means is that the calculations underlying the fiscal rules of the misleadingly named

The right instrument in the wrong hands

The case of the macroeconomic imbalances procedure

In 2011, as part of its reform of economic governance, the EU adopted a new procedure to identify and correct macroeconomic imbalances. In principle this is a sensible exercise. As this chapter has argued, macroeconomic imbalances – notably trade imbalances among Member States – were at the root of the Eurozone's vulnerability in the wake of the global financial crisis. Yet its implementation shows how it is possible to take a sensible policy principle and turn it into a recipe for disaster. We give just a few illustrations.

To a reasonable observer, the imbalances which need most urgently to be tackled include:

1. a massive shortfall of aggregate demand, marked by high unemployment, depressed output and investment, and high fiscal deficits and public debt.
2. a major dichotomy between the 'periphery' countries that had large current account deficits pre-crisis and those 'core' countries, notably Germany, that had big surpluses. The first group now face the deepest recessions, the highest unemployment and the most difficult fiscal positions; the latter have a comparatively favourable economic situation (though increasingly under pressure from the enduring recession developments in the first group).

If the aim is to rebalance the economy the policy conclusions are obvious. Expansionary monetary policy. Boost demand in the core group. Try to restore competitiveness in the periphery while stimulating growth by combining domestic fiscal consolidation with an externally (European) financed investment offensive.

But this is far from what the European Commission's first application of the Macroeconomic Imbalances Procedure delivered. For a start, Germany – the country with the most serious imbalance – was not considered at all. Why? Because the definitions were rigged to keep it out - so a country's current account was defined as imbalanced if its deficit exceeded 4% of GDP, but a surplus represented 'imbalance' only if it exceeded 6%, neatly excluding Germany, with its chronic surplus standing at just under 6%.

Similarly, using a biased and inaccurate measure of unit labour cost movements, the Commission falsely accused Belgium and France of excessive wage growth while implicitly treating Germany – which has systematically undershot the wage growth needed for balanced economic growth – as the benchmark. Another off-base recommendation was to chide Finland for failing to cut wages to 'fully reflect the drop of productivity during the crisis'. Sensible wage policy is oriented to *medium-run* productivity developments and does not act in the pro-cyclical fashion demanded by the Commission.

Ideology also shows in the choice of areas for promoting structural reform. Some such as financial sector reform are barely raised, while without supporting evidence, labour market 'rigidities' are wrongly held to be critical in resolving macroeconomic imbalances and explaining unemployment and poor productivity trends.

Stability and Growth Pact should exclude investment. The effect would be to give all governments more budgetary room for manoeuvre, and to help reverse the worrying long-term drop in levels of public investment in most of Europe, which is eroding our ability to compete with the best in the world in cutting-edge industries and in research and education.

The EU's fiscal framework should also be redesigned to take symmetrical account of the dangers of weak aggregate demand and over-deflationary budgetary policies, along with the dangers of fiscal laxity which until now have been its single focus.

And the EU's fiscal and economic governance needs to be radically democratised. There must be a far greater role for national Parliaments – in approving National Reform Plans, for instance, before their submission to the European Commission – and in defining the negotiating mandate on major issues, as the Danish Parliament already does and as the House of Commons does not. And the European Parliament should, as it is demanding, be given co-decision over the EU's annual economic and employment policy guidelines (see below). And in addition the unaccountable Troikas of Commission, Central Bank and IMF officials which are imposing savage austerity programmes on the EU's most crisis-hit countries must be dissolved, to restore accountability to the European Parliament and to the national parliaments of the countries in which they operate.

How the system works, and how it could work for us

What the EU's role in coordinating economic policy adds up to in the Treaty is a set of rules limiting budget deficits and public debt; and a procedural framework for coordinating national economic policies through the adoption each year of EU-wide Broad Economic Guidelines and Employment Guidelines. Eurozone members (but not other EU countries) can face sanctions for having excess deficits or debt, or for breaching the Economic Guidelines.[13]

In the Treaty, the Guidelines – and the annual procedure built around them, now known as the European Semester – are policy-neutral, but in subsequent legislation the right has been able, through its majorities in all three EU institutions, to define the preoccupations and targets of economic policy largely in accordance with their own vision – albeit with the thumbprints here and there of the centre left, thanks to the need now and then to win over an obstinate social-democratic minister or two in the Council, and to some significant (but not transformative) victories won by social democrats in the European Parliament.

The European Semester is a hugely flexible, if largely untested, instrument. Among other things, this process defines the objectives of EU economic policy, requires each Member State to set out a National Plan for meeting them, monitors their progress and can – in the case of deficits and debt – applies sanctions if they miss the targets.

The right has used the European Semester to set objectives primarily concerned with fiscal prudence, promotion of flexible labour markets, wage restraint and market liberalisation – reshaping the European economy in keeping with their ideological preferences. Since 2009, they have used it to coordinate the implementation of pan-European austerity. But social democrat majorities could and should use the same mechanism to target the real problems of the European economy, some of which this chapter has already highlighted – such as lack of growth, unemployment, inequality, trade imbalances and chronic under-investment. In a social-democrat-led Europe, these could become the chief targets of economic policy – and so contribute to the progressive reshaping of Europe's economy which is the subject of our next chapter.

Coordinating economic policies, not policing them

Nevertheless, the European Semester, even under social-democrat leadership, would still be essentially about coordination and benchmarking – and there are limits to what it can achieve. As the right has found, even supposedly binding European targets can be ignored by Member States. And to rely on ever tighter rules and heavier sanctions – as the right has done in response to the Euro crisis – sets up an immediate conflict between European objectives and the independent democratic mandate of each Member State government. On democratic grounds, it would be a mistake for progressives to react to the neoliberal and deflationary harness that the right has imposed on European countries by aspiring to construct an over-ambitious progressive harness, binding on 28 governments of every political colour and backed by sanctions for non-performance.

The EU's role of coordinating the fiscal policies of Member States should not be made to bear too much weight. Member States might be expected to coordinate their reflationary or deflationary policies, or their efforts to meet targets on job creation, research or purchasing power, when their governments are convinced of the rightness of that course. When that happens, coordination will enhance the effects of the policies followed by each Member State. But where there are profound disagreements among Member State governments, the EU should not have the role that the right is trying now – on the basis of faulty economics – to give it: to dragoon Member States into adopting a fiscal stance, or a social policy objective, set at the centre. Too much reliance on mandatory targeting could create at best a wide morass of shared competences, where it is not clear to the citizen who's responsible for what; and at worst, a clash of democratic mandates.

Better rules for coordination of fiscal policy should have a more modest, but still important, ambition. So long as the real fiscal instruments of taxing and spending remain – as they are – overwhelmingly in Member States' hands, the key EU role on fiscal policy is to encourage them to coordinate their activities in order to achieve maximum effectiveness.

The first achievement of the changes we have outlined would be that EU rules no longer hinder Member States who want to pursue sensible anti-cyclical policies. Beyond that, by focusing attention on the right economic objectives and indicators, Brussels can send important signals on the direction of economic policy. Under social democratic leadership, the European Semester should be used to set targets for wage movements, poverty reduction, R&D spending and the like, and to benchmark progress. In its co-ordinating role, the EU can encourage a common analysis of the economic situation, help develop a consensus on common goals, and focus attention on the synergies available from – for example – a coordinated fiscal policy stimulus. Non-performing Member States can be named and shamed and a full repertory of 'nudge' techniques deployed. Instead of being an autocratic or technocratic process, the aim would be to make these signals part of a wider political debate and process at European, national and local level.

3. Towards a European fiscal policy

Since there are limits to what can be achieved through closer coordination of Member States' policies, we have to grasp the nettle of what role the EU could or should play directly, through policy instruments of its own, in managing the European economy – given that for the major part of that economy, monetary policy is already fully in ECB hands.

The budgets of Member States, accounting for some 45 per cent of EU GDP, traditionally play an important part in stabilising short-term fluctuations in economic activity. In economic downturns, benefit payments – especially unemployment benefit – increase and tax revenues fall, cushioning the impact of the downturn on businesses and households and preventing a deeper recession.

The EU budget, on the other hand, is far too tiny, at roughly 1 per cent of GDP, to have any significant impact on the economic cycle. In fiscal policy, therefore, the Member States are the only real players, and the most the EU can do is, as we saw above, try to coordinate their action.

There are good reasons why that state of affairs is unsatisfactory. The first concerns stabilisation policy. The further economic integration proceeds, the less effective fiscal policy in an individual Member State becomes. Co-ordination can overcome that problem and give national policies bigger bang for buck – when national governments are willing to be coordinated. But when they are not willing to be coordinated, then Europe lacks powerful instruments of stabilisation, both at national and European level. The difficulties are still greater if some Member States are hit from time to time by so-called 'asymmetric shocks', which affect them much more than the rest of the EU. For smaller and weaker economies in particular, budget constraints may make it difficult for the automatic stabilisers to work.

The second powerful argument why progressives should be arguing for some independent fiscal capacity at European level is distributional. Economics tells us that economic integration, such as the single market or the single currency, potentially yields substantial economic benefits by encouraging trade and investment. But it also tells us that there are likely to be both winners and losers. The political legitimacy, and in the longer term the viability, of the project relies, however, on ensuring a felt-to-be-fair distribution of benefits, including where necessary compensation of losers. Within the Eurozone moreover, as we have seen, economic as well as political stability is at stake, since the Eurozone will not be economically stable if means are not found of achieving convergence in real economic performance.

Within richer industrial countries, the effect of public expenditure and taxation is on average to reduce regional inequalities by around 40 per cent. By contrast, the redistributive power between Member States of the EU budget is very small indeed, probably not wildly different from the 1 per cent estimate in the classic Macdougall Report way back in 1977.[14] The overall size of the EU budget as a percentage of GDP has changed relatively little – from 0.7 per cent to 1 per cent – in the subsequent thirty-six years, despite a radical increase in the tasks transferred to European level by Member States and the enlargement of the EU, from nine European countries of relatively similar levels of economic development to 28 countries with a dramatically wider disparity in living standards. Average income in the UK, for instance, is €27588 per head, compared to €16450 in Poland, €11470 in Bulgaria and, at the other extreme, €68869 per head in Luxembourg.[15] The right may put its faith in market forces and the benefits of open borders to close the gap, but as we have seen, that has not worked so far for the Eurozone. Progressives may want to put less faith in market forces and to demand the creation of more effective policy instruments.

Finally, perhaps the most straightforward argument for a bigger direct EU role in economic governance is the benefits this would bring from economies of scale. In some areas of government activity – major infrastructure or R&D projects are often cited – operating at European level instead of as 28 national governments could deliver major cost savings, cut out duplication and ensure that the technologies employed are interoperable across borders.

Europe does not have the policy instruments needed to tackle underlying economic imbalances. Most acutely, it does not have effective means of promoting real economic convergence, without which monetary union in particular is doomed to instability, with profoundly negative consequences for the whole European economy. Needless to say, the EU certainly does not have effective means of reversing the growth of economic inequality which, we have shown, played a key role in the financial crash of 2008. Nor would most of Europe's present leaders see this as any of Europe's business. But the starting point for progressives should be that all of the structural weaknesses which contributed to the Eurozone crisis, and to the long recession affecting the EU as a whole, need to be addressed as part of the solution.

Almost forty years ago the Macdougall Report found that, to play a significant stabilising role, the EU budget would need to be of the order of at least 5-7 per cent of GDP. The least that can be said about that figure is that it is far from the current political agenda of any Member State. Macdougall also outlined, however, a transitional stage, with an EU budget of 2-2.5 per cent of GDP, with expenditure focused particularly on structural, cyclical, employment and regional policies, with a prime objective of reducing inter-regional differences in capital endowment and productivity. This would be backed by limited powers of borrowing and repayment, to ensure, at the least, that EU budgetary policy did not actually reinforce economic fluctuations. If we want a more stable, growth-oriented European Union, with less economic inequality between the richest and poorest regions, something on this scale is probably a minimum first step.

There's just one problem. Even at 1 per cent of GDP, the EU budget is considered to be such a toxic political issue in Britain that all parties are falling over themselves to call for cuts. If we want a better Europe, it's going to need a bigger budget, but first we have to find a way to detoxify the issue.

British politics and the EU budget

The Labour Party needs urgently to change the terms of the UK debate on the EU budget. So long as the only issue that counts is the size of the budget, Labour will be on the losing side. The winter of 2012-13 is instructive. In October 2012, Labour joined the Tory eurosceptic right to defeat the government, voting for a cut rather than a freeze in the EU's seven-year budgetary framework. Yet a few weeks later it was David Cameron who was lionised by the press for securing cuts in that long-term EU budget – cuts far greater than his own government had imposed at home. Labour will never come first in any EU-bashing contest with the Tories.

The argument that 'if everyone else is tightening their belt, then of course so should the EU' may have powerful doorstep appeal, but it ties Labour in ideological knots. Labour's central economic case against the government is that their austerity politics is damaging and wrong-headed. So how can euro-austerity be seen as a good thing?

Labour's argument should be that, in its present shape, the EU budget is a budget for the past, not the future. In particular it should argue for a reduction in the CAP budget. For historical reasons, 40 per cent of EU spending currently goes on agriculture – down from 70 per cent in the 1980s, and falling to 32 per cent by 2020, but still too much for a sector that creates less than 5 per cent of European jobs. Worse, over 70 per cent of the money goes to Europe's biggest farmers, landowners and agri-industrial conglomerates. HM the Queen is, notoriously, one of the big beneficiaries of this largesse. Add in the environmental damage done by the CAP and the effect of subsidised EU competition on millions of third world subsistence farmers, and the case for radical reform is unanswerable.

The next biggest areas of EU spending, the regional and cohesion funds, get a more mixed press. They are a strategic investment instrument for sustainable growth and competitiveness, designed to even out macro-economic imbalances and promote convergence, but they are often criticised for bureaucracy and poor cost control. This is a result in part of sheer ungovernable scale – the EU structural funds help finance over 600,000 projects, from bridges across the Danube to vocational training in Dublin.

The revenue side of the EU budget is also a dog's breakfast. Contrary to the Treaty, which prescribes that the EU should be wholly financed from its own resources, failure by Member States to agree on a suitable revenue source has led to the situation where by far the major share of the EU budget is funded by an opaque, complex and deeply inequitable system of transfers from national budgets.

The result is an annual EU budget battle geared to the lowest common denominator of national budgetary interests – by no means the same as wider national interest, let alone common European interest – and a polarisation between net payers and net contributors. This foments mutual distrust and encourages some of the runaway beneficiaries of the single market, such as Germany, to see themselves as benighted paymasters of the Union. The European Parliament and Commission have in recent years developed detailed proposals to give the EU its own revenue base and stop it leaching off national budgets. The proposals focus on taxes – like a carbon tax and the FTT – which would target not citizens but polluting industries and the overweening and undertaxed financial sector. The Labour Party has to date been reticent to back these strongly progressive ideas.

Modernisation of the EU budget can become a powerful issue for Labour. The Tories have shown no interest. Their internal war is between 'less Europe' and 'no Europe': their party is no longer able to engage with the project of making a better Europe. The Labour Party needs to lay out a vision of a reformed EU budget, with its own revenues, in which spending is focused on those things that can be done better at European level, whether because of their cross-border impact or because pooling resources reduces duplication and inefficiency and delivers economies of scale. Labour should make clear its ambition to bring CAP spending down; refocus and de-bureaucratise cohesion spending; and shift a far larger share of the EU budget towards investment designed to promote the smarter, greener, more inclusive European economic model outlined in chapter three.

Labour should then be ready to argue that a reformed EU budget needs also to be bigger. Despite all the psychodrama of Cameron's great budget victory, the EU budget of 1 per cent of GDP is in reality tiny compared to the UK budget, at 37 per cent of GDP, or the US federal budget, at 24 per cent. On economic stability, efficiency and redistributive grounds, Labour should be championing a bigger and better EU budget.

We should not, however, put all our eggs in one basket. The intellectual case for a bigger and better EU budget is strong, but the battle to change minds will be long and tough. Faster progress may be made by picking a fight on specific policies where the issues are clearer and more concrete and the case for action more easily understood. That is why, in the last two sections of this chapter, we propose two areas – unemployment benefit and corporation tax – where a European initiative would help tackle the urgent problems of the European economy and where progressives should be ready to engage the debate.

An EU-wide minimum employment benefit

To improve economic stability in the EU, and above all to reduce the risk and severity of future recessions, we need stronger anti-cyclical mechanisms at the European level.

As economies become more closely integrated, national monetary and fiscal policies (even without a single currency) become less effective in counteracting economic fluctuations. A national government in the EU which cuts taxes or raises spending, for instance, to boost economic activity, sees much of the money flow straight out of the national economy in the form of increased imports. And national stimulus action can worsen the budget problems created by the downturn.

Within the Eurozone, of course, there is no national monetary policy, and the potential disadvantages of a single currency are magnified if Member States are in different phases of their business cycle: that's when one size of monetary policy doesn't fit all. The loose monetary policy that suits an economy in a downturn will cause overheating and inflation in a neighbour that's already close to full capacity. So EMU requires powerful mechanisms to synchronise the business cycles of its members.

Many possible ways could be envisaged to strengthen the EU's defences against business cycles and economic shocks, but one of the most effective, and most progressive, would be a Europe-wide minimum employment benefit. This idea has already been placed on the EU agenda, by François Hollande among others. And detailed work has been done on the design of a possible scheme in the European Commission's Directorate-General for Employment, under the leadership of one of the few socialist Commissioners.[16]

This is not the place for detailed blueprints, but an EU-wide core benefit for short-term unemployment would have many advantages. Payments to unemployed workers would rise in states suffering high unemployment and fall where unemployment was low. Each Member State would be free to supplement the EU benefit in keeping with national traditions – higher rates, longer eligibility etc.

An EU unemployment benefit would work automatically and immediately to dampen economic fluctuations, without delays for political negotiation, legislation or budgetary changes. The protection available to citizens would become less vulnerable to the budgetary difficulties of a Member State in recession – and a minimum benefit would be guaranteed to Europeans in even the poorest Member States. Because the money would go straight to one of the neediest groups it would be both socially progressive – a dramatic change in the way in which the EU impacts on people's lives – and a highly efficient economic boost, since the less well-off tend to spend rather than save.

At present, Britain is not part of the debate that is developing around ideas for an EU-wide anti-cyclical instrument, because under a Europhobic Cameron government British participation is unthinkable. But a more stable EU, which offers greater protection to its citizens in time of hardship, is something we should be fighting for. The Labour Party could and should become a strong voice in favour of an ambitious and socially progressive solution.

A common European corporation tax – an end to bidding wars for investment

Between 1995 and 2011 the average rate of corporate taxation in the EU fell from 35.3 per cent to 23.1 per cent, continuing a trend which the EU statistical office Eurostat traces back to the 1980s, and reflecting a comparable, but less marked, trend worldwide. Eurostat reports that the tax burden on labour, by contrast, started growing strongly in the early 1970s and has continued to grow, albeit more slowly, ever since.

These trends come as no surprise. With the dramatic opening of global markets and the dismantling of tariff and regulatory barriers in recent decades, and the growth in the scale of corporate cross-border activity, companies enjoy an unprecedented freedom either to site production in the most favourable location, or to use transfer pricing and other accounting practices to shift taxable profits to low-tax jurisdictions.

The change is particularly marked in the EU, with its highly integrated single market. With corporate taxation a wholly national responsibility, and any EU action needing unanimous support of all 27 Member States, the pressure on governments to compete for footloose capital by lowering company taxation has been intense.

The result has been a shift in the tax burden from capital towards labour. This needs to be reversed by putting an end to fiscal bidding wars among European governments. As one part of a rebalancing of the tax system – along with support for a Financial Transactions Tax and a major onslaught against tax evasion and tax havens – we need a European framework for corporation tax, establishing a common tax base and setting EU-wide minimum rates. With a stronger tax base, we strengthen the power of public authorities to reshape the economy in pursuit of a wider political, social and environmental vision.

WHAT KIND OF EUROPE?

What sort of economic governance we want depends ultimately on what sort of Europe we want. This chapter has set out the outlines of a reformed governance which would remove the deflationary bias of present fiscal rules; curb the power of financial markets to derail economic recovery; address the problems of inequality and diverging real economic performance that underlie the vulnerability of the

European economy; and bring both monetary and fiscal policy under more effective democratic control. Every proposal made is already the subject of fierce scrutiny and debate in Brussels. Some, such as 'Eurobonds', the financial transactions tax (FTT) or a European unemployment benefit, for which social democrats have argued in vain for years, are now at the centre of political debate. The FTT, once derided as impractical and of the loony left, is now being introduced by eleven Member States, including seven with centre-right governments. Arguments can be won in Brussels and the political ground is shifting. It is time for British progressives to join the debate.

NOTES

1. Figures were not available for Greece.
2. The 'German solution' to the lack of domestic purchasing power has been, in addition, to seek to gain demand via rising net exports. This too merely postponed the problem, as it laid the foundations for the Eurozone trade imbalances, which, as we shall see, have played a big part in the Eurozone crisis.
3. When the Bourbon kings returned to the throne some years after the French Revolution, they were famously said to have learned nothing and forgotten nothing. In the same spirit, the speeches of EU Economics Commissioner Ollie Rehn today echo perfectly the spirit of Herbert Hoover in 1929.
4. For which quarter their respective GDP is set at 100 in the graph.
5. The most recent and exhaustive of these, from the IMF, is available at: www.imf.org/external/pubs/ft/wp/2013/wp1301.pdf/. For an analysis of fiscal austerity in Europe see the *Independent Annual Growth Survey*, ECLM, IMK and OFCE 2013: www.iags-project.org/documents/iags_report2013.pdf/.
6. This is the relationship that economists call the fiscal multiplier. The IMF famously admitted in 2012 that it had substantially under-estimated this multiplier – and therefore under-estimated the damage done by austerity. The European Commission is still in denial.
7. For a more detailed explanation and discussion see A. Watt, 'A role for wage-setting in a new EU economic governance architecture after the crisis', in FEPS (ed), *Austerity is not the solution! Contributions to European economic policy*, 2012: www.feps-europe.eu/assets/9549a450-68b1-479f-9ab9-9bba1bdff0c0/austerity-is-not-the-solution.pdf/
8. For more detail, see the *Independent Annual Growth Survey* 2013, chapter 4.
9. In the critical years 2010 and 2011 even social-democratic governments in Spain, Greece and Portugal were, given the situation facing those

countries, powerless to oppose the diktats issued by the EU institutions and conservative-led Germany and France and their allies.

10. The no-bailout clause was inserted in the Treaty to guard against 'moral hazard' – the risk that governments will overspend if they know that at the end of the day the ECB will bail them out.
11. The European Stability Mechanism is a financial institution set up in 2012, primarily to provide financial support to Euro area governments in difficulties, and backed by capital from all Eurozone states.
12. To overcome the vulnerabilities in the European banking sector and the negative feedback loops between individual Member State budgets and some of their banks, and to respond to the cross-border operations of many banks, the EU is developing a banking union, whose main elements are a common rulebook for European banks, a single supervisory mechanism, a common deposit guarantee scheme and a common system for winding up failing banks.
13. But not the Employment Guidelines, which are purely voluntary.
14. Report of the Macdougall Study Group on the Role of Public Finance in European Integration, 1977. The report was the outcome of three years of analysis by a group of independent economists appointed by the European Commission and chaired by Sir Donald Macdougall, the former head of the UK Government Economic Service.
15. Figures are adjusted for differences in purchasing power. Source: World Bank
16. DG Employment, in effect the EU's employment ministry, is led by one of the European Commission's few socialist Commissioners, Laszlo Andor of Hungary.

3. Reshaping the European economy

Derek Reed

Radical change is needed in the European economic model, to ensure that growth, once restored, will be sustainable, and will help build a better life for all. The European Union, in partnership with the Member States, has an important contribution to make to that economic shift, but its policies will have to change dramatically.

Two decades of thwarted efforts

At the turn of the millennium, the EU set itself ambitious goals of industrial, social and environmental transformation. The Lisbon Strategy, launched at a time when a majority of EU prime ministers were Socialist, had the huge ambition of making Europe 'the most competitive and dynamic knowledge-based economy in the world capable of sustainable economic growth with more and better jobs and greater social cohesion'. The strategy prioritised R&D, innovation, the knowledge economy and social and environmental renewal, but it relied to a very large extent on coordinating action at Member State level, rather than focusing on those things which the EU itself could do, and it quickly fell victim to changing priorities, as majorities in the EU institutions shifted to the right. Since 2010, the Lisbon Strategy's successor, known as EU 2020, has fared no better, and for the familiar reasons – lack of political will, insufficient resources and the absence of the tools to do the job.

For millions of Europeans, life was not improving even before the 2008 financial sector meltdown. That is why we need an economic model that serves a wider vision of human welfare than the bottom-line obsessions of neoliberalism. The European Commission, like the Tories at home, tells us that globalisation gives us no choice, that to compete in the global economy we need to work harder and longer and accept the erosion of social norms – like secure jobs and good pensions – that were won by previous generations in times of lesser prosperity. But globalisation is just the excuse, the real problem is politics.

Policy-driven changes such as labour market reform and financial deregulation, together with the increasingly transnational scale of big business, have produced a shift of power and wealth from workers to employers and from public authorities to private firms. And within the corporate sector, the size and power of finance have grown at the expense of manufacturing and non-financial services.

This is a model which has encouraged the pursuit of short-term profit to the detriment of social responsibility and jobs. Investment, both public and private, has fallen across much of Europe: from 23 per cent of GDP in Germany in the early 1990s to 17.5 per cent now; from 25 per cent in Spain to 18 per cent now; and from 26 per cent in Finland to 19 per cent now;[1] while R&D represents a pitiful 1.9 per cent of GDP for the EU as a whole. Little wonder that Europe and Britain are falling behind our international competitors, when most of our trading partners spend close to 3 per cent or more of GDP on R&D – 3.5 per cent in Japan, 2.8 per cent in the USA, 3 per cent in Switzerland. Growing corporate power has delivered an era of excessive profits, the emergence of a new class of super-rich; corporate rip-offs of the consumer; tax evasion on a global scale; and opportunistic relocation of production in pursuit of quick profits and tax breaks.

The neoliberal economic model has delivered insecurity, instability and inequality, culminating in the global disaster of 2008. Even by its own narrow economic criteria it has performed worse, not better, than the less market-oriented welfare capitalism that it replaced. Europe needs a different vision, in which the objective of economic policy is both a stronger economy and a better society. That will require a rebalancing of the economy, above all in two dimensions. We need to rebalance the goals of economic policy, in order to find a better balance between economic, social and environmental objectives and between the short-term and the longer-term. And to achieve that we need a second rebalancing, this time of economic power.

A WIDER VISION – PURSUING A *EUROPE OF EXCELLENCE*

In our vision for Europe, social and environmental progress are not a cost which must be cut in the interests of competitive success; they are an essential element in Europe's strategy for competitive success. To achieve this vision requires an economic model which embraces a wider range of interests and objectives – through counter-acting short-termism and developing a strategic framework for key industries; through changes in the tax system and in corporate governance to favour long-term investment over short-term speculation; and through enabling a range of stakeholders – businesses, employees, communities and public authorities – to work together for solutions to economic challenges.

Europe must, of course, make its way in the world. Economic models which fail to compete do not generally endure. But our Europe would base its competitive strategy on the pursuit of excellence. Investors would choose Europe for its skilled workforce, its vibrant universities and research centres, its first-class communications and public services, its efficient public administration, its social peace, its quality of life. These are the source of Europe's competitive edge and can help build the agile, fast-moving companies of the twenty-first century. Europe has no future trying to compete as a low-cost producer in a global economy, with a race to the bottom of social and employment standards and with poverty incomes.

TACKLING CONCENTRATIONS OF POWER

Increasing concentration of economic power creates new scope for abuse. In a global world of powerful and footloose multinational corporations, and a growing dominance by international financial markets, the citizen relies more than ever on strong public institutions to ensure that abuses are curtailed, democracy safeguarded, and growing prosperity widely shared, and that rising wealth leads to higher social and environmental standards and a better quality of life for all.

Action at European level is our best shot at tackling the abuses and the excessive power of global corporations. A single European country, acting alone, will struggle to confront the power of the capital markets and credit ratings agencies to cow governments; the power of over-mighty press barons to erode a free and plural media, intimidate politicians and put themselves beyond the reach of the law; or the power of Google and Facebook to invade privacy and accumulate vast quantities of data on our private lives. Through common action at European level, the balance of forces can be decisively changed. Putting everything on hold until some elusive global agreement is reached at the G20 and then implemented is nothing more than a gambit for procrastination. The choice is action at the European level or it is inaction.

Reshaping the European economic model is not a job to be done at the European level alone. Many of the necessary policy instruments are rightly at national level, and what is done at European level must respect the political choices of each Member State, whether governed from the right or from the left. An extension of EU powers is not on the cards and is not absolutely necessary. But the EU's existing powers, used in the service of a more progressive economic vision, could begin to build a more inclusive, more sustainable and also more prosperous Europe. The strongest argument for action at European level as being crucial to achieving real change is that business has become European. The single market is not the product of Brussels bureaucrats, but the natural evolution of industrial society, driven by the decisions of thousands of managers and entrepreneurs who have recognised that they can only be competitive through European integration.

There is a question of urgency here as well. Shoring up Europe's social and economic model and seeking to promote internationally higher standards is easier when you still account for between 20 per cent and 30 per cent of global wealth and a very high proportion of international trade. As our economic pre-eminence shrinks, so our 'soft power' to reshape the relationship between economy and society and to push for responsible capitalism will diminish.

SIX POLICIES FOR A NEW ECONOMIC MODEL

The theme of rebalancing needs to be reflected in many areas of EU policy – in R&D and innovation; in a more diverse, plural and independent media; and in higher standards of data protection – to give just a few examples. Big changes are also needed at both EU and national level in corporate governance, to open up boardrooms to a wider range of voices, to give statutory effect to issues of corporate social responsibility, and to raise standards of company reporting and transparency – notably regarding the profits made and taxes paid in each tax jurisdiction in which they operate. An important first step was achieved in February 2013 when the European Parliament pushed through new rules imposing these requirements (from 2015) on the banking sector – in the teeth of opposition, needless to say, from the UK government. More is needed and can best be done Europe-wide.

There is not space here to examine the changes that a progressive European majority should make in every area of policy, but the rest of this chapter sets out what could be achieved in six areas crucial to the construction of a better socio-economic model:

- Regulation of financial markets
- Cracking down on tax evasion and avoidance
- Labour market reform
- Research and development
- Energy strategy
- The digital economy.

The first three of these are horizontal issues which condition the mode of operation and terms of engagement of capital and labour as a whole. The fourth, also horizontal, is a key to modernisation and rebalancing of Britain's industrial base. The last two are sectoral strategies, for two sectors whose role in the modern economy gives them wider significance, and which illustrate the role the EU could play in a new strategy of re-industrialisation, in Britain and across Europe.

On most of these questions the battle lines have already been drawn in Brussels. On some, the transparent failure of conservative orthodoxy has begun to shift the terms of debate. And in each of these policy areas an achievable shift in the balance of political forces offers real hope of much more substantial progress.

TAMING FINANCIAL MARKETS

After the catastrophic outcome of their tenure as masters of the universe, financial institutions need to rediscover their humbler historical role as a secure repository of savings and as providers of funds to finance productive investment, mortgage finance and the like.

Chapter two catalogued the reasons for the financial sector's growth to overweening power and the disastrous consequences of its excesses for the rest of us. It reminded us that in 1929, the last time the world experienced a comparable crash, it marked a political turning-point on both sides of the Atlantic: the New Deal in the USA, the rise of Keynesianism and the mixed economy in the UK and Europe. These were the foundation stones of a political settlement that endured until the late 1970s and produced the longest sustained economic growth and greatest narrowing of economic inequality in history.

The crash of 2008 has by comparison been followed by something like business as usual, or almost. On one level, that might seem paradoxical. The European Union, for example, is in the middle of – by any standards – a massive programme of legislation to strengthen supervision; to make banks safer by raising capital and liquidity requirements; to bring in stricter rules for credit ratings agencies; to clamp down on market abuse and insider trading; to regulate hedge funds and private equity; and to improve transparency and investor protection, notably for complex and exotic investment practices like credit default swaps and collateralised debt obligations, which, it turned out, even the financial markets did not understand.

What has been achieved in the EU's reform of financial sector regulation and supervision was urgent and necessary and should be saluted. It establishes a new regime which covers the whole EU, the biggest single economy in the world and home to twelve of the world's twenty top financial centres (including London, by many measures the biggest of all). No prizes for guessing how much of this would have been achieved if we had relied on action in Britain alone, in thrall to the City of London.

And yet. The sheer size of the financial sector continues to be at a historic high, swollen by a massive implicit subsidy from taxpayers – labelled the 'too big to fail' subsidy by the Bank of England. In Britain alone the subsidy is estimated at £34 billion a year. Banks and financial institutions continue to be over-leveraged because tax systems and remuneration practices encourage high-risk behaviour. Pay and profits in the financial sector have bounced back from the 2008 crash, and are wildly out of line with those in other sectors, in large part rewarding what Lord Adair Turner, the last Chair of the Financial Services Authority, has called 'socially useless activities'.

Moreover, the power of financial markets is now the explicit and avowed justification for pan-European austerity policies. That deserves a moment's reflection. In the 1970s and 1980s Labour and social democratic governments were told that they could not pursue economic stimulus policies because they would cause inflation, or provoke a balance-of-payments crisis. Even the right can no longer make this case with much conviction. In April 2013, the IMF's World Economic Outlook said that the risk of serious inflationary problems in Europe was remote and that a temporary overshooting of central banks' inflation targets was not cause for concern. Instead, Olli Rehn – European Economics Commissioner, arch-priest of austerity, Paul Krugman's 'Rehn of terror' – offers only one reason to oppose an economic stimulus which could finance investment, create jobs and restore hope. It can't be done, says Olli (and Angela, David and George), because it would spook the financial markets. Another fine mess he's got us into. Only the power of the financial markets stands between Europe and growth.

Clearly, reform of financial markets is unfinished business. Christine Lagarde, head of the IMF, said in April 2013 that the oversized banking model of too-big-to-fail is more dangerous than ever, and called for more comprehensive regulation. The European social democrats, who have taken a lead on this issue since well before the 2008 crash, are calling for more radical action to separate the casino banking of the investment banks from high street banking; to clamp down more effectively on remuneration patterns that incentivise excessive risk-taking; to fully regulate shadow banking; to eliminate the tax and regulatory havens which are integral to the business models of much of the financial sector; and to establish a bank resolution and recovery regime that allows failing banks to be wound up without taxpayer bailouts.[2]

British progressives should back this agenda, and they should insist on Britain levying the Financial Transactions Tax. Once it is established, and the wolf-cries of the vested interests have been exposed as bogus, the FTT can become a powerful tool to reshape the financial sector and to generate truly substantial revenues for causes better than funding bankers' Learjets. And Britain, with the biggest financial sector, would reap by far the biggest revenues, to ease budgetary problems and fund investment and world-class public services.

CRACKING DOWN ON TAX EVASION AND AVOIDANCE

Thanks to globalisation, light-touch regulation and the disproportionate growth of the global financial sector, we are living in a golden age of tax evasion and avoidance. A report produced in February 2012 for the social democrat group in the European Parliament estimated that it was costing national governments in the EU €1 trillion a year – far more than the combined budget deficits of all 27 EU Member States.[3] A determined attack on tax fraud by corporations and the super-rich would go a very long way towards restoring public finances across Europe without the austerity which is destroying jobs, killing hope and laying waste to living standards and public services.

The European social democrats used the tax report to launch a campaign calling for a halving of the €1 trillion tax gap. By the end of 2012 the European Commission had produced a cautious but useful action plan on combating tax fraud and tax havens. The Parliament's response, drafted by Slovenian social democrat Mojca Kekuš, pushes for more radical action – proposing that financial institutions which assist their clients in tax fraud should lose their banking licences; calling for stronger EU legislation on taxation of offshore accounts; requiring companies to publish their revenue, profits and taxation figures country by country; and strengthening registration of companies and trusts.[4]

Britain and some other Member States have done their best to obstruct even the Commission's modest action plan, but a leak in April 2013 from the UK's oversized offshore financial industry, revealing the names of thousands of high-profile tax dodgers from the worlds of business and politics, has put defenders of the status quo on the back foot. Within a week of the front-page revelations of tax-dodging, the EU's five biggest Member States, including Britain, had signed an agreement on increased exchange of tax information, and pledged to push for this increased cooperation among tax authorities to become a worldwide standard; and Labour MEP Arlene McCarthy had succeeded in pushing through a tough new European law on accounting standards for multinationals which will help expose both corruption and tax evasion.

Since action across national borders will inevitably be the key to tackling tax evasion and tax havens, progressives should be clamouring for the European Union to take the lead. We should be asking for common European criteria that identify tax havens and serve as the basis for a public blacklist. Strict standards of transparency should be required of any tax haven, on pain of heavy economic sanctions. Companies operating in Europe should be subject to a code of conduct on tax transparency, and those which breach the code should be barred from access to state aid, research funds or public procurement contracts. All beneficial owners of companies or trusts, and all nominee intermediaries, should be disclosed, along with the names of all directors. Full company accounts should be on public record for all companies, and there should be an online European register of companies and trusts, available for public inspection. The European Union should be responsible for negotiating all bilateral tax agreements with third countries, so that those, like Switzerland, with secretive banking laws are no longer able to play off one EU country against another.

Any serious attempt to ensure that the rich pay their taxes like the rest of us will provoke howls of outrage, massive lobbying and threats to relocate outside Europe. Progressives must face down this blackmail. There is a long history of threats of self-imposed exile by high rollers, which is par for the course whenever there is a prospect of social or economic change. The Emirates, the Cayman Islands and Belize may themselves begin to feel the pinch now that the political world is waking up to the massive scale of tax avoidance. And European governments should show solidarity when they start tackling the problems of evasion, not offer to roll out red carpets to spivs and rock stars past their sell-by date.

There is also a reputational issue here for the UK. London is now widely recognised as by far the largest European centre of sophisticated corporate tax avoidance, making Cyprus and Malta seem like exemplars of financial probity and transparency. In the long run the tainted image of the City will make its viability – currently so central to the UK economy – vulnerable.

NOW THAT'S WHAT I CALL LABOUR MARKET REFORM

Reform was once a left-wing word. But mention labour market reform in a Labour Party or trade union meeting today and people shiver and cross themselves. That's what decades of market liberalisation and social democratic 'triangulation' (that Clintonite memorial to short-term advantage and long-term disaster) will do.

For years neoliberals have made the running on labour market issues in London and Brussels – though not, for instance, in the Nordic countries, whose more progressive and more successful model was first ignored, then co-opted and denatured, by the European Commission.

It wasn't ever thus. For much of its history, the European Union was a driving force of progress in the workplace. Groundbreaking European laws have brought big advances for Europe's citizens, regardless of where they worked: 1975, equal pay for men and women; 1989, health and safety at work – derided now but responsible for saving thousands of lives; 1994, the European Works Council Directive; 1996, protection (of a sort) for workers posted across EU borders; 2000, race and sex discrimination and equality at work. British workers have benefited doubly: directly, where European law has raised UK employment standards; and indirectly, where it has raised standards in the rest of the EU to UK levels, preventing downward competitive pressures in Britain. European law is a vital tool to shield a common industrial strategy based on high workplace standards against cost-cutting and short-term profit. That, of course, is why so many Tories and so many British tabloids just hate the EU.

But things have changed since 2000. With a shift of political control towards the right, the flow of progressive legislation has largely dried up. Unemployment, precarious work and inequality are on the increase. Competitive pressures at work are ever more intense. More and more migrant workers are employed under abusive conditions. Real wages in many occupations are stagnating or falling. Young workers, denied proper jobs, go from one work placement to another, without a proper employment contract. Instead of the serious apprenticeships which have proved indispensable in sustaining the productivity of the German workforce and that country's competitiveness, all that many others seem to offer is unpaid or ill paid work experience stacking shelves at supermarkets, which is good news for the stores' short-term profits and for government employment statistics, less welcome for the experienced staff whose livings are threatened or for the young 'trainees' who gain no new skills and no income for their pains.

The European left has an alternative labour market agenda, in tune with our values and in tune with the modern *Europe of Excellence* competitive strategy outlined above – a strategy built on the recognition that in a world of global competition, Europe's one enduring competitive edge is its labour force, and that the cornerstone of our competitive strategy must be a labour force which is highly educated, trained, adaptable and motivated. What is lacking, at least until the 2014 European elections, is sufficient votes to make the left's alternative agenda count.

A progressive programme of labour market reform would serve crucial economic and social objectives. It would empower workers, open up access to the labour market, raise living standards and improve working conditions; enhance Europe's global competitiveness; improve macro-economic stability; and make it harder, in a future economic crisis, for the burden of adjustment to be imposed on working people.

Keeping up with a fast-moving world

In a world of ever more mobile capital, the most durable source of competitive advantage is the labour force. Europe's most precious competitive asset is therefore a workforce which is well educated and trained, and has the autonomy and motivation to respond to constant change. This, and the need to overcome the barriers which keep many people out of the workforce, should be the guiding principles of European workplace and labour market policies.

It is no accident that the Nordic countries are among the EU's highest economic achievers. They have sought to provide real job security by keeping skills up-to-date, while investing heavily in active labour market policy, social dialogue and a social security system that does not leave anybody behind.

Under conservative leadership the European Commission has appropriated from the Nordic model its ugly name of flexicurity, while filleting it of those elements which provided security, and turning it into a hated euphemism for erosion of employment rights. The left needs to get behind a progressive model of active labour market policies, income support and life-long learning which would make a reality of the security enjoyed by Nordic workers.

Modern competitive conditions require a rethink of the concept of flexibility. In a fast-moving global economy the most successful companies will be the most agile. Those which rely on shifting pools of short-term workers, on detailed rulebooks and limited workforce autonomy, will lose out to companies whose workers have ties of loyalty and motivation, based on job security and decent working conditions; who have the experience, training and authority to show initiative and exercise creativity. That is why the most successful companies will be those which have built high-trust industrial relations systems.

The obsessions of old-fashioned deregulators – freedom to hire and fire, short-term contracts, minimising employers' obligations to the workforce – are incompatible with the workforce adaptability, initiative and responsibility which are now the key to success. To equip the British and European labour markets for this new world will require action both on individual rights and on the collective voice of employees in the workplace.

Secure jobs at decent wages

One part of the labour market reform programme needed in Europe concerns the pay and conditions of individual workers, and a good place to start is wage levels. European social democrats rightly call for a European framework agreement on minimum wages. This would leave Member States free to choose their own instruments – whether statutory as in Britain or through collective bargaining as, for example, in Sweden – but each national minimum, after a transitional period, would have to reach at least of 60 per cent of average earnings. In Britain, for instance, that would mean a phased rise from £6.19 per hour to around £7.80.

The most pervasive and retrograde change in the British and European labour markets has been the emergence of a dual labour market of haves and have-nots, through the proliferation of all sorts of precarious employment – casualisation, agency work, short-term or zero-hours contracts, internships often unpaid, bogus self-employment, use of sub-contracting chains to evade employers' obligations.

Young workers are the prime victims of insecure employment and of sheer lack of jobs. Faced with mounting evidence of mass youth unemployment, the Council of Ministers in February 2013 finally acted on another longstanding social democrat demand, adopting a European Youth Guarantee, to give every under-25, after four months unemployment, the right to either a job or training. It's a start, but not much more, because the ministers voted only €6 billion for a programme which the ILO has calculated would cost a minimum of €20 billion a year – to tackle a problem that's costing the European economy €130 billion a year.

To reshape the labour market in favour of employees Europe needs an ambitious legislative programme: to extend to all employees the main rights and protections enjoyed by those with a standard full-time contract;

define a common core of workers' rights, independent of contractual status; clarify the responsibilities of contractors to their workforce through joint and several liability; and establish a quality framework for internships and apprenticeships. In many countries, including the UK, we need greatly improved standards of enforcement, to clamp down on abusive employment and breaches of employment law.

Progressives should also give a new priority to better work-life balance, through more ambitious parental leave and maternity leave provisions. Above all, Britain needs to reverse its position as the chief opponent of the EU directive on working time, on which the European Parliament submitted widely applauded and flexible proposals in 2008. Their adoption – supported even by conservative governments elsewhere in the EU – was regrettably blocked by the then Labour government, under pressure from the CBI and after systematic misrepresentation in the media.

A European voice for employees

The second pillar of labour market reform must focus on strengthening the collective bargaining position of European workers. Trade union activity at national level is undermined by the ability of multinational businesses to play off one national workforce against another. Proposals from European social democrats and trade unions to extend rights to cross-border information and consultation have been gathering dust for many years now.

Industrial relations systems must be re-oriented towards anticipating and managing change, to create a faster-moving European economy and a new confidence among Europe's workforce that change is not a threat but an opportunity.

An EU law of 1994 provided for European Works Councils in transnational corporations above 1000 employees, but only by agreement of both management and unions. Of the 2400 companies potentially covered, only around 900 currently have Works Councils, and their powers are limited. Progressives should insist on a revised law to give workers a stronger voice and to ensure the spread of Works Councils to all eligible companies.

In January 2013 the European Parliament adopted proposals developed by the Spanish socialist MEP Alejandro Cercas to create a European legal framework for the anticipation and management of industrial restructuring, ensuring early information and consultation, retraining where needed for employees, and economic regeneration for blighted communities. There is no prospect that the current Commission or Council of Ministers will act on the Parliament's proposals. They should be a priority for progressives after the Euro-elections of 2014.

Common rights come before a single market

Changes are also needed to ensure that the principles of the single market cannot be used to over-ride fundamental rights at work, or to permit different terms and conditions within a single workplace for workers of different national origins. In a series of judgements starting with the notorious Laval case of 2007, the European Court of Justice has upheld the principle that companies operating across EU borders and bringing in workers from another Member State could employ them on the terms and conditions of their country of origin – bypassing those that applied in the host country.

The ECJ ruling put the principle of the freedom of cross-border commerce above the principles of equal pay and conditions, rights of collective bargaining and the right to strike and picket. For trade unionists, this has become a deeply negative symbol of the EU's values, and has helped make cross-border migration and the undercutting of local labour markets into a toxic political and social issue – much to the detriment of the Labour Party and progressive parties throughout Europe, but catnip to UKIP who have found it their strongest issue on the doorstep.

European trade unions and progressives in the European Parliament have worked together on proposals for a European Social Progress Clause which would safeguard the inviolability of fundamental labour rights and the principle of equal pay and conditions for equal work. Similar protections should also be extended to workers coming temporarily from outside the EU, for example as seasonal workers or through postings within multinational firms.

The issue of defining the limits to single market rules goes wider. Where the European Commission or the Court of Justice invokes single market principles to over-ride the wider objectives of mutual support, collective security and solidarity; to undermine local autonomy in the provision of public services; to put at risk national labour market traditions; or to curtail fundamental rights such as the right to strike – social democrats should legislate at European level to curb this interference, restore local autonomy and preserve the strength and diversity of Europe's social model. The left should always argue that where regions and Member States take measures to create jobs, they must not be thwarted by superior principles of the internal market and opposition to state aids. Neoliberals have forgotten that the internal market should be the instrument of policy not a pagan deity before which all must genuflect.

PLAYING TO OUR STRENGTHS – EUROPEAN R&D POLICY

The damage done to Britain's productive base by Margaret Thatcher has still to be undone. It is true that, following the crisis, Peter Mandelson as Business Secretary revived the idea of an activist industrial policy, and the Coalition has continued in the same vein. But the resources made available are so limited that it amounts to little more than rhetoric. Britain's manufacturing sector is not as weak as people think; but its export performance remains muted, despite a massive devaluation of the pound since 2008.

A future Labour government will want to tackle this problem with greater vigour. A broader, stronger productive base will be essential to reducing Britain's corrosive over-dependence on the financial sector. The European Union will be a huge ally in this process. European R&D policies, in particular, play to one of Britain's greatest strengths. They can provide a big boost to the efforts of a Labour government to develop in Britain the high-value, knowledge-based industries of the future.

The Tories, and even some Labour front-benchers, have at times argued that the EU's state aid rules, which prevent governments from distorting competition in the EU by backing their own businesses, are overly restrictive – and they may need to be finessed, through the normal legislative processes, to give nation states more room for manoeuvre. But the bigger picture is of EU policies and instruments which complement national efforts, and indeed are essential to them.

In its bid to create a modern productive economy the UK starts with a big advantage. It has an outstanding research and science capacity. With 1 per cent of the world's population and 4 per cent of its researchers, it produces 6 per cent of the world's academic articles, and crucially, 14 per cent of those which are most highly cited. Its research-intensive universities are among those topping the world rankings. This is a huge national asset – one that any government would want to nurture – and it is increasingly dependent on EU funding. For example, the EU currently provides 12 per cent of Cambridge's research funding and this is expected to rise to around 20 per cent. The situation is similar for other Russell Group universities.

The EU awards its funding on the basis of excellence alone. Because of this, due to the strength of its research base, Britain receives more funding per head of population than almost any other Member State. It has received around £3.2 billion so far under the current EU research framework programme (FP7). Indeed, when it comes to this part of the EU budget, Britain is a net recipient, not a net payer.

And it's not just about the money. No country today can be a research leader without a dense web of connections with centres of excellence in many parts of the world, including Europe. Moreover, because the selection pool is bigger, competition for European funding is greater. Winning so much of it hugely enhances the international profile of UK universities and helps to attracts top researchers to the UK.

The new EU research funding programme, which is called Horizon 2020, will potentially do even more to underpin British industrial policy. Due to be launched at the beginning of 2014, it will support close-to-market activity, such as demonstrators and pilot lines, as well as public private partnerships in areas such as nanotechnology, biotechnology and innovative medicines.

Britain has often struggled to capitalise on its own inventions. For example, the new 'wonder material' graphene was developed at Manchester University but, up to now, the vast majority of patents relating to it have been filed in the US, China and South Korea. The EU's new 1 billion euro academic-industrial partnership – the 'Graphene Flagship' – should help to get the UK and Europe back into the race.

So, if used strategically, EU instruments can support a renewed drive to rebalance the British economy. But the story does not end there: because modern industrial policy is not just about the supply side – i.e. increasing the flow of new technologies; it is also about the demand side – i.e. ensuring that there is a ready market for these technologies. With public finances under pressure, it is vital to persuade private finance to invest. Companies are sitting on large piles of cash but do not have the confidence to invest. They need to be persuaded that, if they develop new technologies, there will be a big, integrated, European market into which they can sell them. This means putting in place the right regulations and standards, commonly agreed at EU – or world – level. It can also be achieved through a much bolder and imaginative use of public procurement budgets across the EU. If Britain loses its influence in Europe, it will not be able to make any of this happen.

In short, if Britain distances itself from – or leaves – the European Union, the task of reviving its industrial base and finally escaping from the Thatcher legacy will be a great deal more difficult.

A TRANSFORMATIONAL ENERGY STRATEGY

Europe is at an energy cross-roads. A small number of strategic decisions, which must be taken in the next few years, will have long-term consequences for our future competitiveness and prosperity.

Today, Europe and the UK are reliant on huge quantities of expensive imports of polluting fossil fuels, and at the mercy of volatile and rising global prices; and the UK's reserves of North Sea oil and gas are rapidly depleting. In the last ten years Britain has gone from being a net energy exporter to being 25 per cent import-dependent – a loss of over £20 billion to our balance of payments. For the EU as a whole, imports of fossil fuels are running at €350 billion a year – that's €700 a year per head of population.

The choice facing Europe is stark. One option is to carry on with business as usual, becoming ever more reliant on imports, and more vulnerable to world energy prices and political shocks – and beholden to the unstable and despotic regimes of many resource-rich countries. This will mean spending trillions of Euros a year on energy imports, propping up undemocratic regimes, soft-pedalling on human rights abuses and compromising our foreign policy autonomy. The massive expenditure on imported fuel will contribute little to investment, jobs or growth at home. That is the path Britain and Europe are currently on, supported by right-wing majorities among EU governments, the European Commission and the directly elected European Parliament.

We need a better way. Starting with the European elections in 2014, the election of a progressive majority would open the way to a greener and smarter European energy strategy and greater energy independence. A more dynamic European energy strategy has the potential to create many thousands of new jobs – in the energy sector itself, in energy-related R&D, and through the wider impact on European industry. The billions currently used to pay for imports could be invested in the domestic economy to reduce our demand for energy by raising energy efficiency, giving a clear and decisive push for widespread deployment of renewable energies and putting in place the modern infrastructure necessary to implement these goals.

This massive investment would mark a step-change in our economy, stimulating the construction, automotive and high-tech industries and their down-stream suppliers, and creating high-quality, high-skilled jobs. European energy strategy would become the backbone of a new re-industrialisation of the UK and Europe, ensuring we compete on high-value-added and are not dragged into a race to the bottom in labour costs, social standards and working conditions, which Europe cannot hope to win.

A determined Europe-wide push for renewables will yield economies of scale and breakthroughs in technology and pricing, resulting in an unlimited, affordable, clean energy supply for the future. However, we should urgently tackle the many barriers to renewables development which currently exist. One such barrier is the lengthy planning and authorisation procedures – currently averaging ten years – for cross-border energy projects. Recently adopted legislation aims to reduce this process to just over three years by streamlining authorisation procedures and ensuring key projects are given priority status, but it has not tackled the current burdensome requirements set out for environmental impact assessments. We should ensure that a root and branch review of the environmental impact assessment directive eliminates unnecessary requirements and barriers for renewable energy projects.

Another significant barrier to renewable energy projects is the high cost of capital. Power generation from fossil fuels has high running costs in the form of gas and coal, but is less capital intensive than renewable energy projects. These projects are extremely capital intensive at start-up, whereas the running costs are low and the inputs (sun, wind, waves) freely available. The current economic and financial crisis has pushed up the cost of capital, hitting renewable energy projects particularly hard, so one way to ensure such projects can proceed would be the creation of a European green investment bank (or at least a significant strengthening/reorientation of the EIB), to attract private funds for investment in renewable energy and energy efficiency projects, and make best use of new and innovative financial instruments such as project bonds.

Our alternative energy strategy will also deliver high levels of energy efficiency, through increased R&D in energy-saving technology for home appliances, vehicles, industrial processes and energy production;

and through an ambitious programme of refurbishment of existing buildings, with stringent requirements for new buildings.

The combination of the push for renewables and investment in energy efficiency will give British and European industry an extra global competitive edge – and drastically reduce energy poverty among our citizens. Conservative politicians continue to drag their heels, arguing that Europe cannot afford to shift to a greener energy strategy in the absence of global deals on climate change. Regardless of collective global action, we cannot afford not to make this shift; and it would give our industry a game-changing first-mover advantage in the global marketplace.

Two key actions

1. Experience has shown that the most effective way to achieve common goals in energy policy is through binding national targets for each Member State, agreed at EU level, leaving each national government freedom to decide how to meet the targets, in the light of their specific national context. To provide investor certainty and stimulate investment, we need a new 2030 energy package with ambitious targets for:

- greenhouse gas emissions – a 40 per cent reduction from 1990 levels
- renewable energy – to meet 45 per cent of Europe's total energy needs
- energy efficiency – 30 per cent energy savings on 2005 levels.

2. A progressive-led EU should launch a huge infrastructure investment programme, to adapt and modernise Europe's creaking infrastructure and interconnect the energy grids of all Member States. Interconnected grids would finally create a true internal energy market and allow the input of greatly increased quantities of renewable electricity to the grid. Long-distance electricity super-highways should connect North Sea wind to the main centres of population and the industrial heartland and bring solar energy from Southern Europe, North Africa and the Sahara to central and northern Europe.

THE DIGITAL AGENDA

The economic future of both the UK and the rest of Europe lies increasingly in the knowledge economy, with the digital economy at its heart. New opportunities are abundant and the UK in particular is well-placed to harness the huge potential for high-end job creation, sustained growth and rising productivity.

There are over 4 million ICT workers in the EU, a number that has been increasing by 3 per cent a year even during the current crisis. Britain has more ICT graduates than any other European country and is one of Europe's largest ICT markets, with consumer spending of £140 billion a year. As a software development powerhouse, attracting £1 billion a year in international investment in R&D, Britain is uniquely placed to benefit from the creation of a real digital single market throughout the EU. Its achievement must be a priority.

Despite warm words and impressive goals at the European level, real progress has been slow. European governments and EU institutions, under right-wing leadership, have found that rhetoric is cheaper than action. In the EU budget negotiations, for example, oral support for a shift in spending towards investment in jobs and growth was unanimous, and the European Commission's proposals actually moved cautiously in that direction. But that shift was the first casualty of negotiations in which governments were more concerned with either slashing the EU budget, or defending vested interests, or both.

The Connecting Europe Facility is Europe's flagship programme of industrial modernisation. Its telecommunications component, a €9 billion investment in broadband and e-services, saw its budget slashed by 89 per cent by the prime ministers meeting in the European Council. Allocation of the 4G spectrum is another sorry tale of foot-dragging, delay and investor uncertainty.

Progressives should bring new dynamism to the digital economy. Creation of a true digital single market across Europe would bring huge rewards for British consumers and businesses. European Commission estimates show that over the next eight years it could raise GDP by 5 per cent, creating 3.8 million new jobs. Wider use of online procurement would bring big efficiency gains in private and public sectors alike. Coupled with the creation of an interoperable European system, savings could be €100 billion per year.

A single market for everybody – the roaming case

Progressives should not regard the creation of a true single market across borders as an interest only of the business community. The efficiency and welfare gains can be huge – but who benefits depends on who is making the rules. In 2012, for instance, the European Parliament adopted legislation to curb profiteering by telecoms companies on cross-border mobile phone calls, but the gap between domestic rates and EU roaming rates is still far too high, especially for data or the internet.

The proposal from the social democrats – highly practical, but also powerfully symbolic – was to abolish mobile roaming charges within the EU altogether, so that people can call to and from any EU country at the same rates as domestic calls. The benefits would not only be for people living, studying or holidaying abroad: the biggest beneficiaries would be small firms, for whom costs of communication are a huge barrier to access to the EU market.

The story on roaming charges is far from unique: social democrats in the European Parliament have already achieved a lot on many consumer protection issues, but for more radical action Europe needs a left-of-centre majority in the next Parliament.

Consumer rights will be a key political battleground in coming years, as consumers bear the brunt of the scams and mis-selling of unbridled capitalism – from privatised energy utilities ripping off customers, to supermarkets throttling the life out of our inner cities, the food and drinks industry's toxic activities, pharmaceutical firms bankrupting our health systems and airlines playing fast and loose with safety rules. Increasingly, the battle will be fought across borders, as the importance of internet service providers and cross-border online shopping continues to grow. Defence of the consumer needs to be part of the core business of social democrats, and the EU is potentially our most effective instrument.

Common consumer standards across the European Union not only provide consumers with peace of mind; they represent a massive regulatory simplification for business, who will face one set of rules in place of 28. Already, in the face of an unhelpful balance of political forces, social democrats in the European Parliament, often led by Labour MEPs like Glenis Willmott and Linda McAvan, have succeeded in getting it to make some big stands for consumers. It now needs a new generation of aggressive regulation to confront corporate abuse.

EU-wide interoperable e-government – using the internet to provide government services to citizens – could also bring big savings in service delivery, easing the strain on public finances and cutting administrative costs by 20 per cent. But these systems need to be carefully designed to ensure better, not reduced, public services. The left needs to lead on this, not only to deliver efficiency gains, but also to ensure that the new systems are imprinted with our values of fairness, social equality and justice, and to avoid misuse of e-government as a fig-leaf to mask reduced levels of protection and a roll-back of the welfare state.

Progressives should also be champions of high levels of cyber-security and data protection. No one country can achieve this alone: the rationale for strong, coordinated EU action is overwhelming. By giving citizens confidence in their online safety, we can encourage take-up of both broadband and e-commerce – another area where the UK leads the EU field and stands to gain most from EU-wide promotion of e-commerce. If single market barriers were eliminated, the Commission has estimated that growth of e-commerce could deliver consumer welfare gains of around €204 billion, or 1.7 per cent of GDP. But dismantling single market barriers for the digital economy will mean we need stricter tax laws to prevent avoidance by multinational retailers. That will only happen with a stronger left presence in European decision-making.

NOTES

1. In the UK, for once ahead of the trend, combined public and private investment started low – 19 per cent of GDP in the early 1990s – and has edged just slightly lower, to 18 per cent.

2. See for instance *Hedge and Private Equity Funds – a critical analysis,* by Rasmussen and van den Burg (Socialist Group in the European Parliament, April 2007).
3. It was €764 billion in 2011.
4. This would extend to all multinationals the rules on transparency which, as noted above, the EU will apply to banks from 2015.

4. Social policy for a competitive Europe

Nick Costello

The welfare state is under attack across Europe as never before. This is true in terms of policies to reduce provision. It is also true in the battle of ideas.

Most of the policy changes are not full-frontal attacks, because social provision is difficult to attack directly. The undermining process is usually conducted in two ways. Firstly, at the margin, by implying that a huge proportion of social benefits are being fiddled – the logic of 'strivers' versus 'scroungers'. One can demonstrate till blue in the face that the proportion of the welfare budget claimed fraudulently is 0.7 per cent whereas people believe it is 27 per cent, and that the sums involved are far less than those for tax evasion by companies and the rich – but the endless stream of anecdotes with photos and names in the media is almost bound to stick more in people's minds. The second way is more indirect. Social spending is about 30 per cent of Europe's GDP and half of government spending. So the policies of austerity that mean slashing overall spending are bound to also mean cuts in social spending, which can then be portrayed as an unfortunate necessity.

Social provision across Europe is also under attack as a result of attempts to privatise anything that moves, thereby both reducing the role of public provision and giving the private sector as much of the action as possible through the contracting out of provision, and through public-private partnerships (where the emphasis is on giving as much as possible of the partnership to the private side, with the public side mainly there to cough up when things don't work). This is made worse by wider moves to reduce the level of provision in all areas. We are familiar with this in Britain, but it is true across most of the continent, corresponding with the prevailing right-wing hegemony.

Angela Merkel summed up the right's argument best: 'If Europe today accounts for just over 7 per cent of the world's population, produces around 25 per cent of global GDP and has to finance 50 per cent of global social spending, then it's obvious that it will have to work very hard to maintain its prosperity and way of life.' The implication is clear – social spending is seen purely as a cost, almost as a luxury, which Europe 'has to finance' and probably needs to cut.

The truth is very different: social investment is key to competitiveness on the basis of a skilled and highly-trained workforce. Without social investment, the economy could compete only through a race to the bottom, with falling wages and conditions the only way left to compete with the world's emerging economies – and they would have to fall a frighteningly long way to 'match' those of China or India. With social investment, there is a much sounder route to growth and competitiveness, but one which does not offer the same short-term rich pickings to the banks and low-value-added firms that have too much influence on policy-making today.

This approach is not something theoretical and untried – it is working today in several European countries. Even Barroso, the right-of-centre President of the European Commission, has to admit this: 'It is precisely those European countries with the most effective social protection systems and with the most developed social partnerships that are among the most successful and competitive economies in the world.'

He is of course talking especially about countries like Sweden and Denmark, which do offer a model of how to stay competitive on the basis of high levels of social provision.

There is nothing paradoxical about this. After decades of hearing the messages of belt-tightening austerity, telling us that we can only make the economy better by suffering, it is sometimes difficult to remember that people in a good state – well-educated and trained and healthy – are also better able to contribute to the economy. People prefer to be active and healthy, well-educated and skilled, and generally in control of their lives. And these same active and healthy, well-educated and skilled people are much better placed to contribute to society and to the economy, and less often have the need to call for help from social services or from the health system in order to be able to cope with life's ups and downs. So the social investment approach works to supply the tools for people to avoid life's vicissitudes or to cope with them when they arise. If followed through it means there is less often the need for much more costly intervention when problems arise with which people are ill-equipped to deal. This is the way forward towards the kind of society that is organised along lines that people can accept.

We need to achieve two objectives, using both economic and social policy. Firstly people need to be employed – hence the agenda on the economy described in chapter three is about putting people in a position where they can earn a decent living: where there are jobs, and where people have the education and skills to do highly-skilled jobs. Social policy is also needed to facilitate this, to make sure people have the education and training to be able to do the skilled jobs that a modern economy needs.

Secondly, social policy must also be there for people for the periods when this doesn't work out, most obviously, to provide unemployment benefit and social assistance when needed.

As the quotation from Barroso above suggests, policy discussions in Europe are starting to open up to this more progressive approach, influenced by the increasingly desperate social situation in more and more Member States. In February 2013, the European Commission came out in favour of this social investment approach – but without being able to argue for the resources needed to make it work properly, since this would contradict the overarching austerity policies which remain in force. Nonetheless this is an important advance. In a sense it provides the tools but not the power to operate them. This is pointed out in the opinions of the European Parliament, as well as the Economic and Social Committee representing the social partners, both of which support the approach but argue that it needs to be accompanied by a large-scale programme of investment along the lines called for by the Parliament in its 2012 proposal for a Social Investment Pact.

THE SITUATION ON THE GROUND

Social protection expenditure fulfils three vital roles for society and the economy, but current neoliberal policies are undermining all three of them. The first role is social protection itself – supporting people at different stages of their life (e.g. providing early childhood education and care, or pensions and care in old age), and when different life risks materialise (e.g. benefits for people without jobs, healthcare). The second function is social investment – helping prepare people for the challenges they will face in life, through early childhood education and care, education, training and retraining, assistance in searching for jobs and preventive health policies. The third function is automatic stabilisation – when a crisis occurs, many forms of social expenditure automatically rise and reduce the impact of the crisis on living standards, spending and growth.

That's the theory – or rather the potential – of an effective social policy. The reality may be somewhat different. The diminishing and undermining of the social dimension is weakening the ability of welfare states to protect people in the crisis. In its first phase, social benefits were able to keep incomes from falling in 2009 and into 2010. Since then, they have no longer been able to do so – partly because people's periods of entitlements have run out, but, even more worryingly, because cuts have been reducing the levels of benefits at the very time they are needed most. This is one of the factors behind the soaring levels of poverty and inequality we are now experiencing.

Secondly, social policy should be investing in people's capacities – making sure people are well-educated, well-trained and healthy – both to provide a better life for people, and to offer conditions for economic success based not on driving wages and conditions down, but on a skilled, productive workforce that can do the jobs of the twenty-first century; but mass unemployment is causing millions to stop acquiring new skills and experience at work, and cuts are whittling away at the provision of training, education and health services, thereby compounding the damage inflicted by the crisis.

Thirdly, although social spending has a naturally counter-cyclical Keynesian effect to stabilise the economy – unemployment and many other benefits automatically go up whenever the economy goes into decline, so they compensate for the fall in growth and incomes – the current rounds of cuts across the board, introduced at the very time that unemployment is soaring, are reversing this automatic stabiliser effect.

So current policies are failing the people on all three fronts. They are making people worse off, and harming Europe's competitiveness at the same time, all in the name of obeisance to an intellectually discredited model of austerity.

As outlined in chapter two, the policies of austerity are now intellectually discredited in their own terms, including from the least likely source, the IMF, whose studies have shown that the 'fiscal multiplier' is far higher than had been assumed in mainstream economics. What this means is that the cuts in public spending have produced much larger falls in private consumption and in economic activity than had been expected, thus slashing tax revenues and boosting the need for spending on unemployment benefits and social assistance. The net result is that these cuts are not even succeeding in their official aim of reducing the deficit. Previous chapters also demonstrate how the facts have completely undermined academic theories which purported to show that controlling public expenditure would lead almost miraculously to stimulating growth.

But we should not expect these conclusive rebuttals to lead the current management to change policy, because one of the real motivations of the austerity continues to be to roll back the sphere of public provision and leave everything possible to the market. This is the same philosophy which put security at the 2012 Olympics in the hands of Group 4, with a fiasco only averted by public service being called in at the last moment; in this case, the British army – which not even the Cameron government is yet proposing to privatise.

The damage that neoliberal policies have been inflicting across Europe is so widespread and flagrant that even Barroso now says that there is a 'social emergency' today in Europe. But there is an unavoidable and crucial link between the past decade of more right-wing control in Europe and the choice of which powers to move to Brussels and which to keep at national level. The EU's power to impose austerity has been increased with the six-pack that allows it to limit public deficits; while the power to soften the impact of austerity is in theory left at national level (social policy subsidiarity). In fact, the budgetary straitjacket forces Member States to weaken their social provision, especially in 'programme countries' – shorthand for those countries subject to the 'Excessive Deficit Procedure', currently Greece, Portugal, Ireland and Romania.

The fiscal austerity decided and imposed at EU level inevitably increases inequality, deprivation, exclusion and under skilling, while it puts Member States in fiscal straitjackets that impede them from funding properly the social policies needed to soften or reverse the impact of these policies. Then Member States have to implement the cuts in social policies, and take the blame for them, since social policy is supposedly their prerogative rather than that of Brussels. This is the same mechanism that sees Labour councils taking the blame for implementing cuts that are made inevitable by Tory central government's spending limits. But when people see through this, and trace the cause of the cuts to budgetary restrictions partly decided in Brussels, it feeds euroscepticism: Brussels comes to be seen, not as the defender of people's rights and conditions, but as the threat to them – especially in programme countries where the troika of the European Commission, the IMF and the European Central Bank very visibly defines the cuts to be made, but also more widely. Instead of 'Europe' being seen to be 'on our side', it opens itself to the caricature of being the regional branch of the IMF, the bailiffs in grey suits.

New instruments are needed to give meaning to the social dimension of the internal market. We must not buy the argument that this discussion somehow only concerns the euro-zone: Britain is also suffering the effects of the Stability and Growth Pact in terms of austerity, along with the other 27 Member States. We need a rebalancing exercise, and to give as much weight to social issues as economic issues in the European semester procedure that sets the framework each year for the EU's economic and social policies.

Cutbacks in social provision across Europe are an integral part of the trend towards the reorientation of European economies to the benefit of short-term profits that we have seen since the 1980s and the start of Thatcherism. Inequalities have grown, while the social safety net to help people at the bottom to cope has been progressively weakened.

The need for a progressive approach to social policy in Europe is greater than ever, for two main reasons.

The twelve new Member States that joined in 2004 and 2007 are mostly much poorer and have lower levels of social provision than the fifteen they joined. Their membership has increased the degree of internal inequality between the different countries of the EU and contributed to much wider gaps in income distribution. Enlargement has therefore accelerated the threat that increased integration poses to wages and conditions if it is not accompanied by measures to level up standards, and transition periods to allow these measures to work; indeed, certainly some on the right saw this tendency – a downward pressure on incomes through cheaper labour gaining early access to the labour market – almost as a central justification for the most recent enlargements. Meanwhile the right-wing dominance of European politics throughout this period has ensured that the needed accompanying measures have ground to a halt.

Without these accompanying social policies, purely market-based integration is bound to undermine, and has undermined, the popular legitimacy of the European Union. Only a radical progressive social agenda can restore previous levels of popular acceptance of European integration, by changing the reality to one where common European approaches actually start to improve people's lives once more. This has been shown time and time again: one of the key factors behind the French no vote in 2005 on the proposed European constitution, for example, was the unpopularity of the Bolkestein directive – even though the directive itself had nothing to do with the constitutional vote. (The directive, which sought to open up a single European market for service providers, was seen as a threat to workers' conditions since it proposed that workers could be employed under the conditions of their Member State of origin when working in another country.) Europe can only advance – and only should advance – on the basis of popular support and legitimacy. But that support is bound to be jeopardised if the right is able to use Europe to undermine social standards.

This is true more generally: when the EU opens markets between Member States without doing anything else, it undermines the ability of countries with stronger social provision and better wages and conditions to maintain these conditions; and at the same time it undermines the possibility for countries with weaker provisions to improve theirs. So even maintaining social conditions requires that the development of social Europe keep pace with the development of economic integration. This can take different forms, including: minimum requirements at European level; the slanting of European programmes towards Member States with lower average incomes and more poverty.

Examination of the 2005 referendum vote in France also shows that what ultimately led to the changes in the Bolkestein directive was not just debates among politicians, but – much more importantly – mass mobilisation, with demonstrations, strikes, petitions and leaflets.

In the long term we need to work towards a future where the conditions of Polish, Portuguese or Bulgarian workers are moving in the direction of those of Dutch or Swedish workers, not vice versa. That is not going to happen overnight, but it must be the general trend in order to safeguard the ability of the Netherlands or Sweden or other more prosperous Member States to keep their more decent social provision and working conditions and to avoid a race to the bottom.

The British discussion of social Europe focuses almost exclusively on the question of British opt-outs at the expense of the wider picture. Debate often takes place without people knowing what it is that Britain is opting into or out of. In fact the first set of shared workers' rights were developed in the 1970s, with the explicit justification of keeping pace with the growing freedom of firms to move around Europe. They covered areas like equal pay for men and women (1975); the need for consultations on mass redundancies (1975); maintaining workers' rights when firms were transferred (1977); guaranteed payment of unpaid wages when firms went bankrupt (1980); and a general framework for health and safety at work (1989), which subsequently gave rise to over thirty implementing directives. The 1990s saw the beginnings of a European labour code, including obliging employers to supply a written labour contract within two months (1991).

We need to take further steps to strengthen social Europe in line with this approach.

Here European funds, and especially the European Social Fund, can provide important help. All of the ESF funding can legitimately be seen as social investment, since it is directed at improving workers' skills and tackling other barriers that exclude people from the labour market (including obstacles as varied as discrimination against Roma, and insufficient support for working mothers). The ESF needs to increase in size – it currently represents only 1 per cent of European social spending – and to begin to address social policy needs beyond the workplace. Furthermore, the matching funds from Member States should be considered as what in fact they are – investment – and therefore exempted from the fiscal limitations set under the Stability and Growth Pact. It makes no sense to cut back on people's skills and ability to work – the very things that will make the economy and productivity grow in the future – in the name of a strategy for stability and growth.

A second improvement would be to ensure that, when deciding policy on such areas as posting of workers, there is a basic underlying logic that integrating market access proceeds only in line with integrating social provision. More Europe can only be popular if it is more of the kind of Europe that makes people better off – not more of the kind of Europe that threatens people's conditions.

The general long-term approach must be one of working towards the levelling up of provision in Bulgaria, rather than the levelling down of provision in the UK. And this must be accompanied by a social investment approach, so that safeguarding or increasing social provision is carried out in a way that enhances competitiveness rather than undermining it. Social investment needs to be seen as a way of contributing to reductions in equality – and performance in this area should be part of the annual Brussels assessment of national economic and social policies in the European Semester.

5. Why the right is plain wrong on environment policy and climate change

Linda McAvan

Environment policy is the one policy area where all bar the most eurosceptical have accepted the need for cooperation between EU neighbours. That pollution, plant disease and the health of our coastal waters need cross border, not simply national solutions, was recognised in the early years of the EU. The first European Environmental Action programmes date back to the 1970s, long before there were any formal provisions in the EU Treaty for joint action. More recently, the imperative to tackle climate change, the most pressing environmental problem of our time, has led to a raft of joint policy measures as the EU has tried to show global leadership to kick-start talks on a successor international treaty to the Kyoto protocol. But progress on the green agenda is stalling at European level. The economic crash has broken the political consensus, as some governments and MEPs of the right have tried to block further action to tackle climate change. This comes at a time when climate scientists are telling us that we are on track for a world that may be simply too hot to handle, with temperatures 4 degrees centigrade above current averages. The European Commission has said repeatedly that switching to a low carbon economy is essential to break our dependency on increasingly expensive imported fossil fuel and has published research showing that if we implement existing policy measures on renewable energy, energy efficiency and resource efficiency we could generate up to 8 million jobs.[1] Yet green measures are all but absent in the austerity programmes in the countries which have sought EU bailouts, reinforcing the view that green policies are only for the good times. The challenge for the left in the coming years is to re-establish both political and public support for coherent European climate, environmental and energy policies, and to embed them into Europe's plans for economic recovery, growth and jobs.

OPTIMISM IN THE GOOD TIMES: COPENHAGEN AND THE EU CLIMATE PACKAGE

When European leaders met for their regular spring summit in March 2007 it was in an atmosphere of optimism. Europe was going through a golden decade. Economic growth at 3 per cent was solidly outpacing that of the USA and Japan. Unemployment was low in most countries and averaged 7.3 per cent across the EU 27 (compared with 12 per cent now). It was the era of the Celtic tiger and unprecedented growth and change in Southern Europe. Three years earlier, enlargement to the East had gone smoothly and the Euro was seen as a strong currency, as low interest rates and cheap credit spread a feel-good factor across much of the continent. In a speech to the New York Stock Exchange that spring, Commission President Jose Manuel Barroso spoke proudly of Europe's recent economic performance – which showed that 'we still know a thing or two about high performance engines' – and of Europe's return to healthy growth and potential creation of seven million jobs.

It was in this benign economic climate that European leaders met in Berlin at a Summit hosted by Angela Merkel, German Chancellor and President in Office of the European Council. There they launched an ambitious plan to transform the European economy from one heavily dependent on fossil fuels and imported energy to a low-carbon economy based on renewable energy and green innovation. Setting targets to cut the EU's carbon emissions, expand the share of renewable energy and improve energy efficiency, all by 2020, it was hailed as the biggest advance in Europe's green agenda for a generation; the aim was to give the EU a solid negotiating platform for the upcoming UN climate change negotiations due to deliver a new global agreement in Copenhagen at the end of 2009.

Tony Blair, then in his last months in office as British prime minister, can claim particular credit for the EU deal. His government had published the landmark Stern report on the economics of climate change the previous autumn. Stern warned that while it would cost money to tackle climate change – around 1 per cent of GDP – failure to act would cost much more; at least 5 per cent of global GDP. Blair recognised that only action by the EU as a whole could influence the global debate on climate change, as the EU negotiates as a bloc of nations in global climate talks. At an informal EU summit in Finland in October 2006, he and Dutch prime minister Jan Peter Balkanende presented a joint letter to fellow leaders stating that the world would reach catastrophic tipping points on climate change within fifteen years unless serious action was taken to tackle global warming. They urged the EU to make the transition to a low-carbon economy in what they called a 'once in a generation opportunity for Europe to mobilise the political will and resources to transform and modernise our energy system'.

In the eighteen months that followed, the EU institutions began translating the warm words of EU leaders into concrete policies. The European Commission, the body at EU level responsible for initiating legislation, put a series of draft laws to tackle climate change on the table in early 2008. The race was then on to get political agreement on this 'climate change package' before Christmas that year, during the French EU Presidency and before the European elections in 2009. A period of intensive negotiations between Europe's legislators, MEPs and ministers followed. Negotiations were far from easy. Countries were at very different stages, both in terms of recognising the climate change threat and their preparedness for a low carbon economy. Czech President Vaclav Klaus was a self-confessed climate sceptic. Poland generated most of its energy from coal. The UK had hardly any renewable energy. But despite these difficulties, and the emerging threat of economic downturn, in December 2008 MEPs and ministers were able to sign off on a series of new laws: a revamped European Emissions (carbon) Trading System (ETS); an overall target of 20 per cent for renewables, with an individual legally binding target for each Member State; national emission reduction targets; laws to curb carbon emissions from cars; and a commitment to invest in carbon capture and storage and to deliver a 20 per cent improvement in energy efficiency. These plans meant that by the start of the Copenhagen climate change summit, the EU was the only region in the world to have adopted not only binding legal targets to cut its carbon emissions but a batch of policies to deliver on those targets.

For the United Kingdom, signing off on the climate package presented a number of challenges because of our heavy dependence on fossil fuels. While countries like Sweden produced almost 40 per cent of its energy from renewables and France generated 75 per cent of its electricity from nuclear energy, the UK remained heavily dependent on coal (despite having closed much of its domestic coal industry) and gas for its electricity generation. Energy from renewable sources – at 1.3 per cent in 2005 – was at one of the lowest levels of any EU country. The UK committed to increase this ten-fold in order to reach a target of 15 per cent by 2020. While other countries had higher targets, the UK faced the steepest increase. The UK also agreed to cut overall domestic carbon emissions by 16 per cent by 2020. In other words, the shift to a low-carbon economy would need big changes and hefty investment. The Labour government therefore introduced the Climate Change Act, which empowered the Secretary of State to put in train a series of measures to cut greenhouse gas emissions by 80 per cent by 2050 through a series of legally binding national carbon budgets, the first of their kind in the world, to be overseen by an independent Climate Change Committee. A plan for more low carbon power generation was also put in place, including – controversially for some in Labour's ranks – a new generation of nuclear plants to replace the country's ageing reactors, alongside a huge expansion of wind, wave and solar panel alternatives. When the Labour government lost office in 2010, the new Tory/Lib Dem coalition pledged to stick with Labour's climate policies and to be the 'greenest government ever'. For the Tories, this green agenda was a central plank of the detoxification of the Tory brand, to the extent that they changed their traditional logo from the torch of liberty to a green tree against a blue background. Subsequent policy decisions would later show this blue to green conversion to be largely an optical illusion.

This new EU climate change policy complemented a series of other environmental protection laws that the EU had adopted over many years. The first Environmental Action Programme was agreed in 1973, and by the time environment was included in the EU Treaties (Single European Act 1986) dozens of environmental protection measures were in place. Environment policy is also one area where there is clear public support for EU action: recent Eurobarometer polls show that 74 per cent of people in the EU (71 per cent in UK) agreed that fighting climate change and improving energy efficiency could boost the EU economy and jobs, and 73 per cent (74 per cent in UK) think we will be using more fuel-efficient cars in 2050. Companies too are often strong advocates of joint EU action on the environment. Minimum standards mean a level playing field, and, although some companies may wince at the prospect of a new EU environment regulation, most prefer one EU law to having to comply with twenty-seven different laws when they trade across borders.

A British audience may well remember a time when raw sewage was being washed up on our beaches, fish life was dying off in our rivers, acid rain sometimes fell, and holiday makers got 'Spanish tummy' from drinking water abroad – among other problems. EU law has consigned many of these problems to history, leading to major environmental improvements and ironing out differences in standards across the continent. A notable development in recent years is the REACH Directive, which requires registration of all chemicals on the EU market and restrictions on the use of dangerous chemicals, which must ultimately be replaced with safer alternatives. Another area where EU law has led to major changes is management of waste, particularly in the UK, which until 2001 was 80 per cent dependent on landfill for disposing of our waste. This has now been brought down to 49 per cent. Along with Greece, it was given an extra four years to meet EU targets on reducing landfill, as it came from such a high starting point. Today it recycles 25 per cent, and while far from being a leader in recycling – that honour goes to Germany – there has been real progress.

THE ECONOMIC CRASH: DISAPPOINTMENT IN COPENHAGEN

But if the years since the 1970s were mainly ones of increasing ambition in Europe's environment policies, the economic crash is putting progress under strain. By the time MEPs and ministers were finalising agreements on the climate package in the autumn of 2008, Lehman Brothers had collapsed, Alistair Darling had announced a £50 billion bail-out of British banks and the lessons of 1929 and avoiding depression were the topics of the day. Some governments and MEPs, mainly on the right, began to question the wisdom of the EU pursuing its climate change agenda. Even Germany, despite Merkel's role in chairing the original summit that had launched the climate package, began to behave equivocally. But a combination of French leadership in Council, a broad political consensus in Parliament and a renewed sense of hope for a deal on Kyoto following the election of Barack Obama in November 2008, meant that talks remained on track. By the time parliament rose for the elections in spring 2009, the climate package was fully in place and governments were setting out national programmes to deliver on the targets.

This is not the place to rehearse all the reasons for the failure of the Copenhagen December 2009 climate talks to produce a new binding international Treaty to tackle climate change, but the fallout of that failure is being felt today in Europe's climate policies. It has certainly prompted some, though by no means all, business voices to argue that European companies cannot bear any additional costs arising from implementing green policies – from which they claim their international competitors are shielded. And as Europe's share of global emissions falls (the EU represents just 11 per cent of emissions today), while those of China, India and the emerging economies grow, those same voices question whether the EU can really aspire to be a global leader on climate change. Both these lines of argument are debatable, but the critics are undoubtedly right that, despite being the best prepared region for the talks, the EU somehow failed to use its clout in Copenhagen.

The first lesson is that if the EU is to be a leading voice, it has to speak with one voice: despite the single negotiating mandate for the EU 27, too many prime ministers went to Copenhagen determined to make their own mark, rather than sticking to the EU script, leaving their fellow negotiators unsure about who exactly was leading for the EU. Lesson number two is not to put all your cards on the table on day one, as the EU did, the result being that the EU was not seen as a 'player' in the final talks. At the close of the summit, the EU representatives were not even in the room when the watered-down set of commitments – the 'Copenhagen Accord' – was agreed between Obama and the BASIC countries (Brazil, South Africa, India and China). The Accord did at least keep the UN climate process alive, and there is talk now of another push to get a global agreement in 2015 at the Paris talks. But the deadline for agreeing a second round of the Kyoto protocol in 2012 has now ended, with only the EU and Australia, Croatia, Iceland, Norway, Switzerland, Kazakhstan, Belarus and Ukraine signed up to a new commitment period – and the last three countries have warned that they may not implement it.

THE FALLOUT OF FAILURE: FADING GREEN AMBITION

Fast forward almost four years and Europe's climate policy is under even more pressure. The 20 per cent cut in emissions by 2020 could only ever have worked as a driver for low carbon investment against a background of growth and higher demand for energy. Instead, the economic slowdown has meant that the EU is now on track to reach its target early – we are already 80 per cent of the way there – not because of greener policies, but simply because of the economic slowdown. Without a meaningful target to drive behavioural change, Europe's wider climate policies are under strain. The Emissions Trading Scheme in particular is struggling; with surplus allowances on the market and reduced demand pushing the carbon price down from a forecast €30 per tonne to figures in the low single digits. A high carbon price was supposed to incentivise investment in low carbon technologies and energy efficiency, particularly in the third phase of the ETS (which started in 2013 when companies began having to buy their allowances at auction, rather than receiving them for free). Revenue generated by these auctions was also supposed to provide every government with an income stream for investment in low carbon technologies, as well as creating a source of funding for the installation of carbon capture and storage projects to cut emissions from fossil fuel power stations and heavy industry. By mid 2013 not a single CCS project had been funded.

The collapse in the carbon price clearly requires corrective action. The European Commission recognises this, and has tried to open a debate on adopting a more ambitious emissions reductions target. The original climate package sought a 20 per cent emissions reduction by 2020, increasing to 30 per cent if other countries signed up to a climate deal. The Commission, with backing from progressive MEPs, has supported making that move to 30 per cent now irrespective of other countries' performance. It has also put on the table proposals to boost the carbon price by delaying or 'backloading' the sale of carbon permits at auction. But just as the right has failed to respond with the right kind of policies to tackle the financial markets, so they have consistently blocked policies to sort out the carbon markets. In the European Parliament, right-wing MEPs have become increasingly hostile to climate policies: in a landmark vote in Parliament in April 2013, they voted to reject the Commission's proposal for modest adjustments to the Emissions Trading Scheme system, wreaking havoc on the carbon markets. Companies which were planning to invest in renewable energy and other low carbon technology, seeing the collapse of the political consensus on tackling climate change, are now losing confidence and interest. Levels of investment into renewable technologies in Europe fell last year for the first time since the financial crisis. The kind of transformative investments needed to create Commission President Barroso's 'most competitive and dynamic knowledge-based economy in the world' are stalling. And all this is happening at a time when EU dependence on imported fossil fuel is increasing: in 2011 the EU was the world's largest energy importer, with 54 per cent of our energy coming from third countries.

Ironically, as the EU hesitates, other countries are beginning to wake up to the climate-change threat. Both China and the US, though not committing to international binding agreements, have begun domestic action. China's twelfth Five Year Plan includes commitments to almost halve the carbon intensity of GDP by 2020: to grow strategic green industries such as electric cars; and roll out pilot carbon emission trading systems in five cities and two provinces, with the aim of scaling up to a national carbon market in 2015.In the US, individual states on both the East and West coasts, including California, are also developing carbon-trading schemes; and at federal level there has been big investment into renewable energy projects as part of Obama's stimulus package.

THE UK GOVERNMENT'S AMBIVALENCE TO EU ACTION

Despite its increasing hostility to many aspects of EU law, the UK government has, to date, sided with those who want to defend the EU's climate policies – at least that is the official line. But this official line has been undermined on more than one occasion by senior Conservatives – and the fact that since the start of the coalition government, climate and energy policy has been headed up by a Lib Dem Secretary of State no doubt reinforces the idea in Tory minds that somehow climate change policy is not a 'real' Tory policy. This despite David Cameron's frolics with huskies in the Arctic and pronouncements that he would lead the greenest government ever. George Osborne, in particular, has made statements tipping the wink to climate sceptics on Tory back benches that climate policy does not rank high in his priorities. At the 2011 Conservative Party Conference he pledged to 'cut carbon emissions no slower but also no faster than our fellow countries in Europe' – a dig at his own government's policies.

In the European Parliament, attitudes among Tory MEPs on climate change issues have mirrored this evolution and ambiguity.

Whereas in the 2004-2009 European Parliamentary term Tory MEPs played a constructive role on the climate change package, steering their colleagues in the EPP Group, of which they were then members, towards agreement, Tories in the 2009 Parliament have taken a very different line. Having left the mainstream EPP to create their eurosceptic ECR (European Conservative and Reform Group), a majority have become increasingly climate sceptic and hostile to European environment law. On a number of crucial votes, they have seemed determined to use their muscle in Brussels to undermine official government policy. Not only have they voted against moves to increase the 20 per cent target to 30 per cent, but in the April 2013 crucial ETS backloading vote, they voted against by a large majority. Both times their votes made the difference as to whether or not the measure got through: sixteen Tories voted in July 2011 against the 30 per cent target, lost in Parliament by just nine votes. And twenty-one Tories voted to block backloading, lost by nineteen votes.

If Osborne's careless words and the growing climate scepticism of Tory MEPs were no more than political bluster, few would pay attention. However, there is growing evidence that government ambivalence on climate policy is costing the UK investment and jobs. Investment in wind power has fallen: dither and delay have meant that there has been no progress on developing CCS – a technology where once Britain hoped to become a world leader. The most recent reports from the European Commission do not inspire confidence that the UK will meet its 15 per cent renewables target by 2020, given that the current figure is 3.3 per cent. The government itself has estimated that replacement of aged coal and nuclear power stations, and upgrading of the grid, will need around £110 billion of investment over the next decade. Yet since this government came to power, the UK has fallen behind Brazil and India in investment in green growth, slipping from third to thirteenth place internationally. Instead of investing in renewables, Osborne has nailed his colours to the shale-gas mast, despite the unproven nature of its potential in the UK or its carbon footprint – and some would argue without thinking through potential public opposition. If Tory MPs have whipped up opposition to wind farms, are they prepared for the scale of the public outcry should shale-gas developers start prospecting in rural England? With Britain still generating around 80 per cent of its electricity from fossil fuels – roughly 50/50 gas and coal – much of that imported and none of it abated through CCS, little wonder that David Kennedy, the chief executive of the Committee on Climate Change, has said that Osborne's plan for a dash for gas should be 'Plan Z', as it is 'completely incompatible' with the UK's legally binding carbon emissions targets.

A NEW IMPETUS FOR EU GREEN POLICIES – A CHALLENGE FOR THE LEFT

If the right has allowed climate and environment policy to slip down the EU agenda over the past 5 years on environmental issues, what can the left do during the next European Parliament and Commission term (2014-2019) to give it new impetus? The first step is to be clear in our own minds that George Osborne and his ilk are totally wrong. Investment in tackling climate change, energy efficiency and the environment are not policy add-ons for the good times. Tackling climate change must be an urgent priority, because while politicians dither, climate scientists are warning that the planet is warming faster than we thought. Whenever ministers and MEPs undermine climate policies by delaying implementation dates, or watering down commitments, they are not saving money; rather they are storing up problems for the future. Nicholas Stern, now a member of the UK House or Lords, told the World Economic Forum in Davos recently: 'I got it wrong on climate change – it's far, far worse'. So we on the left need to get that message out to the electorate and ensure that both our domestic and EU policies are up to the challenge.

Another area where we need further work is on spelling out the benefits and not just the costs of taking action. An EU law that cuts CO2 emissions of the average car does not just mean a greener car, it means a car that is cheaper to run: current plans for further car emission reductions by 2020 would save drivers £3,300 (€3,800) over the lifetime of their cars.

Similarly, technical advances introduced under the Eco Design legislation, be they in low-energy light bulbs, energy-efficient kitchen appliances, TVs that turn off the standby mode or more efficient boilers, have rarely been sold as money savers to a public increasingly sceptical about whether anything good can come from EU law. And if energy efficiency measures save money for individual households, those savings can be multiplied many times for manufacturing. In an EU which is 54 per cent dependent on fossil-fuel imports, investment in renewables and energy efficiency should be seen as self-evidently sensible, even to those unconvinced by climate science.

To those who argue that, given the economic circumstances, it is inevitable that green issues fall down the political agenda as concerns about the wider economy dominate, the European left should also have an unequivocal response. Yes, jobs and growth must be our top priority in the coming years, but sticking with the climate change agenda and active environment policies can generate growth, indeed can offer more growth potential that many of the so-called 'traditional sectors'. A top industrialist recently pointed out to a group of MEPs that two thirds of growth in British exports to China is in 'green' products. Maybe we should also be looking again at our own use of language when we talk about climate action. Mathias Groote, German Socialist chair of the Environment Committee in the European Parliament, pointed out recently that our tendency to talk about 'green jobs' has reinforced the view that there is a 'green' economy – suitable for the 'good times' – and a 'real' economy which needs our urgent attention now in the crisis. Rather there is, he argued, only one economy, pointing out that the wind industry is the second largest consumer of steel in Germany. In his strongly industrial region of Lower Saxony in Germany, approximately 22,000 employees are currently engaged in the wind industry sector, and this number is expected to increase over the coming years. Are these green or brown jobs? So maybe the left should stop talking about the 'green economy' and start arguing instead that, just as we reject the austerity policies of the European Right in favour of a more Keynesian economic policy, so we reject their policies which weaken Europe's climate and environment policies, because they are central to any growth strategy.

Turning to the prospects for the international climate talks, we need the EU to play a full role in discussions in the run-up to the Paris climate change summit at the end of 2015, which is the next critical phase for the UN talks and another opportunity to contain global warming. It will simply not be credible for the EU to turn up in Paris armed only with its existing 2020 targets. We should accept an immediate new interim target of 30 per cent emission reductions by 2020, and start work urgently on more ambitious targets for the medium and longer term. In March 2013, the European Commission published a green paper *Shaping the 2030 framework for climate and energy policies*. Our response to the green paper should be to call for a clear set of binding targets to cut emissions, to increase our share of renewables and to improve energy efficiency, backed up with concrete policies to keep the EU on a clear trajectory to cut carbon emissions by 80 per cent by 2050, in line with existing commitments. Interim targets, possibly at five yearly intervals, up to 2050, should be considered in order to provide the kind of certainty business needs to underpin their investments. Failure to agree now a longer-term framework for climate policy will heighten the risk of 'carbon lock-in' – governments and businesses taking decisions today, such as investment in fossil fuel power generation, which are hard to reverse and result in a growth in carbon emissions in the medium to long term.

But the green paper also presents the left with the opportunity to re-evaluate some of Europe's policies, such as energy liberalisation, and ask whether these policies have delivered what they set out to do. One area where energy policy is clearly failing is in the area of fuel poverty. MEPs from the Socialist Group, led by then Labour MEP Eluned Morgan, fought hard to get the concept of fuel poverty included in laws on liberalisation of energy markets. But the average European consumer might well be wondering what price-liberalisation means if domestic energy prices keep rising, and bills are becoming unaffordable for many. One in five UK households is now in fuel poverty, which is more than in any other EU country. The Netherlands, for example, has half the levels of fuel poverty that we do. We need more active measures to tackle fuel poverty, and we could start by doing far more to tackle energy efficiency in homes. The new EU Directive on energy efficiency provides an ideal framework for action. It requires governments to set national energy-efficiency targets, draw up a strategy by 2014 for renovating all housing stock, and renovate a certain percentage of buildings owned and occupied by central government every year. Making homes more energy efficient should be a flagship policy of the next European Parliamentary term. EU regional funds coupled with social funds could be used to train a new generation of workers in energy-efficiency technologies, creating much-needed jobs, particularly for young people. An added bonus is that ordinary people would see Europe making a positive difference to their every day lives.

A future Labour government elected in May 2015 would come to power at a critical time in the development of the next generation of EU climate, energy and environment policies. A new European Commission with a new President will just have taken office. A new

European Parliament will be finding its feet. As a party with a track record on climate policy and a leader, Ed Miliband, experienced in the issues and in global climate diplomacy (having served as Secretary of State for Climate and Energy policy at the time of the Copenhagen Summit), Labour would be well positioned to shape an ambitious EU climate policy for the 2015 Paris talks. We can also hope that elections taking place across the EU in the coming period will return more sister parties to government, and that the Obama administration, in its second term of office, can make some progress in the US and use its influence on countries such as China, India, Russia and Brazil, to come back to the climate change negotiating table.

CONCLUSION: A U-TURN THAT MUST BE AVOIDED

Politicians on the Right, many of whom never supported climate action before Copenhagen, are now using the lack of a UN deal as an excuse to hamper implementation of Europe's climate package. But theirs is the shortsighted view. Climate scientists are certain that climate change remains a clear and present danger, and while the public may, it is true, have their minds more focused on jobs and the economy at present, they will not forgive those politicians who ignore the evidence and refuse to put in place measures to mitigate the dangers. Businesses too, particularly those looking to invest in innovative technologies, are losing patience with politicians unable to create the kind of stability for environmental policy they need for investment. The left in Europe should therefore make a clear commitment to integrating climate and environment policies into their plans for European recovery. Keynes famously said if the facts change, then he changed his mind. But the facts on climate change have not changed, except in the sense that global warming is speeding up and its threat is more imminent. We should therefore not change course from the one adopted back in 2008 – we must continue to set out a clear trajectory to a low-carbon Europe.

NOTES

1. http://ec.europa.eu/europe2020/pdf/themes/green_jobs.pdf.

6. International trade: our jobs, our values

David Martin

The economic crisis did not begin in Europe in 2008. Even before the crisis the European Union's growth performance was weak, and Europe was already perceived as a rapidly declining industrial region propped up by a buoyant service sector. Now that the service bubble has burst, most notably in banking and finance, Europe faces the prospect of low growth for years to come. Without action to reverse this situation low growth will lead to even higher unemployment and continued pressure on public services, and will threaten the sustainability of Europe's social model.

There is no single route out of this crisis, but the EU's continued clout in international trade offers a way forward. In the 1980s the creation of the single European market was seen as a way to halt Europe's relative decline. It certainly succeeded in mitigating the decline, and it allowed some European nations to achieve higher growth than would otherwise have been possible, but it did not halt that decline. For the foreseeable future the fastest growing economies will be outside Europe's borders. Today the challenge is to use the attraction of a market of half a billion people to negotiate market opening for European goods and services in these rapidly growing economies.

However, for progressives this must be about more than trade liberalisation: it must reflect our values and principles. This chapter will argue that properly managed international trade can have a significant positive effect on economic growth and development, and should be seen as a key tool of any left agenda for post crisis recovery both at home and in developing economies.

At first glance, the value of EU trade policy has the dubious honour of being the only shard of common ground between the left and right, and between eurosceptics and europhiles, in Britain today. The pro-European left champions our single EU trade voice on the global stage, underpinned by Social Europe, as the bedrock of our jobs and growth strategy at home and abroad. The Tories obsess over the Single Market while crying out for more Free Trade Agreements with emerging economies. And even the hardened eurosceptics – the 'fruit-cakes, loonies and closet racists', to quote that unimpeachable source the British prime minister – admit that their first priority after wrenching Britain out of the EU would be to negotiate a preferential trade agreement to get it back into the Single Market.[1] (The flaws in this back-of-the-napkin proposal are too numerous and self-evident to explore in the course of this chapter.) Nonetheless, the value of being part of this powerful trading bloc in international trade negotiations, and of the UK jobs that are dependent on it, continues to be the Achilles heel of the populist eurosceptic movement.

One commonly trotted-out argument from moderate to extreme eurosceptics is that Europe is holding the UK back from a golden age of trade with emerging economies. They point to newly-coined groupings of emerging economies, such as the BRICS and CIVETS, as markets that the UK should be focused on instead of ailing Eurozone countries.[2] This is a baffling argument. Far from being a barrier to trade, the EU is in reality the UK's best opportunity to boost trade with emerging economies. There is nothing which prevents or restricts UK trade with these countries, but it is EU-negotiated trade deals that will secure the preferential market access for UK businesses that can significantly boost trade. As is argued throughout this collection of essays, the EU is not an either/or policy choice for the UK: there are clear value-added benefits in being part of a powerful trade bloc.

KEY PRINCIPLES FOR REFORM

A refocused trade policy could play a major part in Europe's recovery from the financial crisis and in alleviating global poverty. This chapter identifies four broad areas for reform, where embedding social-democratic values can temper the right's crude free-market agenda and build a fairer trade policy:

- focus on exogenous growth
- work within the multilateral framework

- put binding sustainable development at the heart of trade policy
- build a pro-development fair trade policy to last.

TRADING OUT OF THE CRISIS: EXOGENOUS GROWTH

The importance of a strong European trade policy has moved centre-stage as the global recession has deepened. Quite simply, we must trade our way out of the crisis. Twenty years ago Gordon Brown told the Labour Party Conference – to the perplexity of many delegates – that endogenous growth was our future. Michael Heseltine was quick to pointed out that this was not 'Brown but Balls', but twenty years ago, when Ed Balls wrote that speech, it was in fact a plausible option. Today, even after the current failed austerity measures are brought to an end and the Eurozone turns the corner into marked economic improvement, endogenous growth will not be enough to generate sustained economic recovery. The UK now needs an exogenous growth strategy, and we do indeed need to focus on these emerging markets. For the foreseeable future, over 90 per cent of global economic growth is expected to be generated outside Europe.[3] To be sustainable, economic recovery will need to be consolidated by stronger links with new global growth centres where the UK has tended to trade little in the past (for example trade with Ireland exceeds total trade with all the BRICS). To assert this is not to deny that the bulk of our trade is and will remain with our continental neighbours, which makes the single market the most important trade agreement of all. But growth in the next decade from a very low base will have to come from closer economic cooperation with the emerging economies. To achieve this, a coherent EU-level trade policy is indispensable, because growth in trade with these fiercely competitive economies necessitates a strong regulatory framework, and only a regional approach gives us a position of strength in negotiations.

In this regard, the rise of regional and global supply chains gives Europe a strong selling point. European regional value chains have been evolving thanks to the deepening of the single market. iPhones are designed in California and manufactured in Shenzhen, China, but they have a 12 per cent European contribution. Nokia smart phones are made in China but contain 54 per cent European value-added. Even individual components of a Nokia phone reveal the layers of added value: the supply chain for the main phone processor alone stretches from France to India, Japan and the US. The same pattern is repeated from children's toys to passenger jets. Traditional analyses of trade patterns and job creation have focused on the flow of goods and services across borders. But today, in recognition of the importance of value-added global trade flows to economic growth, the WTO is increasingly working with organisations such as the OECD to get a clearer picture of the economic effects of this value-added.

The lesson we have to learn from this is that in many sectors in a globalised world, no single country any longer has the capacity to make products on its own. Trade is more and more about adding layers of value, from research and development and design to the manufacturing of components, assembly and logistics. We need to differentiate between 'made in China' and 'made by China'.

DOHA ON LIFE SUPPORT: MULTILATERAL V BILATERAL

To help expand exogenous growth in the EU and attract value-added investment, a successful conclusion of the Doha Development Agenda would be ideal. It should remain the long-term goal of the EU to show flexibility in these world trade talks, to achieve a rules-based global trading system that works for developed and developing countries. However for the time being Doha, if not dead, is certainly on life-support.

The second-best option is to engage with regional trading groups or individual countries to negotiate comprehensive bilateral trade deals. The EU has pursued this with vigour over the past decade. Ever-increasing lists of countries and trading groups have signalled their interest in pursuing free trade agreements with the EU, which the European Commission has enthusiastically embraced. While the lack of progress on Doha is regrettable, Free Trade Agreements – which secure not only reciprocal market opening but deeper agreements on regulatory standards and non-tariff barriers – are clearly the medium-term future of EU trade policy and a key component in economic stimulation and job creation. But while pursuing this policy, the raw liberalisation agenda of the right must be tempered by a comprehensive vision from the left, which must place high common environmental, labour and human rights standards at the heart of trade agreements, and ensure trade agreements with developed countries do not have an adverse effect on the world's poorest regions.

It is inconceivable that any EU Member State acting alone would have the clout to negotiate such deals. It is therefore not surprising that each Member State has ratified EU Treaties which give the Union the competence to negotiate trade deals for the bloc. The EU is the world's largest trading bloc. It is worth reiterating this to stress the absurdity of the idea that the UK could negotiate market openings with partner countries at anywhere near the level of intensity – or of safeguards – that the EU pursues and achieves. In the food and drink export category, for example, Scotch whisky accounts for a quarter of total UK food and drink exports.[4] In one of its biggest potential markets, India, it faces tariffs of around 150 per cent. Negotiations for a significant reduction on spirit drink tariffs are challenging for the EU, but would be nigh-on impossible for the UK acting alone. This challenge is multiplied across sectors and partner countries. This is where our membership of the EU can provide real added-value. The single market of 500 million people is a massive pole of attraction to other economies, and the lure of preferential access to this market encourages countries across the globe to covet an EU trade agreement. And in comparison with other areas of foreign policy, the EU is most often coherent in speaking with one voice on trade policy on the international stage.

As noted, the European Commission is engaging with a wide range of countries and regions to negotiate free trade agreements. It is fair to say that attempts to negotiate with other regional trading blocs have not been as successful. Original ambitions to conclude an FTA with the ASEAN bloc disintegrated when the differing levels of ambition within the ASEAN region became apparent.[5] Since then the Commission has pursued deep and comprehensive FTAs with individual countries, such as Singapore, Thailand and Vietnam. Similarly, negotiations with the MERCOSUR region have, at the time of writing, all but stalled, although no individual FTAs within the bloc have so far been pursued.[6]

Despite the setbacks, region-to-region negotiations should not be abandoned. The slow geopolitical shift towards regional trade powerhouses currently has renewed vigour – as seen in the launch of negotiations in the Asia-Pacific region for a Trans-Pacific Partnership, a free-trade area including the United States, Japan, Australia and

Canada. Meanwhile the Commission is committed to renewing engagement with ASEAN as a bloc within the next few years, and has concluded an agreement with the Central American region.[7]

The challenges for other regional blocs are substantial, in terms not only of speaking with one voice in trade negotiations, but also of attempting to align regulatory standards and dismantle internal non-tariff barriers. The EU is not simply a world leader; it is streets ahead, and perceived of as the model of successful economic integration to which the rest aspire. Its natural comparative advantage in speaking for one harmonised single market gives it an unparalleled head-start in trade negotiations, and allows it to pursue key European demands – ranging from high food safety standards to comprehensive Geographical Indicators that give additional legal protection abroad to traditional European produce that is recognised to come from a specific EU region. The scope to use this natural advantage should be fully realised, and, crucially, should be used as a force for good, setting the bar high on global standards for sustainable development chapters in trade agreements. In the Doha limbo there must be coherence between the EU's various trade fronts; including in mitigating any damage to the multilateral trading system, and pursing pro-development as well as pro-competitive policies.

But while these region-to-region negotiations have stalled, the EU has turned its attention to bilateral agreements with individual countries, with the launch in 2006 of the Commission's strategy *Global Europe: Competing in the World*, by then-Commissioner for Trade Peter Mandelson.[8] The conclusion and implementation of the FTA with South Korea in 2010 – the first of the 'new generation' deep and comprehensive trade agreements – was looked upon enviously by neighbouring countries in the region, particularly by the Japanese, who launched a vigorous and successful campaign to persuade the European Commission to open trade negotiations with them. Meanwhile the Commission has continued negotiations for, and in some cases concluded, free trade agreements with Canada, India, Singapore, Colombia and Peru, amongst others. The inclusion of the prospect of a free trade agreement between the US and the EU in President Obama's State of the Union address caused much excitement in Brussels and no wonder. Such an agreement would cover over half of world trade, and generate a predicted 0.5 per cent increase in EU GDP.[9] Such economic optimism should be taken with a pinch of

Atlantic sea salt, but given the size of the economies involved, there is no doubt that even a moderate boost to GDP and job creation in the EU would be appreciable.

SUSTAINABLE DEVELOPMENT AT THE HEART OF TRADE

But trade is not an objective in itself, and trade liberalisation is not the end of the game. Rather, trade is a means to an end to secure jobs, high living standards – both at home and abroad – help alleviate poverty, and engender strong sustainable development in our economic relations; it is an instrument of peace, and a factor in discouraging unmanageable migration. The challenge for the left, while we are in the minority across Europe, is to embed our social-democratic values in external trade policy. Equality, freedom and social justice need to be at the heart of our trade relationships if we are to consolidate them at home, promote them abroad and work to entrench them in the multilateral system.

Investing in green technology must be prioritised, not in spite of the economic crisis but because of it. The renewable energy sector is one of the fastest growing industries in the EU. Focusing investment on alternative energy sources can create jobs in this sector in the shorter term, and develop thriving European businesses in the longer term. But the UK is lagging shockingly far behind on this. Of all the EU Member States, the UK has the lowest rate of employment in the renewable energy sector.[10] As the UK's global position on green growth freefalls, the left must mount a convincing argument for investment in green jobs; not only to place environmental protection firmly within our trade policy objectives, but also to stimulate the European economy and create jobs in this rapidly expanding industry.

At the core of the left's sustainable development trade policy is human rights and labour rights. We cannot turn a blind eye to sweatshops in areas of Southeast Asia, or trade unionist assassinations in parts of Latin America, when trade agreements are signed. The protection of wages, decent working conditions and the right to collective bargaining are all too often protected on paper only. The benchmarks and monitoring undertaken by the ILO must be enhanced, and a greater emphasis placed on partner countries not only ratifying but also fully implementing key Conventions. The long-term objective of the EU should be to achieve agreement on regulation on labour rights at the level of the WTO, in order to set a high global standard and provide an established dispute resolution mechanism. Meanwhile, we must do it piece by piece, one FTA at a time.

If the aim is to prevent social dumping, there must be coherence in the EU's demands on partner countries: if socialists do not champion a race to the top then the race to the bottom becomes all too inevitable. The competitive lead which countries achieve by weakening workers' rights is an unfair as well as unjust advantage, and enforceable labour standards can go a long way towards levelling the playing field.

Responsible investment

In this respect, Corporate Social Responsibility (CSR) is slowly transforming from buzz speak of the left to a solid plank in the EU's external trade policy. We need to go much further. A comprehensive CSR policy should be in place for all European investors in third countries, and there should be a mandatory CSR clause in all sustainable development chapters of FTAs.

A responsible investment regime has been shunned by the right in favour of laying out the red carpet for investors, both foreign and European. In response to the lifting of sanctions against Burma by the ILO, the Commission swiftly proposed reinstating trade preferences, as European investors clambered to get access to the exceedingly vulnerable country. Carefully managed, responsible investment can help to rebuild Burma and consolidate its economic recovery and democratic transition. But without a strict, binding and closely monitored CSR policy, including mandatory CSR reporting, Burma's natural resources, labour force and burgeoning democracy all risk exploitation. And if the EU doesn't demand this of European investors in Burma, then where else would it do so? The response of the European left to reform in Burma is in interesting contrast to the approach of David Cameron, who saw tentative reform as the excuse to seek arms contracts and an opportunity for mineral exploitation, even if that only serves to enrich the military regime.

There is a long way to go in opening up corporate activity to real scrutiny, but socialists have managed to make gains in this area in recent years, notably by championing new regulations on obligatory disclosure of payment to governments by companies operating in the extractive industry. Payments made by multinational oil, gas, mining and forestry companies to governments, often in developing countries, have been cloaked in secrecy for too long. By bringing transparency to the process of corporate payments to governments, not only will it shed some light on the powerful role of multinationals; it will also empower the citizens of these countries to follow the money trail and hold their governments to account.

The role of civil society: we really are all in this together

Indeed the role of citizens and civil society is crucial if Europe is to build a fairer trade policy. As the plethora of FTA negotiations bear fruit, monitoring compliance of human and labour rights in partner countries will increasingly rely on civil society input, including the work of human rights organisations and trade unions.

A precedent was set with the South Korea FTA, in which the EU and South Korea both committed to establishing respective Domestic Advisory Groups (DAGs); these would create permanent channels between civil society and the European Commission/South Korean government, in order to monitor implementation of the FTA. The requirement to create Domestic Advisory Groups was set out in the sustainable development chapter, explicitly drawing a link between civil society participation and the enforcement of labour rights and environmental standards. The hope is that these DAGs will not only monitor the implementation of the sustainable development chapter and the impact of the FTA, but will also act as soft power in the broader context – for example encouraging partner countries fully to ratify and implement all ILO conventions on labour rights.

Measuring the success of the DAGs will help strengthen future civil society provisions in FTAs. To be effective in monitoring implementation of the FTA, these Groups must have a broad representation of stakeholders, including not only the business community and academia, but trade unions and other civil society organisations. Given the limited resources which NGOs and trade unions often have, consideration should be given to further budgetary assistance for capacity-building, particularly where civil society organisations are expected to contribute significantly to implementing and monitoring human and labour rights provisions in partner countries where this activity is challenging. So far the Commission has been reluctant to commit to this, but without such engagement there is a real danger that sustainable development chapters of FTAs will fade in importance, for want of resources or teeth.[11] The left needs to make this a sticking point both in future negotiations of FTAs, and indeed when it comes to the scrutiny and approval of the next Trade Commissioner.

The role of the Parliament

The European Parliament has generally been acknowledged to be the most progressive EU institution in safeguarding of human rights, labour rights and environmental protection. And since the entry into force of the Lisbon Treaty, the Parliament has been on an equal footing with the Council on most decisions, including international trade and on practically all legislation. All FTAs require Parliamentary consent before they can enter into force, and all other aspects of trade policy are adopted through the ordinary legislative procedure. The scope for influencing the formulation of trade policy by the left has therefore never been greater, even taking into account the right-wing majorities in both Commission and Parliament, and the appointment of liberal Commissioner for Trade Karel De Gucht from the classically neoliberal Flemish party, following the departure of the socialist Commissioner Cathy Ashton to take on the role of High Representative for Foreign Affairs and Security Policy.

The left has already flexed its trade muscles across the range of open negotiations, from the pre-launch mandate to the final approval required on completed FTAs. The opening of negotiations with Japan was the first FTA to be launched under the terms of the Lisbon Treaty, and the intention of the Council to issue a mandate to the Commission before the Parliament had adopted its position was swiftly rectified by MEPs. The Parliament subsequently adopted a resolution on its priorities for negotiations, including key socialist demands for a robust sustainable development chapter with core labour rights, and specific reference to animal welfare standards (which called for the abolition of the Japanese whale hunt and trade in whale products). The precedent has been set for full parliamentary involvement in the formulation of trade objectives, and socialists must continue to fight tooth and nail to ensure the adoption of holistic and progressive mandates.

Indeed, policy coherence across foreign policy, trade and development has been central to the left's demands in the parliament, and must continue to be so. Thus socialists opposed a trade upgrade with Israel in the context of ongoing settlement-building and the blockade of Gaza; and though this position failed to achieve the necessary critical mass in the Parliament, it nonetheless framed the debate over a so-called technical upgrade in the geopolitical context of the Union's starkly mixed messages on the Middle East. Similarly, a socialist-led block on an upgrade with Uzbekistan on the trade in textiles – opposed due to its blatant contradiction with EU condemnation of forced and child labour in the Uzbek cotton fields – brought much-needed scrutiny of a supposedly technical measure. In this case the left won out, and the Parliament delayed the approval of the agreement until the ILO assessments of this modern-day slavery can confirm real change on the ground.

Perhaps the biggest opportunity for the left to flex its muscles in trade negotiations was over the FTA with Colombia and Peru. Colombia has been widely acknowledged to be the most dangerous country in the world for trade unionists, due to extraordinary levels of labour activists' assassinations.[12] When negotiations for an FTA were launched in 2009 – in what was to become another failed attempt at a regional agreement with the Andean Community, but resulted in a multiparty agreement with Peru – the left launched a campaign of opposition. The results were mixed. In a 'one step forward, two steps back' approach, the moderate gains achieved by progressives over key demands for a road map on labour rights were overshadowed by a split in the socialists on whether to accept or reject the ultimate agreement. The final agreement – the first comprehensive FTA with a CIVETS country – was widely welcomed by the right, which initially placed no demands whatsoever for human rights conditionality. The achievement of the left in annexing a Memorandum of Understanding to the FTA with the Human Rights Road Map, even though it was in a minority, was certainly a victory. But this real achievement will only yield results if it is underpinned with civil society monitoring, and a willingness in the Commission and Parliament to maintain pressure for change on the ground. This is easier when there is the promise of a trade agreement, less so when agreement has been reached.

The carrot-and-stick approach to trade is a powerful tool of the Union, but it has been mismanaged by the right. Its enthusiasm for launching trade negotiations on multiple fronts, with only finite resources available to the Commission that has to do all the heavy lifting, has not been matched by a willingness to exploit suspension clauses in trade agreements for violations of human rights. Such mechanisms are only effective when partners believe they will be used. While Sri Lanka has seen its trade preferences suspended for failure to uphold certain UN Conventions, no such suspension was launched for Colombia or Uzbekistan. Indeed the Commission proposals to upgrade the Union's trade relations with both countries have struck a blow to the Union's credibility on human rights standards. Progressive forces must bring more coherence to the EU's rhetoric on trade policy and human rights, if there is to be any hope of changing the situation on the ground for those facing human rights violations.

TRADE AND DEVELOPMENT

To say that development should be at the heart of trade policy seems almost trite as neoliberal economic policies sweep through Europe, the financial crisis and political repercussions weaken governments' resistance to protectionism, and the chasm of inequalities between rich and poor grows wider every day. The devastatingly cavalier attitude towards domestic inequalities demonstrated by the right Europe-wide, through its unashamed attempts to dismantle the welfare state, gives a glimpse of the value conservatives currently attach to global inequalities and international development.

But the economic and ethical arguments for using trade as a development tool must remain central to the left's principles if it is to prevent global trade policy lurching from protectionism to wanton liberalisation, neither of which is to the benefit of the developing world.

Aid for trade is a key component in order to support capacity-building in developing countries. Long-term support to help developing countries diversify their economies and expand trade opportunities can finally fully integrate the developing world into the global trading system, and expand the pitiful 1.12 per cent of world trade for which the 49 Least Developed Countries (LDCs) currently account.[14]

Without assistance to diversify, LDCs will remain exceedingly vulnerable. On average each country relies on just three products for over 70 per cent of their exports; at the height of the financial crisis in 2009, LDCs saw their exports fall by 28 per cent in a single year.[15] This would be challenging enough for developed and diverse economies, but it is devastating to developing countries.

But if the left is serious about strengthening capacity-building and integrating developing economies, it needs to play fair. The Common Agricultural Policy in the EU grossly distorts the market and seriously disadvantages the agricultural sector in developing countries. Those in favour of export subsidies and sugar quotas continue to lavish money on European agri-business while shutting out developing countries from the European market. Recent revision of the CAP fell shamefully short of meaningful reform, with the dominant right concentrating on headline cuts rather than qualitative reform. There will be no policy coherence in trade and development until the outdated agricultural regime is tackled.

To help strengthen not only the agricultural sectors but manufacturing and R&D, aid for trade must include policies which promote south-south trade. Greater trade within developing regions is crucial to reduce aid dependence and consolidate regional integration. The trend is towards more south-south preferential agreements, and this must be enhanced, with the EU working closely in support.

Sustainable development must be inherent in capacity-building. Backing for good governance, transparency and human rights protection is the only way to ensure the race to the bottom becomes a thing of the past. The left must ensure that with the integration of developing economies into the global trading system, the norm is for standards to be strengthened, not weakened.

The Generalised System of Preferences system

The solid framework of EU trade and development policy has so far largely survived the financial crisis, but key elements have been chipped away. The starting point was substantial: the EU has the most generous trading scheme in the world for developing countries. Through historical colonial ties and more recent attempts to use trade to extend the EU's strategic foreign policy interests, the Generalised System of Preferences (GSP) regime until recently afforded preferential market access to all LDCs and middle- and low-income countries. LDCs benefit from the Everything But Arms (EBA) regime, which grants duty-free, quota-free access to the EU market for all goods excluding arms and ammunition. The standard GSP regime provides reduced-tariff access for non-LDC developing countries, while the 'special incentive arrangement for sustainable development and good governance', known as GSP+, provides additional trade preferences to vulnerable developing countries which have implemented key aspects of good governance, and of sustainable development ILO Conventions.

But the GSP regime has not been immune from recent reforms to refocus trade and development to the poorest countries. Upper middle-income countries have been removed from the scheme, despite efforts of the socialists to nuance the criteria, with more consideration being given to levels of diversification. This has chimed with the general trend across European development policy to reduce aid to middle-income countries.

Only time will tell if a refocusing of effort on the poorest countries will stimulate economic growth and diversification without vulnerable middle-income countries seeing their growth stagnate and inequalities rise. But certainly the current instrument for reform is too blunt. Far greater attention must be paid to levels of diversification and inequalities *within* developing countries as well as *between* them before further aid and preferential market access is entirely withdrawn.

Furthermore, the current trend to withdraw preferential access in order to encourage countries to pursue an FTA must stop. Many of the upper middle-income countries removed from the scheme, particularly in Latin America, were in the process of negotiating FTAs when the GSP was reformed. But this should not be seen as a viable policy pursuit with middle-income developing countries. Standard FTAs are not, by nature, development tools, and the left must resist any further efforts to weaken the GSP regime. It is vital that all partner countries, particularly developing countries, pursue FTAs only if and when they wish. Any attempts to push developing countries into negotiating an FTA purely from lack of any other market access opportunities would be an abuse of EU power, and would undermine the central principle of equal partnership.

Conversely, the more generous GSP+ is a trade preference the EU should be strongly promoting with vulnerable countries. The scheme remains the most effective carrot and stick approach to trade policy that the Union pursues. The scheme, which offers further trade preferences in recognition of implementation of 27 key ILO Conventions on human rights, labour rights and environmental standards, must remain at the heart of a progressive EU trade policy, not only to promote better working conditions worldwide, but to encourage diversification in vulnerable countries and advance fair economic growth.

Recent reform of the GSP+ has already reinvigorated the scheme for the better. The relaxation of the vulnerability criterion has opened up the scheme to more vulnerable countries, and months before the changes had come into effect Pakistan had already applied to join. This should be welcomed by the left. Certainly there is a long way to go in strengthening working conditions in these countries, but herein lies the purpose of GSP+. The eagerness of newly eligible countries to join is, at least in part, a testament to its success.

But the more attractive the carrot, the greater the threat of the stick must be. This is particularly true for GSP+. Without robust monitoring of the implementation and consolidation of the ILO Conventions and the human rights situation more widely, GSP+ is rendered ineffective; a generous incentive scheme with little incentive for change. The recent beefing up of the monitoring requirements is welcome, but the Commission has a patchy track record of bringing pressure to bear on GSP+ recipients for human rights violations. The left must focus efforts on robust implementation of a strong GSP+ regime, working with civil society organisations on the ground to monitor the human rights situation, and demanding greater policy coherence from the Commission and EEAS when it comes to suspending preferences.

Economic Partnership Agreements: Time to be a flexible friend

At the nexus of EU trade and development policy are Economic Partnership Agreements (EPAs), and here the Commission could do with showing more flexibility.

Colonial ties have resulted in a unique trading relationship between the Union and the African, Caribbean and Pacific (ACP) region. Essentially the members of the ACP/EU Cotonou Agreement have had non-reciprocal access to the EU market. At the beginning of the century poor countries not benefiting from this arrangement claimed this was discriminatory and took a case to the WTO, which they won. As a result, since 2003 the EU and its ACP partners have been trying to negotiate EPAs which, by opening 80 per cent of ACP markets to EU competition, would make the EU/ACP arrangement WTO-compatible. The aim was to complete EPAs with the Caribbean region, the Pacific region and six African Regions. So far only one full EPA has been signed, and that is with the Caribbean Region.

Believing that a rules-based international trading system is an important safeguard for developing countries, the left in the European Parliament has largely accepted the rationale behind EPAs. But it has insisted that they had to be about more than market opening and as a result all EPAs have development chapters. However, the Commission has used EPA negotiations to put on the table a number of issues that go beyond WTO requirements, most notably on intellectual property, public procurement and financial services. Not surprisingly, given that for many ACP countries these negotiations, at least in terms of market access, are something-for-nothing deals, such EPAs have proven highly controversial and difficult to conclude.

The left should back EPAs as a way to put on a solid legal footing EU-ACP arrangements, but we should insist on a number of conditions. Firstly, the Commission should be told not to press for agreements that go beyond trade in goods. In particular, financial services should be treated with great caution. Surely if there is one general lesson from the financial crisis it is that banking liberalisation needs careful and appropriate regulation. Secondly, through aid for trade and other measures ACP countries must be given assistance to link into the global trading system. Thirdly, nothing in the EPA agreements should undermine the regional integration process already underway in Africa. We must encourage South/South trade to develop. Finally, the speed and extent of market opening must be negotiated between equal partners: the EU should not be forcing market opening for sensitive products or where infant industries could be destroyed.

With the global crisis in full force, African countries, just like EU countries, can ill afford to become inward looking, so that delicately-managed EPAs could be a win-win situation for both continents.

CONCLUSION

The right in Europe believe the world should move immediately and uncompromisingly towards free trade; while on the left, in some quarters (for example among some French socialists) there is a view that the best way to help European workers and developing countries is to shield them vigorously from the forces of reform and liberalisation.

There is, however, a third way (if that term is not now discredited), and that is to manage globalisation in a way that creates jobs at home and aids development abroad. The left should put human rights, workers' rights and environmental protection at the heart of its international trade policy. Ideally these rights and protections should be enshrined in a reformed global rules-based trading system. Given the reality of global trade talks, the European left should insist that at the very least these be contained in all EU bilateral trade deals. We should accept that jobs at home depend on an exogenous growth strategy, and harness the might of the single European market to open up other developed markets to fair competition. We should argue for an industrial policy that enables European jobs to be linked into the global supply chain rather than trying to create national champions or complete products. We should also where possible use trade to reduce global inequalities. Finally we should insist that no trade agreement should have the power to undermine the universal delivery of a public service.

Well-managed international trade has the potential to create and sustain jobs domestically, and to be a powerful statement to the world of Europe's values. Instead of exporting arms, Europe could export a belief in the right to decent work, respect for the environment and dignity of human beings.

NOTES

1. For Cameron comment see http://news.bbc.co.uk/1/hi/uk_politics/4875502.stm.
2. BRICS: Brazil, Russia, India, China and South Africa; CIVETS: Colombia, Indonesia, Vietnam, Egypt, Turkey and South Africa.
3. See WTO: www.wto.org/english/news_e/sppl_e/sppl255_e.htm.
4. See www.publications.parliament.uk/pa/cm201213/cmselect/cmfaff/writev/643/m11.htm.
5. SEAN: Association of Southeast Asian Nations:
6. Mercosur is the Southern Common Market: Argentina, Brazil, Paraguay, Uruguay, Venezuela.
7. Costa Rica, El Salvador, Honduras, Nicaragua, Panama, Guatemala.
8. See http://europa.eu/legislation_summaries/external_trade/r11022_en.htm.
9. See http://trade.ec.europa.eu/doclib/press/index.cfm?id=869.
10. See http://ec.europa.eu/europe2020/pdf/themes/green_jobs.pdf.
11. See www.europarl.europa.eu/sides/getAllAnswers.do?reference=E-2012-006385&language=EN.
12. See www.amnesty.org.uk/news_details.asp?NewsID=15338.
14. www.europarl.europa.eu/sides/getDoc.do?pubRef=- per cent2f per cent2fEP per cent2f per cent2fNONSGML per cent2bREPORT per cent2bA7-2013-0053 per cent2b0 per cent2bDOC per cent2bPDF per cent2bV0 per cent2f per cent2fEN.
15. www.oecd.org/trade/aft/47706423.pdf.

7. An internationalism for the twenty-first century

Patrick Costello

The European project did not start as an internationalist one. The founders were focused on removing the local economic causes of the conflict that had led to the Second World War, as well as looking to build an economic block to act as a bulwark against the Soviet Union and its allies in the east. After the failed attempt in 1954 to found a European Defence Community, integration in foreign policy was put on the back burner. The fact that the EC was not a political actor globally meant that, perhaps uniquely among international actors, its trade, development policies and humanitarian assistance work predated its emergence as a global political player. Since the end of the Cold War, the EU has developed a more global and political role, and the challenge for the left has been to ensure that it develops international policies that also reflect the values and approach of the left.

This sounds straightforward, but the world in the early twenty-first century is not one where those on the left can find easy certainties. In April 1999, Tony Blair was able to say, with little fear of contradiction, that 'no one in the West who has seen what is happening in Kosovo can doubt that NATO's military action is justified'. In a major speech in Chicago, Blair made a strong plea for internationalism and an end to the principle of non-interference in the internal affairs of another country. Those who had been active in the struggle to end apartheid in South Africa, or were involved in the campaigns to end oppression in Central America, East Timor and Burma, applauded the idea that human rights violations could be the basis for international intervention, even if they would have preferred it to be a UN intervention and not a NATO one. Indeed UN explicit approval of intervention was an essential precondition for many on the left; which is why supporting the French action in Mali raises questions not of principle but of practicality.

Yet today, as the death toll rises daily in Syria, there is little appetite for intervention to prevent President Assad's war against his own civilian population. Nobody questions the need to do all possible to protect the people and to provide humanitarian aid, but calls for a just military intervention to stop the killing are notable by their absence. Among the sobering lessons of the Afghanistan and Iraq wars are that we cannot predict the outcome of such interventions, and that we should be cautious about the moral certainty of any such cause. The arming and training of groups purely on the basis that my enemy's enemy is my friend has a tendency to backfire and create even greater problems for human rights and for global security, which often continue long after victory is declared. More recently, the debate within the EU between those keen to amend if not to breach the EU's own current arms embargo has been an important and complex one: some Member States are seeking an elusive breakthrough in the absence of external intervention, while others are concerned about which groups would end up being armed, and fear the situation might develop into a proxy war with Russia and Iran – with immense global security implications.

So if liberal interventionism is problematic, what is the core of a progressive foreign policy? This is a question that David Miliband addressed as a newly appointed foreign minister, at the Fabian annual conference in 2008, when he argued the case for taking the best of the liberal human rights tradition as well as the social democrat traditions of solidarity and social justice. If Blair's vision in Chicago was essentially a liberal one, is there more clarity in the socialist tradition? In foreign policy, this has been most clearly expressed through opposition to the North-South divide. But here too, the easy certainties of the 1980s have vanished. All progressives could unambiguously be on the side of the campaigns for debt forgiveness in the 1980s and 1990s, and against the structural adjustments imposed on the poorest countries by the international financial institutions. That was the easy bit. However, the economic rise of China and India to take a global share of GDP that better reflects their share of the world's population, has, perhaps understandably, generated little enthusiasm on the European left. In part this is because so much of this growth has been powered by international investment at the expense of manufacturing and, more recently, service jobs in the west. But, in addition, one of the strongest attractions of international investment in Asia has been its low labour costs and lower levels of social and environmental regulation. In the absence of enforceable basic international labour and environmental standards, globalisation has been creating a race to the bottom in which labour, which is less mobile, is at the mercy of footloose capital that can invest wherever the conditions are best for maximising profit. One of the less talked about consequences of the enormous growth rates in both China and India has been the dramatic rises in inequality within both countries.

WHAT A PROGRESSIVE FOREIGN AND SECURITY POLICY NOW MIGHT LOOK LIKE

In this uncertain world, then, identifying what a progressive foreign policy looks like should make possible an honest assessment about what role the EU could play in developing it, as well as a clearer critique of the current government's policies in this area. Progressive activists should be thinking in terms of the following four central, though not exclusive, elements.

Rebuilding the state

If it remains clear-cut that progressives were right to oppose the debt crises and structural adjustments of the late twentieth century, it is logical that the left should be working today to rectify the international consequences of this failed neoliberal orthodoxy. Indeed the collapse of the Washington consensus provides a political opportunity to rethink the role of the state internationally as well as at home.

One of the most visible outcomes of those lost decades for development was the collapse of the state in large parts of the Global South in the 1990s. While the links were not obvious at the time, the disintegration of Somalia in the Horn of Africa, the bloody civil wars in Liberia and Somalia in the West, and the tragedy of the Great Lakes launched by the Rwandan genocide, followed similar patterns as – in the absence of effective state structures – groups which could access weapons were able to control both people and resources. The little-explored connections between, for example, the uses of tin and coltan in mobile phones, the abundant supplies in eastern Congo and the continuing conflicts over control of the territory involving the mass rape of women are eloquent testimony to the need to rebuild governance and the state in large parts of Africa. Where the state has remained robust, as in South Africa, or Botswana, to take two very different African examples, levels of insecurity and conflict have been correspondingly lower. (Note that there are also counter-examples: for example, Somalia, in the absence of a strong state, now has many of its services provided by non-state actors, e.g. mobile telephony, energy, finance, airlines).

Across the world, the failure of the state to provide basic services to the poor is what has given terrorist groups fertile ground to work in. To take just one example, the absence of the state from large parts of the Sahel, and the ability of Islamic terrorist groups to find safe havens in these areas, also shows us that rebuilding the state is in Europe's security interests too. This is not to deny the importance of non-governmental aid and civil society in addressing inequality. The point here is that the ability of civil society to make a difference is dependent on the existence of a functioning state system that is able to maintain peace, and assure the provision of infrastructure and a fair and legal distribution of resources. It is cheaper for the governments of the rich world to invest in building institutions than to bear the security costs of terrorism and piracy, which are the result of failing to carry out such investment.

Support for multilateralism, democracy and human rights

Being rightly suspicious of the real motivations of some of those who argue for military interventions to protect human rights and democracy does not make them less valid goals for a values-based foreign policy. What applied in the past to South Africa and to Burma should apply to Egypt, Tunisia and the Gulf States too. It is important to remember that the uprisings of the so-called Arab Spring took place not because of the policies of Europe and the US but in spite of them. For all the talk of reform in the Mediterranean, the reality was that friendly dictators such as Hosni Mubarak in Egypt and Zine El Abidine Ben Ali in Tunisia were fully supported by Washington, Paris, London and indeed Brussels, and the spectre of political Islam was waved at those in Europe who suggested they might not be the best allies. In the case of Egypt, when policymakers were deciding on whether or not to provide military aid, its strategic importance as an Arab ally on the border of Israel tended to outweigh concerns for its people – or about the arthritic authoritarianism of the regime. As a footnote, two years after the Arab Spring, it is worth noting that western governments have been much less supportive of the basic human rights – and uprisings – of the historically repressed Shia in Bahrain and the rest of the Gulf; these regimes continue to receive 'security advice' from the West. It does not seem too wearily cynical to attribute this to concern about the security of oil supplies.

However, if Europe and the US were absent during the fall of the Arab dictators, it is even more important that their governments' policies demonstrate full commitment to the democratic transitions that have begun. Fundamentally, this is about supporting the economies of countries in transition: delivering on preferentially opening our markets to them; facilitating access to top universities; and providing much-needed technical assistance and training to help transform the state structures that were previously the personal fiefdoms of the dictators.

Favouring democracy at a national level goes hand in hand with support for multilateralism. For all its flaws – and its inability to act on Syria has been a glaring example – the UN system is still the best option for addressing global international questions. Europe should be in the forefront of the development of the kind of global governance that is needed to improve world peace and security. Even in the fraught area of military intervention, a comparison between the UN-endorsed French intervention in Mali and the 'coalition of the willing' in Iraq demonstrates how significant the backing of the UN Security Council remains in assuring the legitimacy of actions of this kind, a well as public acceptance and the possibility of structured follow-up.

Markets with progressive rules

For a long time, the negative consequences of globalisation were tolerated by too many because, as is always and correctly pointed out, the absolute number of people in poverty globally has been falling since 1980, for the first time in centuries. But when global inequality reaches the grotesque levels where the wealth of the three most well-to-do plutocrats now exceeds the combined GDP of the 48 least developed countries, we can no longer turn a blind eye to the negative effects of that same process of globalisation, which exacerbates a situation that is morally beyond inequality. The pie has got bigger but it is being divided more and more unequally. Furthermore, global growth, which has been a consistent feature of the last ten years, and which has to a certain extent mitigated the worst consequences of these rampant injustices, is now coming to juddering halt; a pause that could, especially if the climate-change threat is not faced, last a long time.

Some would advocate that all this should lead to the reassertion of national control over the economy, to enable fairer distribution to be achieved through national political action. However this will do nothing to solve the problem. Global inequality is higher than inequality within any individual country; it is twice that of even the UK for example. Protectionism and the restoration of capital controls is the global equivalent of solving the crime problem by living in a gated community. Within large enough markets, such as the EU, it is possible to unilaterally impose certain social and environmental standards, and this is hugely important if Europeans are to prevent the race to the bottom; but if the imposition of such standards operates as a protectionist tool, it will do nothing to stop the declining living standards of those on our borders – with all of the security issues that that brings with it.

A more promising path is to try to achieve core labour, social and environmental standards as part of the rules governing international markets. Ever since the World Trade Organisation was founded, international trade unions have been pushing for the inclusion of these standards as part of the ground rules for trade. As the multilateral WTO negotiations have run into the ground, the same question arises for the bilateral trade deals Europe is negotiating to replace them. Is the EU prepared to include commitment to these core standards as a part of those bilateral deals? Will this be an issue in the negotiations for a transatlantic market launched in 2013, for example? There is, and always has been, a powerful coalition opposed to such ideas, including many of the governments of the European Union, who claim that such measures would promote protectionism, but who in fact are often only the most tepid supporters of the more advanced welfare states of the countries they lead, and have no ideological objection to an erosion of social standards at home. Those involved in the parts of our economy that benefit from the increased profits resulting from unregulated production and cheaper labour are also a powerful lobby against such action. If we want to escape from the implacable global competitive logic to reduce standards and drive down the costs of labour, with all the inequality that this inevitably produces, there is a glaring need for agreement on some basic standards for those in work, wherever that might be. No-one imagines that a global minimum wage, paid holidays for all, and the full panoply of the welfare state can be introduced world-wide in short order, but if the European Union does nothing to develop and promote a social, ecological and welfare dimension for world trade, then no-one else will, and the Union's own model will crumble inexorably.

Broader-based security

Many of today's threats to security are ones that the military has not been historically equipped to defend against. These non-traditional threats, from terrorism to organised crime, cyber-threats, environmental dangers, etc, require a very different approach from the traditional military stance, which is geared to threats posed by another state or states. To be equipped to deal with such threats and to be able to guarantee a measure of security requires that policies be coordinated effectively. Aid, trade, development and communications policy are as central to lasting solutions as the deployment of military and police.

At the same time, the military is still needed. We may not need the Cold War relic of the nuclear deterrent but, as the 2011 intervention to enforce the no-fly zone in Libya showed, the Europeans who provided most of the military assets were still heavily reliant on the United States for capacities such as air-to-air refuelling. This is partly because of an assumption that the US will fill the gaps, but also because of cuts to military budgets as a result of the economic crisis. Since 2008, most big European countries have cut their defence budgets by 10-15 per cent. The Royal Air Force, for example, now has just a quarter of the numbers of combat aircraft it had in the 1970s. As US national security pivots towards Asia and reduces its military commitments and resources in Europe, there is a pressing need to make a virtue out of necessity, and to reshape European military capabilities to reflect the real threats that we face, based on a much more broader-based concept of security.

WHY DO WE NEED THE EU TO ACHIEVE IT?

> For a country like the UK, to make its voice heard in the world, 'Europe' does not work as a damper, but as a megaphone.
>
> Hermann Van Rompuy, European Council President, 28.02.13

The argument for an EU foreign policy is not a difficult one to make. It is simply common sense that we will achieve more, have a greater collective weight on the world stage, and be able to pool our resources more effectively, if we have a common policy. Perhaps it is not surprising, then, that even in this age of rampant euroscepticism, support for this policy has remained high. According to the results of Eurobarometer's regular polling, in autumn 2012, 64 per cent of Europeans were in favour of the common foreign and security policy, with 26 per cent against, a figure that has remained remarkable constant (e.g. 67 per cent to 19 per cent in 2003). Even in the UK, where the policy has not exactly been talked up by our political leaders and mass media, 40 per cent of Britons are in favour of the policy (compared to the 14 per cent of Britons in favour of the common currency).

The evidence in favour of the added value of Europeans working together in the world is also overwhelming. From the robust counter-piracy action off the Somali coast to the success of the dialogue between the Serbian and Kosovan authorities, from the impact of the EU as the largest humanitarian and development aid donor to the adoption by the Chinese of so many more European regulatory standards and measures than American ones, the common sense argument is backed up by solid results. To take just one example, what could Britain do alone to counter the threat of the development of Iranian nuclear weapons? It is EU sanctions that have brought the Iranians back to the negotiating table – in part because the US sanctions regime was already so severe that there was little more that the US could have done. It is not by chance that it is the EU's High Representative who leads the negotiations with the Iranians in the so-called E3+3 talks, in which the UK, France, Germany, the US, Russia and China participate.

The range of foreign policy issues where the Europeans have been able to agree unanimously on a collective approach is also testament to this logic of working together. Of course, there is much more of a spotlight on the EU when its Member States fail to act together. Yet the evidence from these cases also points to the value of a common policy. They show clearly how much less effective Europeans are at achieving foreign policy goals when they are divided. On 21 March 2003, two days after the Iraq war started, Tony Blair was criticised by Polly Toynbee in the *Guardian* for not having gone to Brussels before going to Camp David and signing up to the coalition of the willing. The argument was made that it had weakened his hand in negotiating with the Americans. On the same day, the left-leaning French daily *Libération* was berating Jacques Chirac for the same error, for not having gone to the EU before deciding to oppose the second UN Security Council Resolution that would have provided a legal mandate to the US invasion. The same argument was made that acting unilaterally had weakened his position.

This experience of the problems caused by weakness and division was one of the main motivations when, the following year, all of the EU leaders agreed to set up a stronger EU foreign policy, with its own diplomatic service, as part of the EU's draft constitution. The idea – relatively uncontroversial compared with some of the other institutional provisions of the draft – survived the rejection of the Constitution to re-emerge in the Lisbon Treaty. The European External Action Service was finally set up at the beginning of 2011 under the leadership of Baroness Cathy Ashton, appointed a year earlier as High Representative. One of the objectives was to prevent such damaging divisions in the future, and one consequence has been that the new service's staff come both from the European institutions and the foreign and defence ministries of the Member States.

In the end, no institutional structure or Treaty is going to *force* Europe's nations to work together if and when they disagree. And the unanimity provisions of the Treaty make progress at times slow. But that was what Member States, and particularly the UK, wanted: they cannot therefore turn round now and complain about the painstaking procedures that have to be gone through before positions are adopted. Nor can they pretend that their views are being ridden over roughshod. But as the practice of working together becomes ingrained, divisions are becoming rarer, and disagreements are more often resolved behind the scenes. What creates the impetus for agreeing a common position is knowledge of the political cost of being divided. When, in 2012, the Palestinians took a resolution to the UN General Assembly seeking recognition as a state, the initial expectation was that the EU's Member States would be horribly split and that this in turn would seriously weaken the EU's ability to play any kind of role in re-launching the then frozen peace process. In the end, not only was there only one EU Member State who voted against the resolution (the Czech Republic), but, a month later, in December 2012, the EU adopted the clearest statement of policy it had ever made on the impact of Israeli settlement expansion. The very fear of the impact of division had brought the EU Member States together, in order to avoid losing influence collectively and individually.

So, if progressives can agree that an EU foreign policy is more effective than a purely national one, how would this apply in practice to the four elements of a progressive foreign policy outlined in the previous section? Is it right to say that the internationalist British left can achieve more of its foreign policy objectives through the EU than through Her Majesty's Foreign and Commonwealth Office alone?

A positive case study: back from the brink in the Horn of Africa

At the beginning of 2013, a leading Somali pirate leader, known as Afweyneh (Big Mouth), announced to reporters that he was stopping piracy, and he also encouraged his colleagues to stop. The reason, according to the local Somali administration, was that they could no longer function as they used to, and the profits were no longer good. This little-reported statement reflected a first success in the struggle against piracy that had been waged by the EU ever since it appeared in the middle of the last decade as yet another symptom of the failed state that Somalia had become. From 151 verified attacks on sizeable ships in 2011 to 31 in 2012, the drop in pirate attacks has been dramatic; and it has been a consequence both of taking action against piracy directly, and of changing the conditions on the ground that created it.

The EU's naval counter-piracy mission, EUNAVFOR Atalanta, was established in December 2008. It was the first EU maritime operation, with an initial focus on protecting World Food Programme convoys, though its mandate rapidly developed to become wider and more robust. By the middle of 2012, it was even able to launch an operation against a land-base belonging to pirates, using a helicopter from one of the mission's boats to destroy speedboats, fuel stores and other supplies. The success of this EU mission, led by a succession of

British admirals and with its operational headquarters inside the UK's joint operations headquarters at Northwood, is based on naval assets provided by 22 EU Member States, and with the participation of a number of third countries. EUNAVFOR co-ordinates closely with the other, smaller anti-piracy efforts, including the NATO operation and single country efforts by China, Iran and others, but it is the most important player, not least because it has been able to use the EU's diplomatic clout to negotiate for pirates captured by the mission to be tried and imprisoned in different countries in the region. The mission has also played an important role in encouraging merchant shipping to take the necessary protective measures to prevent acts of piracy and hostage taking.

In itself, Operation Atalanta is impressive, but it is only the tip of the iceberg of the EU's action in the region, which is aimed not just at restoring security to shipping lanes, but also addressing the source of piracy in Somalia. Thus, for example, a new EU Mission, EUCAP Nestor, launched in 2012, is now helping to build an effective local coastguard capacity in the countries of the East African Coast, with the aim of allowing Atalanta to complete its mission and leave behind a solid local counter-piracy capacity. The EU has also provided massive support to the African Union Mission to Somalia (AMISOM), launched in 2007 to create the security conditions that would allow the delivery of humanitarian aid, and enable reconstruction and development. In addition, the EU, through its own military training mission in Uganda (EUTM Somalia), has directly trained nearly 2000 Somali soldiers and officers for AMISOM. This mission is now in the process of moving its activities into the Somali capital Mogadishu, a sign in itself of the improving security environment.

It is worth highlighting the security components of the EU's action in the Horn of Africa because it demonstrates that EU activities go well beyond the more traditional funding of development aid. But of course aid remains a vital part of the EU's work in the region. Apart from the provision of humanitarian aid in the face of recent droughts in the region, the EU has also committed hundreds of millions of euros to development support in Somalia in the areas of governance, education, economic growth, food security, health, environment, water and sanitation. All of this work, from training Somali soldiers to providing water supplies, is operating under a comprehensive EU strategy for the Horn of Africa. In 2011, an EU

Special Representative, Alex Rondos, was appointed to ensure that all of the different tracks of the EU's comprehensive approach pushed in the same direction.

The idea that any other international actor, including NATO – or even the UK alone – could have taken such a comprehensive approach to the problem is absurd. The reports of Westminster's European scrutiny committees make clear the key role the EU is playing in this region. The UN is, of course, the other key international actor, and it is important to note that both Atalanta and AMISOM are the result of a clear political direction and mandates set by the UN Security Council. But the UN could not be successful in achieving its desired results without the concerted policy efforts of the EU.

However, if Somalia and the Horn of Africa is a positive case study, there are also a number of instances where, although the EU could have been the major actor, it has not fulfilled this potential, either because of the political complexion of the governments running the EU, or simply because of missing opportunities.

A less positive example: supporting growth and democracy in the southern neighbourhood

The wealth gap between the EU and the countries in the south of the Mediterranean is possibly the most unequal boundary in the world. Certainly, as measured by GDP per capita differences, the gap is significantly larger (7-10 times poorer) than the gap between the United States and Mexico (around 5 times poorer). Added to these differences, the societies of North Africa are much younger than the ageing ones of Europe. Finally, the additional impact of climate change and the creeping desertification northwards and southwards from the Sahara has also contributed to enormous migratory pressures from the south to Europe, and a great need for economic growth in the countries of the Southern Mediterranean. Indeed the deteriorating economy was one of the major drivers of the 2011 uprisings, adding an extra spur to the popular resentment against the corrupt geriatric authoritarianism of the old regimes, at least in Tunisia and Egypt.

In March 2011, a special European summit was called to decide on the EU's response to the collapse of the dictatorships in Tunisia and Egypt. European support had been largely invisible during these mass democratic movements, but in the aftermath the EU had a unique opportunity to show that it was on the side of the new governments by rewarding them with the things they really needed: financial support, easier access to European markets and easier mobility in order to facilitate business and investment. Helping the new governments to generate employment would have allowed them to show people in the whole region the tangible benefits of democratic change. The approach was summarised by the High Representative as the three Ms: money, markets and mobility.

Unfortunately, for all the fine words in the summit declaration, the EU's concrete response has been too slow. Commitments made then are only now slowly being translated into action. Of course, one fundamental political problem has been that the Arab Spring coincided with the economic crisis in the Eurozone. The EU Mediterranean countries most concerned and in normal times best disposed to EU action in the region (Spain, Italy, Greece) were also those least able to push the case for leadership in its southern neighbourhood, as the need for bail-outs and the conditionalities imposed with them weakened their hand.

As a result, the March 2011 declaration shows strikingly little concern for making a new offer to Egypt and Tunisia; instead it emphasises worries about the possible arrival of refugees and migrants from Libya. The response of Europe's leaders was defensive and unimaginative, and we are now paying for this with the risk of further conflict; a new authoritarianism is developing in Tunisia, the army has taken power again in Egypt, and there is growing popular support for hard-line Salafist Islamism, while Europe's ability to influence the Syria conflict has been reduced, leaving regional actors such as the Saudis and Qataris with much more influence in developments in the region. The strengthening of the Salafist movements across the region will have security consequences that, if they could not have been avoided, could at least have been mitigated.

But if Europe could have been a player and has not achieved it, it is also clear that Britain could never have been a sufficiently key actor to make any difference alone. So we are here talking about a case where, in order to achieve progressive foreign policy objectives, the only policy option was and remains for Britain to work for policy change through the European Union.

United we stand, divided we fall

In the field of trade policy and regulatory practices and standards, Europe has been enormously successful at persuading others to do things the way Europe wants to. The fact that Europe is still the largest single market in the world means that all market players are prepared to play by its rules in order to access it. The same does not apply to foreign policy more generally. The EU has not as yet been able to persuade the rest of the world to sign up to a follow-up to the Kyoto agreement to reduce climate emissions, and there are even fewer signs of the EU being able to persuade the rest of the world to subscribe to even the most basic labour standards, such as an end to child labour or bonded labour. The reason is that – unlike in trade, where the European Commission has been given clear legal powers by the Member States in the Treaties, and where the legal rules for access to European markets are fixed at European level – in most areas of external relations, the ability of the EU to act is in part dependent on the extent to which Member States agree to do something at European level. This makes it easy for powerful countries to play European Member States off against each other in order to achieve what they want. China's punishment of France, and now the UK, for officially receiving the Dalai Lama, and Russia's reliance on its importance to EU Member States as energy supplier and importer of German cars, are two clear examples of this, but there are many hidden ones. In many countries, the bilateral embassies of the Member States prefer to leave it the EU delegation to raise issues of human rights, allowing them to focus instead on cutting business deals for their companies. When the EU leadership has a summit meeting with the Chinese or the Russians, Member States will always insist, perhaps rightly so, on the difficult issues in the relationship being raised. But somehow, that does not quite seem to happen when the same countries meet with China and Russia bilaterally.

There have been a number of attempts in recent years to find different ways of ensuring that the EU and Member States take the same line on a number of sensitive issues in relationships with countries, in order to try to avoid being subject to divide and rule. These are beginning to have results. It is now often the EU countries themselves that are asking for a common line on different issues, because they are beginning to recognise that they are also much weakened by not being united. When, in 2012, Belarus expelled the Polish and EU ambassador from the country, the authorities were shocked when, within 24 hours, and in response, all EU ambassadors left the country, staying out until there was a collective agreement on how to return.

It is obviously much easier for the EU to be united towards Belarus than towards China, since the importance of the economic relationship with China makes it more difficult to hold to a united position. However, the impact of united action, in public action and statements as much as in private *demarches*, is felt both by the country concerned, which starts to recognise that there is a new and much bigger player in town, and by the EU countries that find their ability to achieve results greatly strengthened.

So if a left agenda includes having some core labour, social and environmental standards as part of the ground-rules of global trade, it is clear that if EU governments were willing to take that on, and to deploy some of the muscle of the EU's trading power as a lever, backed up by some robust diplomacy, there could be a chance of achieving it. The chances of the UK achieving this alone are very small indeed.

A rational approach to defence spending

EU Member States collectively spend a huge amount on defence. Despite significant cuts, military spending by EU countries still amounts to around 20 per cent of global expenditure. While this is only half what the Americans spend, it is almost twice the combined expenditure of all the BRICS countries (i.e. including China and Russia). So the idea that Europe is only interested in soft power does not quite reflect the reality. What is certainly true, however, is that the money spent by Europe's states on defence is not providing all of the basic capabilities needed to respond to today's crises. In both the NATO military operation in Libya, and the French military operation in Mali, American military assets were needed to prosecute the campaigns effectively. The reasons are well known in military circles: significant cuts in European military capabilities, combined with serious duplication of efforts by national militaries, working with national defence industries, to produce often the same capabilities.

Solutions to these problems exist and have done for many years. They involve a combination of moving towards a single market in procurement of defence equipment; cooperation to ensure inter-operability of European equipment and capabilities; common research and development programmes for large military projects; and specialisation of Member State armed forces to avoid duplications. Within such a global framework of pooling and sharing, groups of Member States could also then work together to take on major military projects, to produce key strategic capacities such as air to air refuelling, aircraft carriers, etc. EU and NATO defence ministers have at different times signed up to frameworks that would imply taking some or all of these steps, and indeed some steps are being taken. However, at the current pace of progress, Europe's ability to play a global security role, or even to be an effective actor in crisis resolution in its neighbourhood, is going to be seriously compromised in coming years.

There are hopes that a combination of current circumstances may change the calculus on this. First, the United States has been explicit in recent years about its expectation that Europeans will take more of a share of the costs of their security. This, combined with the announced US pivot towards Asia, means that Europeans can no longer relax snugly in an American security blanket. Second, the current age of austerity is going to continue to apply pressure on all budgets, including military ones, and this too can act as a spur to greater efforts on pooling and sharing resources. Third, the Lisbon Treaty itself provides some new opportunities for more planned action in this area. The debate on defence by Heads of State and government, planned for December 2013, has involved more than a year of preparation, something that would have been more difficult to achieve under the rotating six-month Presidency of the EU.

This debate should matter to progressives, because what is at stake goes beyond the hard security question of how to assure national defence. How military capabilities are developed depends fundamentally on the assessment of what threats are out there and need to be countered. If we are entering a period when those threats are non-traditional, then the security response has to be much more complex than the maintenance of standing armies and tanks, or even of a small number of expensive nuclear submarines. The way in which that security response is developed will have an important impact on how the EU is viewed globally, whether as another of the great powers defending its interests or, more like the UN, as an actor capable of playing a role as honest broker in preventing and resolving conflict, as well as in postwar reconstruction. Like it or not, the military plays a part in that, and the left should make sure that its agenda is heard there too. Progressives should therefore ensure that the UK debate on defence is also viewed through the lens of efforts to rationalise defence spending at European level to enhance our collective security. It would certainly help everyone to see through puerile rhetoric such as the idea that the nuclear threat of North Korea is an argument for the renewal of Trident.

THE RECORD OF THE COALITION GOVERNMENT

The vast majority of European decisions on foreign policy are taken through unanimity, but the reality is that there are some Member States who have much greater weight in EU decision-making than others. Specifically, the UK, France and Germany are the only three out of the 28 with a genuinely global reach through their diplomatic networks, combined with significant military assets; and the UK and France have the additional advantage of being permanent members of the UN Security Council, the highest of multilateral diplomatic high tables. So the UK is a really big player in this policy, was instrumental in setting it up, and can usually get what it wants, or at least stymie the goals of its opponents. Indeed, it was the UK and France who, together, launched the idea of an EU security and defence policy through a joint declaration made in St Malo in 1998. Unfortunately, the behaviour of the UK Coalition government does not give the impression of one that is, or aspires to be, the driving force behind EU foreign policy, even with the EU's High Representative being British.

The first problem is that the UK's impact on this policy is an extremely well-kept secret. Few Britons would believe that an EU naval mission, commanded by a British admiral and headquartered in the UK's joint HQ, has successfully countered the piracy threat in the Indian Ocean (an achievement all the greater because of the absence of casualties). Compare and contrast this with British military failures and their costs in Basra and Helmand. It is a sad fact that the existential anti-Europeanism of the back-bench Conservative Party makes it impossible for the government to trumpet even the most unalloyed achievements of the UK if they have anything to do with the EU. It just wouldn't fit the narrative.

The second problem is that the government has been very good at sabotaging European influence even when it has been in the UK's interest to amplify it. One important example has been the way in which the UK has done everything possible to limit the EU's role in multilateral organisations. One of the innovations of the Lisbon Treaty was that it gave the EU legal personality, and this, in turn, gave it the possibility of having additional powers in the UN system, for example, the right to table resolutions and to intervene early at the UN General Assembly. This wasn't exactly revolutionary stuff, but it could have been used as an additional factor in maximising European weight within UN agencies and bodies, where – despite the fact that Europeans are the biggest financial supporters of the whole UN system – the impact on governance of that system is limited by lack of EU representation.

A number of other regional groupings in the UN system, and notably the Caribbean states, were suspicious about giving the EU additional rights even in the General Assembly, and the adoption of the resolution giving those rights involved a long and painful negotiation. The UK, in its wisdom, decided that this delicate moment was the perfect time to enter into a rather petty fight about the precise terms to be used in EU statements in the UN system. For the best part of a year, most EU statements at the UN were blocked, and therefore not issued, because 26 Member States wanted to follow previous practice by using the language 'The EU', while the UK insisted on the term 'The EU and its Member States' – to reflect on the mixed EU and national competences involved. Everyone backed down in the end, but it left a rather sour taste in the mouth, and must have been incomprehensible to third parties. To make matters worse, the UK had lobbied very heavily to limit to the bare minimum the implications for the EU of the General Assembly resolution, in order to lessen its impact on other bodies and agencies. Most Member States were furious, since this was perceived by them to be sabotage from within.

Problem number three is that, even on occasions when the government has been prepared to support a European approach, its ideological instincts take it in the wrong direction. Perhaps the best visible example of this was during the Arab Spring when, in February 2011, David Cameron made a dash to be the first western leader to be in Tahrir Square after the fall of Hosni Mubarak. What he was less keen to highlight was that this was a trip planned some time earlier, involving an official excursion around the Gulf dictatorships in the company of arms firm executives, aimed at selling arms that would, presumably, then help those dictators prevent any troublesome Arab-Spring-like rebellions in their own countries. And when the EU appointed a special envoy in the aftermath of the Arab Spring to follow up on the EU response, it was the UK that made sure that his mandate did not extend to the Gulf. So much for the government's commitment to democracy and human rights!

Problem number four is that even when working with and through the EU is clearly the best option for the UK, this government's instincts will always be to seek an alternative. The best example here is consular policy. In September 2012, William Hague proudly announced an agreement with Commonwealth countries to launch a network of Embassies worldwide that was explicitly sold as countering the influence of the European External Action Service. In other words, an EU Member State was setting up a network that sought to compete against the EU. Little has been heard of it since, and this suggests that it was little more than a eurosceptic gesture, and will have minimal impact other than to convince further the UK's European allies that it cannot really be trusted. The only metaphor for such infantilism that makes any sense is that of cutting your nose off to spite your face.

A more expensive example comes from the defence field. In the first few months of the Coalition government, it surprised everyone by signing a defence Treaty with France that included a shared aircraft carrier group, a 10,000-strong joint expeditionary force and the development of joint nuclear testing facilities. Eighteen months later, the new defence secretary, Philip Hammond, announced that he was reversing one of the key provisions of the agreement, the installation of the catapults on new UK aircraft carriers that would make it possible for France to use them for their fixed wing aircraft. Apart from the damage this inflicted on cross-channel relations, and to broader European efforts in pooling and sharing of defence, this action has left the UK spending vast sums on building aircraft carriers that will now have to wait for up to five years before there are any available aircraft to use them.

A PROGRESSIVE FOREIGN POLICY AGENDA

Foreign policy is one of the few areas of European policy where Britain has the clout to set the direction and the terms of policy. It is also one where there is more public support than in most other areas of policy, since it is so obvious that when Europe speaks with a single voice to the rest of the world, its influence will be so much greater. In an era when the main battles in Brussels have been focused on the defensive shoring up of the basic principles of European integration, it is also an area of policy where there has been some progress in achieving greater integration and more unity of purpose.

In this context, Labour in opposition has a real opportunity to think through and define the elements of an EU foreign policy that would strengthen and contribute to the progressive agenda that is being set domestically. Success in addressing inequality at home requires efforts to address inequality globally. Protection of the social rights of Britons requires the defence of those rights globally. The maintenance and furthering of good relations between the many communities that make up the UK today also requires the UK to play a positive and internationalist role abroad. Little of this international agenda is achievable without the European Union, and there is an opportunity here for Labour to differentiate itself from the opposition in defining an international agenda. If it can be articulated well, this kind of approach could also play its part in taking on UKIP, whose alternative to the EU seems to be a return to a rose-tinted vision of the Commonwealth and an era of British imperial power that is, thankfully, gone for ever.

A bold set of proposals from Labour for the EU in this area would enhance the international stature of the Labour leadership and give them a basis for engaging with European chancelleries and sister parties in a way that could only help in presenting a serious bid for power to the British people in 2015. The left could show that there is an alternative way to defend the national interest – and one that will also reinforce a progressive domestic agenda. That is an agenda that is worth promoting energetically and proudly.

8. The mad, the bad and the sad

Glyn Ford

There has been some premature and immature rejoicing about the prospect that support for the United Kingdom Independence Party (UKIP) and other parties to the right of the Conservative Party in Britain may siphon off enough votes from the Tories to deny them an absolute majority in 2015. They might even let Labour in by default. Yet in the longer term the new, or recycled, populist right poses an equally grave threat to the left in general and the Labour Party in particular. This threat is both quantitative and qualitative.

While these parties have so far been taking a majority of their votes from the right – and the centre – a not insignificant minority come from the left. In fact they have proved capable of mobilising voters whose socio-economic background should logically make them 'traditional' Labour supporters, but who either abandoned the ballot-box a generation or more ago, or never found it in the first place. But the main quantitative danger relates to voting asymmetry. In the next general election a 10 per cent vote for UKIP – along with the remnants of the British National Party (BNP) vote – will translate into a de facto 3 per cent Labour swing; while a 15 per cent vote will translate into a 4.5 per cent swing. (The Conservative Party is all too aware of this looming electoral threat after the results of the by-elections in the current Parliament, and May 2013's devastating local elections, where UKIP polled a quarter of the vote. It was this calculation that was the psephological underpinning of Cameron's promise of the longest referendum campaign in history.) UKIP – and friends – thus threaten to allow Labour to win by default, with barely more than a third of the voters and a fifth of the electorate. At best such an accidental victory would put the left in government facing a broken economy, a demoralised and confused population and a financial black hole, with a radical and inevitably tough programme – yet with no mandate. *At worst we would have a party lacking the authority and self-belief to manage the economy out of recession, while offering hope to the poor, the disadvantaged and the country.* Francois Hollande in spades! This is a recipe for a short honeymoon, painful, unplanned and unpopular choices, and subsequent electoral oblivion. It would also leave a poisoned legacy to match that of the other parts of the political mainstream (who themselves will by then have been unceremoniously voted out of office).

The qualitative threat lies in the four main themes of UKIP's policies: euroscepticism; anti-immigration; a wide range of reactionary social policies (including opposition to gay marriage and trade unions); and exploitation of fear of crime and other insecurities. Their rising electoral support is dyeing the fabric of political debate not only on the right and the centre but to a degree on the left; and the temptation is becoming widespread to accommodate notions of church, order, family, nation and state. The new populist forces pander to the same myths and scare stories – and propagated in very similar ways – as the *Mail*, *Express*, *Sun* and *Telegraph* (the main variation being the level of complexity of the vocabulary used). They are united in their ideological opposition to Brussels and their portrayal of Europe as the problem rather than the solution, in part because ignorance about Europe and the remoteness of its institutions make it the ideal whipping boy for almost every malaise under the sun.

The other nations of Great Britain have their own nationalist parties, of course – the Scottish National Party and Plaid Cymru – but they are of a very different type. Their politics, particularly in Wales, is coloured by a political culture that owes much to Methodism and a little to Marxism. Both create challenges for the labour movement, but that is not the stuff of this chapter. English Nationalism is a very different story. It is driven through UKIP, the BNP and the English Defence League (EDL).

The BNP emerged from the collapse of the neo-fascist National Front in 1982, and its leader Nick Griffin attempted a rebranding to transform its image from that of football hooligans and street fighters to British Patriots. This was, for a time, partially successful, even if it was not helped by the London bomber David Copeland being a card-carrying party member. As the sheen wore off New Labour, the BNP began to win seats on local councils in poor boroughs like Blackburn and Barking in the 'white flight' penumbra of the inner-city core. At one point it had more than fifty councillors, with over a dozen in Barking alone. Organisations such as Unite Against Fascism and Hope Not Hate subsequently put herculean efforts into defeating each BNP councillor, and over a couple of electoral cycles they removed all but a handful from elected office. But this was less by reducing BNP support and more by raising turnout, which boosted the scores of its opponents. Blackburn only became BNP-free in 2013, after more than a decade of presence on the Borough Council.

Griffin himself almost won a seat in the 2004 European elections in the North West of England. Five years later, in 2009, he was elected alongside Andrew Brons, a veteran of Colin Jordan's National Socialist Movement, in Yorkshire and Humberside. The two MEPs have since fallen out – fissiparousness being a distinctive feature of the extreme right – and Brons has now formed a new party, the British Democratic Party, ideologically indistinguishable from the BNP. The likelihood is that both will lose in 2014, although –particularly in the case of Nick Griffin – this cannot be a foregone conclusion. Incumbency and a low turnout election, where 2.5 per cent of the electorate is enough to win a seat, means it's not over until the ballot box closes.

The isolation of the BNP owes much to the 'No Platform' policy, whereby Labour, the Lib Dems and most Tories refuse to share a platform with them (similar to the 'cordon sanitaire' that was operated for a time by democratic parties in Belgium and France, but which has now been ripped apart on the continent by right-of-centre parties competing both for their support, and their supporters). While such parties have, of course, the right to free speech, they have no right to a 'free' platform, and large demonstrations accompanied Griffin's invitation to Oxford University, as well as that of Marine Le Pen to the Cambridge Union.

While the BNP formally dissociates itself from the EDL, it doesn't take a Sherlock Holmes to show the myriad links through individual activists. The EDL stages provocative marches and demonstrations through immigrant areas and outside mosques. The bulk of their activists originate from the milieu of football hooligan gangs. New members attempting to join need to be 'approved' by the relevant 'football firm' to pass muster. The immediate threat posed by the EDL seems to have been seen off by broad coalitions of churches, mosques, trade unions and political parties, who have organised under banners such as 'We are Bristol' to deny them the streets. (The Norwegian convicted terrorist Anders Brevik, who murdered more than one hundred young people, quoted from many of the writers and polemicists endorsed by the EDL's ideologues.)

Politically, UKIP are BNP-'lite', with a rhetoric not easily distinguishable from that of the BNP itself. Their enthusiasm for banning former BNP activists from membership is a reflection of resonance not difference. It is a desperate attempt to deflect attention from those that want to make the connection. Yet if the product on offer is little different, the process is not the same. The most closely UKIP have ever been associated with violence was on the fringes of Countryside Alliance demonstrations a decade ago: for them the ballot box alone is the way forward. That is not to say that were UKIP to be in power life would not be unpleasant for progressives and trade unionists, immigrants and those of a different sexual orientation. Their growth reflects a reaction to the social liberalism of David Cameron, whose impeccably right-wing economic policies of austerity and support for a vastly diminished public provision of service is in contrast to his liberal attitudes towards sexual equality and gay marriage, something which many in traditionalist parts of middle England still find beyond the pale. As Professor Alan Sked, UKIP's own founder and former leader (1993-97), said of the current party, it is 'extraordinarily right wing', 'anti-Islam and anti-immigrant'. Research from Manchester University backed him up, showing that prior to their recent electoral gains UKIP supporters had more hostile attitudes towards immigrants and ethnic minorities than supporters of any other party save the BNP. Such supporters also believed that local councils discriminated in favour of immigrants, and that immigrants were responsible for committing more crime.

At present UKIP seem Teflon-coated against accusations of corruption. The electorate were voting UKIP to protest that politicians were all corrupt while one UKIP MEP was serving his time in jail for benefit fraud. This is simply one example of the extraordinarily easy ride that UKIP leaders have enjoyed with the conservative media, which sympathises with their ideology, shares their anti-European passion, and continues to harbour deep disappointment with what is perceived as the liberal cosmopolitan elite now running the Tory Party. This stance of the British newspapers has many causes; loathing of the coalition and Cameron's metropolitan social liberalism; the fact that saloon bar xenophobia sells copy; and the detestation of the EU on the part of proprietors of 80 per cent of UK media – not least because of the threat it could and should pose to excessive media concentration.

After UKIP gained almost one hundred and fifty seats in May 2013's county council elections in England, simple extrapolation – not the surest method of forecasting – has convinced many in the main parties (initially in private, and now in public) that UKIP will come first in May 2014's European Elections. Whether they come first or second, they are a profound threat to Labour and the left.

We have to be very clear. This is not 'English' exceptionalism. Rather, it is a manifestation of problems increasingly besetting the EU and beyond, that threaten to disrupt the post-war democratic consensus that saw xenophobic and ultra-nationalist forces banished to the political margins of society. Such parties are increasingly a symptom of political ills in nearly all Western-style democracies. They can be seen in the 'Tea Party' Movement in the United States, as well as in the arrival in 2012 in the Japanese Diet of Ishihara Shintaro's ultra-nationalist and militaristic Japan Restoration Party, now effectively the main opposition to the conservative Liberal Democratic Party. It could even be argued that similar issues were involved in the Bo Xilai affair in China.

We are witnessing step by step across Europe the emergence on the electoral landscape of fascist right and fascist 'lite' national revolutionaries and xenophobic populist parties. It is the arrival of the mad, the sad and the bad centre-stage in electoral politics. Some are newly minted, while others are old enemies that have crawled back out from the dark corners of politics. These parties formally range across the political spectrum. A few are downright ideologically schizophrenic. Today no-one with a progressive mind-set would have anything complimentary to say about Italy's Northern League or Austria's Freedom Party. Yet twenty years ago the former was part of the Green Group in the European Parliament and the latter a member party of the Liberal International. While these parties are of varying toxicity, they all pose a serious threat to the continued political effectiveness of the traditional left, as they privilege family, order, race and nation, and as they make inroads into the left's old working-class base (what we used to refer to rather presumptuously as 'our natural supporters'), which tends to be excluded from the benefits – but not the consequences – of social change. Their electoral success has begun the process of shifting the mainstream political agenda.

They have generally grown from nationalist – sometimes separatist – and extreme-right fascist movements that were for a long time confined to the fringe of politics by twentieth century history and the domination of the stand-off between socialism and labour, on the one side, and conservatism and Christian democracy, on the other. Forty years ago these mainstream forces had – depending on the national electoral system – virtual monopolies of position, whether under two labels (UK, Germany and Greece) or many (Italy, France and Belgium). What has now changed is that the populist radical parties are on the electoral map. They share a range of characteristics – although not all exhibit all of them. They are right and extreme-right xenophobic nationalist movements. They are authoritarian, only quasi-democratic in internal and external practices, often with charismatic leadership, and their distinguishing policies are anti-European, anti-immigrant, islamophobic and intolerant. They are anti-political – or rather anti-politician. In this they have been aided and abetted by the many mainstream politicians whose corruption, nepotism and financial and sexual scandals have contributed to public disenchantment with the democratic political process. One subset of these parties marries the ballot box and the battle for the streets – officially or unofficially. Some have linked ballot box and bomb. Currently they can command the support of something between a third and a sixth of the electorate – and this may not be the ultimate ceiling.

They did not spring from nowhere; they grew on fertile soil as a product of genuine concerns in communities under increasing social and financial stress. Yet these kernels of concern have been fanned into something close to mass hysteria by sections of the media, and by these parties themselves as they outbid each other in bigotry, exaggeration and downright lies. At worst this vicious circle threatens to spiral out of control into a collapse of normal politics and civilised society.

What changed that allowed them to creep out of the interstices of politics? The super power confrontation between Washington and Moscow ended in the collapse – under its own contradictions – of the late and unlamented Soviet Empire. This jeopardised the old monopoly of parties that had exemplified the old left/right standoff. Weakening party loyalties – as life-styles were becoming increasingly pluralistic and the collective was giving way to the individual – meant that fewer people were identifying and living within traditional class alignments and mores. With the end of the Cold War these remaining loyalties all but melted away. Voters were freed to explore a wider and multi-dimensional political terrain. This they did, abandoning political, religious and class loyalties in favour of switching, experimentation, single-issue politics and simple abstention. The old battle cries rang hollow and failed to resonate with voters and summon them to the ballot box, as the electoral cycle accelerated.

In an increasingly global world people were deeply ambivalent about what was happening to them. They loved the fashion, food and music. Foreign money, goods and services were welcome, yet foreign labour and neighbours less so. They felt threatened, insecure, and alienated. In Britain West Indian nurses staffing the NHS was one thing, Polish pregnant mothers in the antenatal clinic another.

All this was ratcheted up by two further phenomena. First, post 9/11, came the rise of Islamophobia as press and sections of the public bought into the naiveté and exaggeration of 'The Clash of Civilizations', made all the worse by the atrocious conduct and savagery on both sides during the Iraq War. This melded into the already advanced demonisation of immigrants and asylum-seekers. And it added to the sense of insecurity and fear of crime, fuelled by an ever-spiralling sensationalism in parts of the media which left many feeling that the streets were no longer safe, the police were incompetent in bringing villains to book, and that the justice system cared nothing for the victims of crime. The toxicity of these two parallel sentiments has been to provide the extreme right with a timely new narrative well suited to the angst of the first years of the twenty-first century. Second came the global financial crisis. When times were good governments across Europe – falsely or at least exaggeratedly – took credit for their skilful management of an economy that, in reality, they knew little about and had even less control over – as the consequences of bankers' ramp rapidly exposed. When the crisis hit, the story was hurriedly changed. Now, suddenly, it was all the fault of global forces outside their control – 'a crisis made in America', etc, etc. The public was not impressed and looked first to their national governments for solutions. When came there none, incumbents were dead men talking.

With each election fewer people vote, and of those that do, more vote for 'none of the above'; ever-shorter electoral honeymoons are granted to the one sitting on the cushion when the music stops. In the

Netherlands the Labour Party (PvdA) and the ex-Maoist Socialist Party have between them held the left vote. And in Greece the Socialist Party's (PASOK) losses have been some of SYRIZA's (the radical left coalition) gains. But, with only the rarest of exceptions, the beneficiaries of this move away from the mainstream have been the nationalist, populist or right-wing parties. Across Europe, parties and their agendas have been inexorably driven rightwards as socialist and social democrats have failed to channel popular anger and resentment at the way the pain of the crisis has been so unfairly distributed.

THE POPULIST RIGHT IN EUROPE

There are different dynamics in different countries. These new and emerging parties evolve rapidly. In some cases they are absorbed into the mainstream as it increasingly segues to the right, simultaneously spawning and spinning off newer and nastier parties further and further to the right; and sometimes they have toned down their rhetoric. Despite – or maybe because of – their populist agenda, their appeal takes in wide sections of the left's voters as well as those of the right. The virtual extinction of the French Communist Party is not unconnected with the rise of the Front National, which is now the first party of choice both for the old working-class vote and for students.

The gradual but accelerating emergence of these forces is well chronicled. In Greece in 1984 a solitary representative of the National Political Union (EPEN) was elected to the European Parliament. EPEN were apologists for the Colonels' Regime in Greece and lost their sole seat in the 1989 European Elections. 2000 saw the emergence of the national xenophobes of the Popular Orthodox Rally (LAOS) who absorbed the remnants of EPEN, then known as the Hellenic Front. In 1984, when Golden Dawn was linked with EPEN, their coalition peaked at 2.9 per cent of the vote. Golden Dawn is infamous for its 'vigilante' groups 'protecting' citizens on the streets of Greek cities from the immigrant threat – all too reminiscent of Germany in the 1930s and the Blackshirts' persecution of the Jews. The global financial crisis, as it played out in Greece, began to shatter traditional Greek political alignments. The election of May 2012 saw the viciously anti-immigrant Independent Greeks (ANEL) win 10.6 per cent of the votes, while neo-Nazi Golden Dawn received 7.0 per cent and LAOS 2.9 per cent – giving the populist right the support of more than one in five Greek voters. Little had changed by the time of the re-run election in June. LAOS had by then been absorbed by the traditional conservatives of New Democracy, and ANEL's vote slipped a fraction, but Golden Dawn's level of support remained unchanged.

Italy's pattern was similar, although there has been a continuity of extreme right-wing politics – and periodic bouts of terrorism – since the end of the Second World War. Mussolini has always inexplicably retained a hold on some sections of public opinion at the margins even to this day – rather like the Caudillo in Spain. The Italian Social Movement (MSI) was an avowedly neo-fascist Party that was aligned in the European Parliament with Le Pen's Front National. With the emergence of Berlusconi and Forza Italia in the mid-1990s, the MSI and its leader Gianfranco Fini rebranded the MSI to become the post-fascist National Alliance (AN). Fini's achievement was to glide to the centre-right while not shedding extreme right support, thereby gaining respectability across the political spectrum. It is another example of 'the banality of evil'.

For a period the two political crutches propping up Berlusconi's clientelist government were the AN in the South and the populist Lega Nord above. For a period, before he fell out with Berlusconi, Fini was even Deputy Prime Minister. In the European Parliament the AN, its days with Le Pen forgotten and forgiven, slipped virtually unnoticed into the European Peoples Party. Working with Berlusconi assisted the political fortunes of Lega Nord and AN for few years, bringing their political strength to the point of being crucial for assembling a right-wing majority: for the first time in the post-war Republic extreme right-wing parties were permitted to get their hands on the levers of power. All this was achieved by exploiting popular hankering after stability and law and order, in contrast to the squabbling of mainstream parties, who were seemingly incapable of focusing on the multi-layered crisis faced by Italian society. In February 2013's Italian elections the (ex)-fascists were everywhere. Berlusconi's coalition was a broad enough church to accommodate the openly fascist 'The Right', led by Francesco Storace, while former fascist leader Fini found himself in Mario Monti's coalition with a section of AN. Even Beppe Grillo's Five Star Movement is prepared to associate itself with 'CasaPound' and its Holocaust deniers. On the streets the violent armed thugs of Forza Nuova and Fiamma Tricolore intimidate immigrants and the left almost unchallenged.

In France the Front National had its breakthrough with the Dreux by-election in 1983, when it gained an unprecedented 17 per cent in the first round as a reaction to Mitterrand's right-turn and the continued rejection of the traditional right, thrown out in 1981 after decades in power. Founded in 1972 by Jean-Marie Le Pen, a former Poujadist MP accused of torture during the Algerian civil war, it had barely registered in previous elections. Dreux precipitated their stunning result in June 1984's European elections, when they obtained 11 per cent of the votes and 10 seats. Their MEPs included at least one member who had fought with the Waffen SS. They formed a group in the European Parliament with the MSI and EPEN, but lost both in 1989, when EPEN failed to get any MEPs elected, and the MSI departed with the arrival of the German extreme-right Republikaner Party, whose revanchism claimed part of Northern Italy for Germany, and the Belgian far-right Flemish nationalists the Vlaams Blok.

In the 1990s the FN took control of four cities in the South of France: Orange, Toulon, Marignane and Vitrolles. Here they cut off funding to immigrant hostels and projects, recruited their own members to the security staff, censored libraries and, at one point, offered a 5000 franc (€750) bonus to parents of whom at least one was French (until this was ruled illegal).

In the 2002 French presidential elections Le Pen finished second to Jacques Chirac eliminating the Socialist candidate Lionel Jospin. Le Pen managed 17.8 per cent in the second round. All this was despite his 'Holocaust Denial' and scepticism as to German atrocities in France during the occupation. In the years after 2002, however, the FN was in the doldrums and by the 2009 European elections it was down to three seats.

Age and politics had caught up with Le Pen, and the following year he stood down, triggering a contest between Marine, his daughter, who had carefully and discreetly distanced herself from the more extreme political positions of her father, and his Deputy Bruno Gollnisch. This pitted populism against the national-revolutionary tendencies inside the Party. Marine won with over two-thirds of the vote. The result was a toning-down of the rhetoric, the loss of a few neo-fascist activists and a sharp revival in electoral fortunes in regional elections, in the Presidential election (where Marine Le Pen's 17.9 per cent was the FN's best vote nation-wide ever) and the parliamentary elections where, despite only winning two seats, the FN played a central role in delivering Hollande's majority to further its aims of undermining the mainstream right. The refusal of the latter this time round to collude with the FN resulted in Le Pen keeping her candidates where she could in the second round, where their presence cost the right dozens of seats. This, and the FN's continued high poll ratings, has resulted in calls on the right for a breach in the 'cordon sanitaire' to allow for electoral collaboration with the FN. Earlier attempts to steal the FN's anti-immigrant vocabulary and policies have not proved enough, so that the new Secretary General of the UMP, Jean-François Cope now talks of 'the right without complexes'. Noises can now be heard on immigration and integration, and an unholy alliance with Catholic fundamentalists and extreme-right hooligans has been forged on gay marriage and gay adoptions. Indeed, during the demonstrations against 'marriage for all', UMP politicians and some leaders of the Le Pen movement were practically arm-in-arm – a new form of inappropriate behaviour. In addition, a note of – so far – mild euroscepticism has been creeping into the language of the centre right.

These tendencies are replicated to the same or a lesser degree across the EU and beyond. In Austria the Freedom Party actually finished second (by 415 votes) in the national election in 1999, and went into coalition with the third-place conservatives. The Netherlands elected Pim Fortuyn to Parliament. Denmark has the Danish People's Party (propping up a Liberal government which then pursued an anti-immigration policy so virulent that it fell foul of EU rules). Finland has the True Finns, while Romania has the Greater Romanian Party. Paradoxically, this extreme populism has yet to spread – in spite of economic hardship – to Spain and Portugal, which have perhaps been inoculated by their long periods of right-wing dictatorship. However, the attachment to the mainstream will not endure there either if economic prospects do not improve, and unless the socialist parties in the two countries concerned stop behaving like whipped dogs with their tails stuck firmly between their legs. Germany too, albeit with the benefit of a strong economic performance underpinning support for democratic politics, has so far been sheltered, at least nationally, from the rising populist tide. Nevertheless the newly-founded Alternativ für Deutschland, a strictly eurosceptic party, could easily evolve in a more populist direction, and has already given Angela Merkel's party an attack of the pre-election jitters.

On the other hand Belgium – the self-styled capital of Europe, which has held up economically during the crisis rather well – provides an early depressing example of the way that the centre right's shunning of ultra-nationalism has begun to crumble. For years the extreme-right Vlaams Blok made inroads in the north of the country, playing on a whole panoply of prejudices, backed by street-fighting thugs and placing itself in the vanguard of Flemish nationalism; it won seats in the European Parliament and became the largest single party in Antwerp. But it was blocked from taking control of Flanders' largest town by the 'cordon sanitaire'. But then in 2007 the traditional moderate right-of-centre Christian democrats – well house-trained, pro-European, tolerant, welfare-state centrists, losing ground to the extreme right – formed an electoral alliance with a tiny party, the NVA – a splinter from a defunct Flemish nationalist party. NVA was Vlaams Blok-lite and largely comprised of the less gruesome defectors from the openly neo-fascist Blok.

The temporary respite produced by this alliance enabled the Flemish Christian Democrats, now pushing for radical transfers of power back to the region, to lead an ill-starred coalition until 2010. But above all it handed respectability and success to the extreme nationalist right. The consequence is that today NVA is by far the largest political force in Flanders; it threatens to make Belgium ungovernable, has seized Antwerp for its leader (Bart de Wever), is infiltrating the police and the public service in ways that make the old Falange seem amateurish, and is pursuing a eurosceptic, neoliberal programme, with anti-immigration policies as its principal priority, intolerance as its prime value and extreme regional nationalism as its leitmotif. And de Wever and his cohorts can further congratulate themselves: with the exception of the small Flemish Socialist and Green parties, the whole of the Flemish establishment has followed him like a herd of particularly disciplined sheep. De Wever rules Antwerp thanks to the votes of Christian democrat and Liberal councillors. And the illusion behind his conceit of the viability of a small Flemish state goes without challenge.

But this grisly grand tour of Europe has to conclude in Hungary. The poster child of the tearing down of the Iron Curtain seemed for a brief moment to provide new hope for the left in East and central Europe, despite bitter memories of the Soviet era. The old Communist Party morphed itself into a social democratic movement and won several terms of office for its reconstructed ex-CP leaders. But a mixture of incompetence and corruption weakened their hold, just as the first stirrings of the extreme right were observed. But here the current threat to democracy, human rights, the rule of law, and all the values enshrined in the Treaties and the Charter of Fundamental Rights, is not so much from Jobbik, the street-fighting semi-military anti-Semites who have now won seats in the European Parliament and formed the third largest party in the Hungarian Parliament; rather, the principal danger to freedom and liberty comes from the government itself, led by Viktor Orban, the leader of Fidesz, which has had a large enough majority in the Hungarian parliament to ram through constitutional measures limiting press freedom, undermining the independence of the judiciary, and persecuting dissidents. Orban's mealy-mouthed speech to the World Jewish Congress in May 2013 singularly failed to condemn Jobbick's anti-semitic march and rally in Budapest that had taken place on the eve of the Congress.

Orban's party is a fully paid up member of the EPP, where its MEPs sit in the European parliament, next to German, French, Dutch and Belgian mainstream conservatives. At each successive outrage from Budapest there is some ritual hand wringing from the conservative establishment in Brussels – so wedded, according to their own propaganda, to the basic European values of solidarity, liberty and freedom of expression. Mr Barroso makes a speech and EPP parliamentarians gently wag fingers. But the higher spheres of the EPP leadership in Berlin and Brussels have never been overly choosy when it comes to boosting their ranks in the European Parliament, as was demonstrated earlier with the recruitment of the Italian AN. Despite strident criticism from socialists, liberals and greens, there has been no serious move to put real pressure on the Orban regime, no realistic threat to suspend Hungary from the EU, and no expulsions from the EPP. The presence of the Hungarian hard right at the centre of the current majority party in Europe is a standing rebuke to the Union, and makes hollow all its advocacy of human rights in the world. The danger is, of course, that a precedent has been set; if the ultra-right continues its abuses in Hungary, what is to stop the virus mutating and spreading to other East and Central European Member States, not just on the fringes of their politics, but at the heart of government?

WHAT IS TO BE DONE?

The left in Britain and in Europe should make the indifference of the conservatives to the scandal and danger of Hungarian extremism a central plank of their campaign for the 2014 elections. It should place the issue of Christian democrat/conservative complicity with the forces of darkness at the centre of the public debate.

Against this backdrop, and at this time, what is to be done? The answer is partly organisational: reconnecting with what used to be our traditional base and expressing anger where it is justified at the economic and social policies pursued throughout Europe. Of course, howls of outrage will be insufficient; they must be tempered with some of the proposals outlined in other chapters. But the British and European left must also to say something cogent on the other causes of the malaise affecting large sections of Europe's population – immigration and law and order.

The UK is already largely on the margins of the common European area of freedom, security and justice because of its opt-outs; and now Cameron wants to re-nationalise large chunks of the remaining Justice and Home Affairs agenda. But it is in our interest as socialists to see this agenda strengthened rather than weakened, even in areas where the UK is not currently involved, such as the Schengen arrangements.

Cameron's proposal to opt out of some 130 measures of police and justice cooperation alarms more than judicial observers and police in the UK. Even the generally eurosceptic House of Lords, in their special report of April 2013, drew attention to the consequences for the efficiency of police intelligence and follow-up were this withdrawal from the common policy eventually to take place. Any alternative routes to bilateral or multilateral cooperation would take years to put in place, and would be more costly and less effective. Just as important, the UK would lose its say in the development of further police and judicial cooperation, and the management of the agencies supposed to deliver it. Europol has been increasingly successful in helping to identify and provide intelligence to track down and arrest international traffickers of all kinds; and there is much more that could be done in this area with increased resources.

Apart from sections of the press and Tory eurosceptics, who instinctively believe that British drug dealers and football hooligans arrested abroad have automatically been framed by corrupt and inefficient foreigners, nearly everyone agrees that the European Arrest warrant has proved extremely successful in getting criminals to the courts far more speedily than in the past. After all, it was the European Arrest warrant that helped bring to justice some of the London bombers of

21 July 2005. It is true, however, that the Arrest Warrant system needs further reform: speedy extradition, which now takes a few days instead of many months, will only have clear benefits if those extradited have their day in court quickly and are not held for months in poor conditions. But to take the UK out of the system is incomprehensible for a government that purports to give high priority to law and order, and will only undermine further the credibility of our own judicial system. It is a particularly good illustration of how blind eurosceptic ideology can produce irrational results.

On immigration from outside the Union, there clearly is a need to police Europe's external borders. No one pretends that this is getting easier in the face of a global economic and financial crisis which is acting as a driver of economic migration from outside the EU. Nevertheless that does not provide any excuse for failing to fulfil our obligations under the Geneva Convention to protect the rights of refugees and asylum-seekers fleeing in well-founded fear of persecution. It is in some of the poorest Member States, like Greece, where there is the greatest risk of illegal entry into the EU, yet the consequent problem affects all Member States in general, and the richest in particular. Although we are not in the Schengen area, it is in Britain's interest to make sure that other EU countries are able to protect the external border and so to back the necessary budget increases and operational effectiveness, rather than hide behind the fiction that being outside Schengen somehow makes our borders inviolable.

There also needs to be a comprehensive policy on legal immigration across the EU. Decisions by one Member State inevitably have a knock-on effect on others. One simple example: when Hong Kong and Macau were returned to China Britain made few provisions for its former subjects, who were largely left to fend for themselves. Portugal, on the other hand, offered all residents of Macau Portuguese citizenship. Few have come to Europe. Nevertheless, should there be some unforeseen crisis leading to the uprooting of hundreds of thousands of Macao residents, it is to the UK rather than Portugal that we might expect them to want to go, given that English, rather than Portuguese, is the third most widely used language after Cantonese and Mandarin.

The situation is similar in the case of Spain's treatment of the Algerians and sub-Saharan Africans who cross the land borders into its two African enclaves – Ceuta and Melilla – remnants of its African colonies although part of the European Union. While the Algerians

– some of whom certainly had, a few years ago, a good case to be viewed as refugees and asylum seekers – are quickly repatriated, the sub-Saharan Africans are held in the territories in rather squalid camps for six months or more. They are then decanted across to the Spanish mainland and given one year temporary work permits. The overwhelming majority are from francophone or anglophone countries and promptly disappear northwards never to be seen again as Spain's 'problem' is resolved by being passed on to the rest of the EU. Again these two examples argue for common decision-making at EU level rather than leaving it to Member States individually, or standing aside from such Europe-wide cooperation as exists.

As to migratory movements within the European Union, we have to remind all parties that one of the central features of the EU is the commitment to the four free movements, namely, goods, services, labour and capital, and that this constitutes the underpinning of the creation of a single market. The only one freedom that has regularly been put into question has been the free movement of labour. The 2004 EU enlargement, taking the number of Member States from 15 to 25, saw all but the UK, Ireland and Sweden exercise their right to delay free movement and full working rights by the maximum period allowed of seven years. The consequence was that somewhere close to 600,000 workers arrived over that period of time in Britain (at least ten times the official estimates at the time).

Britain's tabloid press claimed that many of these were welfare tourists (scroungers, unemployed and hooked on social security). Yet figures from the Government's own Department of Work and Pensions showed that while 17 per cent of working-age British nationals claim benefit the figure for non-nationals is 7 per cent. Immigrants can't win. They are simultaneously accused of undermining indigenous labour by working longer hours for lower wages and of all being on benefits. It is only a matter of time before UKIP claims they are doing both. We also need to be aware of the consequences of tabloid hate speech, which at times is in breach of the Race Relations Act. Contrary to what is proclaimed across the right-wing press, immigrants are as often as not the victims rather than the perpetrators of a failure to enforce law and order. Legal Eastern European immigrants suffer discrimination, racial abuse and racial violence that would be the basis of liberal media campaigns and investigations were this to be directed towards other minorities in our society.

However, we have to be upfront in recognising that the sheer numbers of immigrants from accession countries arriving in the UK following the 2004 enlargement did, in some regions, stretch the ability of public services to cope, and this created social tensions in certain communities where numbers were exceptionally high. As a result, when Romania and Bulgaria joined the EU in 2007 Britain played its 'get out of jail' card and, like all other Member States, delayed granting working rights to nationals of these two new Member States until the beginning of 2014. Now UKIP and eurosceptic Tories, surfing on the hysteria whipped up by the *Express*, the *Sun*, the *Mail* and the *Telegraph*, are claiming that the UK is about to flooded, swamped and overwhelmed by the Romanian and Bulgarian hordes who will descend on our shores when the barriers finally fall. UKIP have suggested that up to 7 million may come – one in four of the population of the two countries. (This could mean – with the whole of the 26 EU Member States available for migration – a risk that the last person to leave Romania and Bulgaria might have to be prepared to turn off the lights.)

What is the reality and what should be done? No one should or can pretend that after 2004 there were not genuine problems and tensions from this massive internal EU migration. Unemployed British workers were once urged by Norman Tebbit to 'get on their bikes'; in 2004 the workers of the Accession Eight countries got on Britain's low cost Airlines in their tens of thousands. Eighty per cent were from Poland, as demonstrated by the large numbers of Polish shops that have appeared on our otherwise dying high streets. Forty per cent were under 24 and over eight out of ten were under 34. They were overwhelmingly single and, where they were not, they were generally childless. They worked. Ninety-seven per cent were working full-time. It has been estimated that this East/Central European immigration added more than 1 per cent net to UK GDP; and that the recruitment of highly skilled immigrants from another EU country can open the way for creating jobs for local semi-skilled workers in the same firm. Furthermore, in the last two years, as free movement throughout the rest of the EU has become a reality for Poles and others, and as the Polish economy in particular continues to outperform all others in the EU in warding off the slump, the immigration 'flood' has reversed, and a small exodus has started.

The UK's attempt to measure and curtail the influx was based around the Workers Registration Scheme that ran from 2004 until April 2011. In exchange for registering within a month of taking up employment in Britain, workers from the eight new Member States were able, after 12 months continuous employment, to access social security if they lost their jobs. The reality was the government failed to fund the scheme adequately, and, as a result, the registration process was expensive and time consuming for applicants. Those who tried to register spent long hours, generally unsuccessfully, trying to get through on the phone. The unlucky ones that did were offered appointments weeks or months hence, at venues requiring them to take a day off work and spend hours travelling on public transport. Those that had permanent jobs had nothing to gain from the scheme, while those taking serial temporary posts were not eligible. As most of these, at least initially, planned to stay less than twelve months, uptake was minimal. No one was prosecuted for failing to register.

In 2014, when Romanian and Bulgarian migrants become eligible to work across the EU, the numbers game will be different. In 2004 there was a population of 72 million people in the eight new Member States, who had the possibility of working in three countries with a total population of 77 million. However in 2014 the 29 million Bulgarians and Romanians will have a 474 million population amongst which to disperse. While all 25 countries will not be equally attractive, geographical location, cultural ties and the state of the economy do not particularly favour Britain. And quite a few mobile young Bulgarians and Romanians have already emigrated to other Member States in the six years since the two countries joined the EU. All things being equal, it is likely that less than 50,000 Romanians and Bulgarians will come to the UK over the next seven years, as compared with 2004's figure of 600,000. It should be noted here that only three per cent of the EU workforce is actually employed in another Member State.

While conceding that social services in some areas were overstretched by the post-2004 wave, most evidence would indicate that hyperbole and anecdote have triumphed over facts. The migrant worker 'constituency' was younger, healthier and with fewer children than the indigenous average, and, most importantly, were in work, were motivated, and were self-evidently mobile. These characteristics are a constant, as any serious study on migratory trends confirms. Migrant workers in 2004 paid more tax for less, and made fewer demands on social services, education and health care, and there was no provision for repatriating any their pension contributions. The problem was that the Treasury clawed back the money with glee, seeing no need to trouble itself about addressing local difficulties with additional resources. As for council housing, few migrants were eligible and fewer still were ever placed in desirable housing stock – which in any case had been dangerously depleted because of the selling off of council houses. The problem is the difficulty of getting the facts across in the current political and economic climate and with the UK media.

Beyond these specific questions of immigration, and law and order – where we should highlight the flagrant contradictions of the euro-sceptics without ceding one inch on our principles – we need a wider approach to address the rise of populism, based on legislation, education and organisation. Apart from strengthening the anti-racist legislation we already have, and applying it to those who have ratcheted up the use of xenophobia as an instrument of political warfare, we need further domestic and European legislation. As pointed out elsewhere in this book, we need legislation at a European level to restore the original intention of the Posted Worker Directive, in order to prevent the export of poor and minimum wages and conditions around the European Union. This intention has been undermined by European Court Decisions in the Ruffort, Luxembourg, Viking and Laval cases, amongst others. The judgements themselves cannot be challenged, but the law can be changed to mend the breaches the Court has made to the initial intentions of the Commission and Parliaments. Labour and the left should make a revision and strengthening of the Directive a necessary condition for endorsing the incoming Commission in November 2014.

Equally, although the extent of the problem is grossly distorted, there must be a perception of 'fairness'. Yes, the definition of habitual residence should be changed to prevent job-seekers allowance being claimable within days or weeks of arrival, and no-one disputes that those on benefit should genuinely be seeking employment if there is a realistic prospect of obtaining it. It might, however, be interesting to apply Cameron's English language ability test to the linguistic skills of the Brits on the Costa Brava.

Rather than following Cameron's enthusiasms for opting out of much of the Justice and Home Affairs legislation, we should be tackling the problem at a European level. As Shadow Home Secretary Yvette Cooper has said, other EU countries have to cope with the same problems Britain is facing. For example, it is a shared issue that family benefits, including child benefit, should be paid in the country of residence and not where the father or mother work; and the possibilities of access to social housing should be clarified – although an EHRC survey indicated that 60 per cent of migrants were privately renting, 18 per cent were owner-occupiers and only 11 per cent were in social housing. However, we should not restrict access to the NHS for those working in the UK, any more than we would tolerate UK residents working in France or Germany being denied access to their hospitals.

On the other side of the scale, the regulation on Gang Masters should be tightened up, including by adding a European dimension. It would make good sense to put in place rigorous enforcement of the minimum wage, both through government inspectors and assistance to relevant trade unions – with support for unions to recruit migrant workers and make them aware of their rights, including the right not to be forced to use company accommodation, or to be paid in kind rather than with cash. Here, a campaign for a Europe-wide minimum wage, discussed elsewhere, makes great sense.

In terms of education we need to point out the benefits to Brits and Britain of free movement provision. Hundreds of thousands of British citizens are working or retired across the EU (250,000 in Spain alone). When there was pressure from the trade unions to sack Italian workers at Immingham and send them back home, it quickly became clear that there could well have been be a tit-for-tat response from countries to which British people have migrated. The calls in the past from political and trade union leaders, for British Jobs for British Workers, should be drowned out by the demand for 'Decent Jobs for Workers in Britain'. Equally, we need to show how, in certain areas, filling crucial skill shortages from elsewhere in the EU can lead to the creation of dozens of additional jobs for each worker taken on.

The issue of Cameron's promised Referendum on EU membership is dealt with in the concluding chapter of this book. But no-one in the trade union and labour movement should be under any illusion that if the Tories were successful in repatriating the Social Chapter back to Britain it would be anything other than a retrograde step. After all, it was John Major in 1992 who won the opt-out in the first place. It was only with Labour's victory in 1997 that the UK opted in, and workers in Britain received the same levels of protection as existed in the rest of the EU. The first thing to follow a successful repatriation would be a bonfire of social provisions. The same intention to remove protection underlies the issues of Justice and Home Affairs legislation.

We need to tackle the myriad myths about European legislation – for example the myth that it forces us to recruit non-English speaking doctors. People have the right to come to the UK to work. Equally, and rightly, there is across the EU a mutual recognition of qualifications. Just as it is not discrimination to refuse to employ someone as a driver who doesn't have a driving licence, there is no requirement to employ anyone who fails to meet the necessary standard of speaking English that a given job requires. The myth about benefits 'tourism' also needs to be contested. As Commissioner Andor has made clear:

> EU law also provides that Member States can require that people from other Member States can only stay longer than three months if they are working or are actively looking for work with a genuine chance of being taken on or have sufficient money to not be a burden on public funds.

Organisationally, we need to continue to take to the streets – not looking for a fight, but for an argument, to take away the ability of the 'street soldiers' and the extreme right to deny political space to minorities, Muslims and the left. The left has lost the habit of talking to its traditional supporters. Winning the argument requires progressive politicians to leave the comfort zone of think-tank seminars and make a fair but robust case to communities in the inner cities, suburbs and countryside. Unless we reclaim the streets for our debate then we should not be surprised to find that our 'natural supporters' have indeed emigrated.

9. Flinging the furniture round the room

Julian Priestley

PRECEPT AND PRACTICE

Before summarising the ideas in the earlier chapters it is worth just asking the question: what does being 'of the left' mean today? Not in the sense of some sterile ideological debate but to remind ourselves of certain abiding principles which should form the basis for future action.

Some on the left believe that the inexorable consequences of operating in an economically competitive globalised economy must force progressives to abandon all precepts and succumb to the rules of the jungle, to abandon the welfare state model and accept driving down living standards, removing consumer protections, forsaking environmental standards and throwing away a hundred years of social and labour legislation limiting exploitation and protecting the workforce. The result is either triangulation politics or the autarky of 'Socialism in one country' we hear from the left's eurosceptics. We categorically reject both approaches.

Our contention is that we can learn from countries where outstanding competitiveness and the production and export of quality goods is married with strong social systems and low unemployment rates. The common feature of such countries, mostly to the North of the Union, is world-class public services, strong education systems, lifelong quality training, strict environmental, consumer and employment safeguards, and much more limited inequalities. They have fostered the notion of an interventionist state pursuing active labour market policies, not the reductionist model of the right, which sees labour market reform exclusively in terms of slashing workplace protections and squeezing lower and middle incomes.

In other words, the time-honoured notions of redistribution, social justice and equality should be revived, refined, implemented and communicated, and placed at the heart of the left's appeal. Of course welfare systems should be improved, budgets accounted for, wastage avoided, work when genuinely available and under decent conditions rewarded more than indolence, but not at the expense of fairness, justice and equality. The left should never succumb to the dual myth that the rich work harder with lower taxes and the poor with lower wages.

The key to resolving the economic crisis in the UK and Europe is not to punish pensioners, the unemployed, the sick and the disabled; it is to create decent jobs, reward them properly, and let rising purchasing power kick-start domestic demand – the surest way to long-term cut in the welfare bill. Central to this argument is our contention that high social standards are not inimical to a competitive economy but can contribute to it. For every pound or euro that is saved by stopping cases of abuse by some welfare claimants, there are many more to be produced for domestic treasuries through job creation and effective measures to ensure that taxes owed get paid. Contrary to popular myth, tax avoidance is not some turpitude confined to individuals and companies in third countries or those along the Mediterranean coast. The most powerful engine and the most sophisticated global creative approach to corporate unaccountability and tax avoidance is to be found within the Square Mile.

The alternative to pig-headed austerity programmes – driven by those with a reactionary ideology, and abetted by those too intimidated to challenge it – which are threatening all Europeans with a generational slump, can be found both at home in Britain and more widely in Europe. The alternative requires the shaping of a bold long-term European programme that matches these objectives and resonates and builds on policies put forward by progressives at national elections, before and after the 2014 elections to the European Parliament. What follows is our contribution.

Our contention is that the left must seize the next European elections as an opportunity to regain the political initiative, effect real change in the direction and activities of Europe's governing bodies, and build a new progressive majority in Europe. The elections need to be fought vigorously, around a European Socialist Alternative.

In previous chapters a number of headline points for political and economic reform have been proposed:

- Using the left's position in the European Parliament, whether it be a majority one or even as a blocking minority, to set the political agenda for the next Commission with a set of realistic non-negotiable demands that constitute an absolute prerequisite to endorsing any Commission and its work programme;
- Easing the budgetary constraints on Member States to encourage investment for growth and jobs, with a more gradual return to balanced budgets;
- Prioritising investment in infrastructure, social investment, training, innovation, R&D and an ecological transformation of the EU;
- Making full employment, fair taxation and the reduction of poverty and inequality central policy targets for European economic governance;
- Strengthening democratic control of EU economic policy, including the political accountability of the European Central Bank;
- Creating a European unemployment benefit and reforming labour markets and industrial relations to promote partnership, social dialogue and a stronger voice for employees in workplace decisions;
- Implementing a European-wide financial transactions tax, and instituting a joint European initiative to combat tax evasion and tighten tax loopholes; using Europe's collective clout to impose necessary reform in the tax havens inside and out of the Union;
- Harnessing resources of the European Investment Bank for support for new businesses and for European infrastructure;
- Using all untapped EU revenue for a much larger youth unemployment fund, building up to 20 billion by 2019;
- Making available regulatory-breaks for start-ups and relaxing planning conditions for green investments;
- Implementing rigorous banking reform; tightening the lid on bonuses;
- Reforming corporate governance in the privatised utilities, the large corporations, the airlines and the supermarket chains, so that community interests, job creation and consumer rights take precedence over short-term profits grabs and self-awarded plutocratic salaries;
- Boosting social investment and training in the Member States by

exempting this investment from the fiscal conditions under the Stability and Growth Pact;

- Reorienting social spending to quality training and apprenticeships;
- Setting out a clear strategy to tackle climate change which encourages investment in the green economy, creates jobs and makes our manufacturing industries more efficient, creating global demand for our innovative products;
- Halting the collapse of the carbon market to reduce EU dependence on fossil fuels;
- Setting binding ambitious targets for carbon emissions cuts (30% now; with the aim of 80% by 2050);
- Tackling fuel poverty – where the UK has the worst record in the EU – by effective Europe-wide regulation on the utilities;
- Pursuing a common energy policy with ambitious targets for renewable energy, placing energy efficiency at the heart of the work programme of the Commission and the Parliament for the next legislature, with strict implementation of the EU directive on energy efficiency, to give Europe greater energy security and slash the heavy cost of imported energy;
- Adopting assertive negotiating mandates in international and bilateral trade talks to put effective monitoring in place for the avoidance of social and environmental dumping;
- Placing human rights at the heart of trade policy;
- Using the Treaties and human rights legislation to ensure respect for liberty and freedom within the Union; suspending Member States which flout the founding principles of the Union;
- Isolating in the institutions the emergent racist, xenophobic and undemocratic populist forces; taking the political argument to the communities where their appeal is too often unchallenged;
- Instituting labour market reform, including a revision of the Posted Workers Directive to ensure 'Decent Jobs for Workers in Britain';
- Launching a European Marshall programme to support rapid economic development in the southern neighbourhood; aiding them with major democracy building and public administration reform;
- Strengthening peacekeeping and conflict prevention roles for the Union within UN mandates;

- Promoting defence spending economies and rationalisation through common military procurement and role-sharing;
- Building on the foundations of the European External Action Service; making full use of collective European representation at the UN and other multilateral forums.

WHO PAYS?

Any platform for Europe will have to face searching scrutiny about its funding. And the broader issue of the EU budget has to be addressed.

The institutional stand-off on the midterm financing of the EU is an opportunity missed for reform as is highlighted in chapter two; at times both sides of the argument seem to be more interested in headline figures than in giving priority to policies which will support competitiveness, innovation and, above all, growth and jobs.

This is not the place to rerun all the arguments about the budget wrangle that played out at the end of end of 2012/beginning 2013, and which have just been patched over. The battle pitched the arch-priests of austerity in Berlin and London against those – including many MEPs – who seemed more interested in shoring up CAP spending, and/or were motivated by a version of localist pork-barrel politics. The sterility of the debate will only be matched by the regularity of its recurrence.

As Derek Reed argues in chapter two, it would be better for the left to concentrate on the question of political priorities for the budget than to commit itself simplistically to a particular percentage of GDP as an objective. An opportunity will arise shortly after the elections to return to these resource questions, because the final compromise stitched together includes a mid-term review (in 2015/16). From a democratic perspective, the left should throw its weight behind the idea that these financial frameworks should be decided by Parliament and Council after European elections, and not just before they take place; and therefore they should run for five years not seven. This means spending priorities, and how to pay for them, would form a central element in each European election campaign.

The left must seek to shift fundamentally the spending of the Union to investment, competitiveness, job-creation, research and innovation. All existing policies should have to pass 'the new European economy' test: will they support quality growth? Will they facilitate the creation of quality jobs? Will they provide high quality training and serious apprenticeships? Does the infrastructure they support contribute to long-term regional development? – or are airports to be built in the middle of nowhere only to remain empty as a monument to monstrously wasteful public spending? Is the investment concentrated in regions where the need is greatest, but also where the administrative capacity is sufficient to see projects delivered on time and within budget? For the Common Agricultural Policy, for example, there needs to be both a continuing reduction in its share of EU spending, and a fundamental shift to developing quality European produce and supporting transition towards a new rural economy. The left, even those parts of it whose origins were predominately urban, recognise that supporting European agriculture – on a more modest scale – is a valid objective, but that means root and branch reform and rebalancing of the CAP and its budget.

A budget reform worthy of the name, which focuses EU spending fiercely on those things that can be done best and most efficiently at European level, and which reassures voters, parliaments and governments about the value added of European spending, is an essential first step towards a intelligent future debate about resources – the level and the means. Until then, the endless and rancorous argument among governments and EU institutions about whether the EU budget should be 1.0 per cent or 1.05 per cent of GDP will be both meaningless and offputting to Europe's citizens.

CHANGING THE TERMS OF BRUSSELS REALPOLITIK

The shift in power we seek will not happen by a neat switch from strong centre-right majorities to socialists sweeping all before them. The nature of politics in general, and European politics in particular, is that electors now, seemingly spoiled for choice, refuse the binary left/right choices of old, and thus withhold strong majorities from individual parties, almost whatever the electoral system. So alliances will have to be built. The left will just have to learn to live with that, or accept hand-wringing irrelevance on the side-lines of power. But a return to the old left-right consensus politics, with the two elephants dividing the spoils, must now be inconceivable, given the right's record and the promotion by the left of radical alternatives. Our supporters will have been cheated and disempowered if the crisis elections of May 2014 simply result in business as usual.

But for this fundamental change in the way of doing business to be perceptible – and, more importantly, to work – requires negotiating a programme for Europe with other political forces: the Greens almost certainly, some truly democratic parts of the radical left and, if and where necessary, centrist forces, including those of the more traditional, 'social' Christian democrats (themselves perturbed at the rightward shift of their political family) who are prepared to back a sharp change of direction in economic and social policy – as the full disaster of the consequences of the right's approach hit home.

European socialists should be upfront about their preferred partnerships before the elections, not after. Installing the new Commission in 2014 will be a complicated operation. If the left's nominee wins, then he or she will need a workable majority in Parliament for the new team and the new Commission programme; and a stable majority to run the full five-year term.

Chapter eight highlights the clear risk that at some point representation of a dangerously xenophobic ultra-nationalism could grow beyond the current rump to the point of making the institutions unmanageable; and if that happens, and if the institutions are unable to deliver and achieve a modicum of effectiveness, the hand of the extreme right – hostile to its core to democratic institutions, and European ones in particular and aiming specifically for institutional gridlock – will be further strengthened.

For this reason, whatever the final outcome of the elections there is no realistic scenario in which cooperation between the two largest political forces, the left and the right simply comes to an end. Under the Treaties, for the European Parliament to maximise its legislative and budgetary powers requires solid majorities in committee and plenary. The point of winning is to shift the fulcrum where compromises are struck as far as possible to the left, tilting outcomes toward those that are compatible with our core principles: cooperating with the right is not the default mode but something to be considered maturely on a case-by-case basis. The left's success will principally be judged not by the political colour of the next Commission or European Council President or the High Representative or the college as a whole, but by whether or not the Parliament and the new Commission drive through job-creating, growth-stimulating, innovation-promoting programmes, with stronger safeguards for employees, consumers and for the environment. In the negotiations policy must trump personality. Such a result would indeed be a radical shift, starting to turn the page on the age of austerity. To this noble end, making some political deals and compromises would be worthwhile if the ends were always to the fore. To create a Europe capable of delivering for people makes getting hands dirty a worthwhile sacrifice.

And if the converse happens, the left must be similarly lucid and hard-headed. If the EPP were to be the significantly largest group after the election, and provided that their nominee were to be from the centrist tradition, free of all association past or present with the extreme right, then the left should be prepared to bargain its support in exchange for policy commitments. Outright refusal to cooperate under those conditions would seem to defy the voters' choice, and would incapacitate the European Union, thus playing once more into the hands of the populists.

But – more than has been the case in the past, and reflecting the vigour with which the campaign should have addressed European questions – the left should be clear as to its minimal conditions for supporting the new Commission. Drawing up a shopping list now is neither practical nor sensible. But no-one would understand how the left could support a new Commission if it were to continue promoting dead-end austerity politics, and undermining and hollowing out social and environmental standards. The easing of budgetary constraints on Member States, to encourage investment, research and development and training, must be part of any deal. Giving the new Youth Unemployment Fund adequate resources should also be non-negotiable. Minimum demands should also include the appointment of a new Trade Commissioner prepared to fight Europe's corner to promote ILO standards, and to link trade agreements with human rights. The next Commission must also come forward with an economic regeneration plan for the south-bank of the Mediterranean. And it must spearhead Europe's global leadership on climate change: a common energy policy based on security of supply and energy efficiency is both economically and environmentally indispensable. And the next president of the Commission must make clear commitments about the need to suspend any Member State which undermines freedom and liberty at home.

There is nothing dishonourable in a political force offering support to a 'minority' government so that the business of the state may be carried on; but the bargain must be a hard one, and the left must not be distracted by questions of patronage. The bargain must be about policies not about persons. Legislative action, support for Europeans feeling the pain and change and reform for the many trump the trappings of office for the few.

LOOKING AHEAD FOR THE LEFT: FROM TECHNICAL CLEARING HOUSE TO A BROAD-BASED POLITICAL MOVEMENT

Beyond the immediate electoral horizons, the British and European left will have to address the question of their structured cooperation. While we all accept in principle that the globalisation of economic power and the increased decision-making role of EU institutions require the left to organise politically, progress has been slow. The main vehicle for this cooperation is the Party of European Socialists (PES), which will be put to its greatest test to date in the 2014 elections when, for the first time there will be significant European content for what has previously been an aggregation of national campaigns jumbled together. In future the European elections will have a quasi-presidential focus.

The national parties have hitherto been reluctant to cede any organisational or political autonomy to the PES; hence the lowest common denominator policies of the past, largely ignored by national party leaders; the lacklustre campaigning; decision-making by consensus; and the disinclination to involve party members and sympathisers directly in the work of the European party. When a few Labour MEPs twenty years ago started to campaign for individual membership of the Party of European Socialists they were promptly disavowed by national party officials.

Despite incremental reforms, the European parties remain essentially clearing houses for organising the division of the spoils after the European elections, rather than the motor for the elections campaign. The debacle Europe-wide for the centre left in the 2009 elections was the clearest signal yet that the end of that road had been reached, and reform has since begun; we are told there is to be democratic involvement in the nomination of the 'Commission presidential candidate' for 2014; national party members can now be linked in to a network of 'PES activists'; the 2014 manifesto will in all probability be more trenchant than its predecessors, if only because consignment to opposition has given some parties greater freedom of manoeuvre, and the political and economic situation has deteriorated to the extent that the old platitudes will no longer pass muster.

But these incremental changes will not confer on the European Socialist Party the democratic vitality that will only come about when *individual members* elect party delegates, decide by majority on the programme, and the party leadership, and select the candidate for the President of the Commission after primaries, preferably open ones. To those who say that this democracy could open up division and ideological tensions, the only answer must be 'bring it on'. Why should internal debate, vigorously fought, often on ideological lines, be acceptable in Brighton, Bad Godesburg or Rennes, but not in Brussels for the PES? At least its congresses would attract more interest than some recent gatherings, which have had about as much spontaneity and animation as Kremlin line-ups towards the end of the Brezhnev era.

The authors fully understand that the period immediately prior to the 2014 elections is not the right time to open this campaign for democracy in the European socialist movement, but after the elections any further procrastination must cease. The Labour Party should embrace reform and place on the table an internal reform agenda for the European left's principal organisation. A force to change the politics and the economies of the continent cannot be confined to committee rooms in soulless buildings in the Belgian capital; or to the rarefied atmosphere of think tanks and research institutes. Democratic socialism in Europe can only be vigorously promoted if the structure which underpins it resembles less a network of technocratic committees and more a movement. And that requires members, systematic links with progressive associations, raucous argument, periodic division and then decision; a world away from what we have known until now.

All of this may sound grimly daunting to some activists on the British left. The Labour Party is gradually finding its feet after a disastrous electoral setback; working out plans for government – and the difficult inheritance from the Cameron/Clegg years will leave it little room for manoeuvre. The party is making heavy demands on its activists for support, loyalty and contributions. Winning back power in Britain seems already the steepest of mountains. And now the activists are to be told that they have to work their socks off in European elections to a Parliament they don't fully understand, to change an executive they don't fully trust. And even then that's not the end of it. Just to add to the challenge we tell them that for the left to gain greater influence in Europe requires not merely a strong showing in these EP elections – necessary precondition though that is – but also a change in government in Britain and at least some other national capitals, in order to tilt the balance in the EU, and create a new momentum for growth, jobs, combating climate change, and protecting our welfare system.

Some may claim that the effort is too great and the chances of ultimate success too remote. They will point to the French example – a freshly minted socialist government having to start off its term with cuts in public spending to meet Brussels targets. Perhaps, they may think, we might be better off just concentrating on 2015 (although a poor result in the EP elections, and possibly trailing UKIP, is scarcely the soundest springboard for national electoral success twelve months later). They might believe that we could achieve progressive goals on our own, outside a Europe which in their view would only place extra roadblocks on our way to the irreversible shift of power and wealth which should be our goal. This was once called 'socialism in one country' – and would be as likely to succeed now as it did then. Can any socialist seriously believe that political transformation in an era of economic globalisation is to be carried through by a medium-sized country dependent on international trade but acting alone?

A siege economy of the kind that was postulated in the 1970s is not simply unrealistic: it is impossible.

If we were to withdraw, our trade with Europe would start to wither, our attractiveness for inward investment would evaporate, and we would, as David Martin points out, be absent from the key bilateral and multilateral trade negotiations which will shape the planetary organisation of trade in the coming fifty years. Our political influence, which, as Patrick Costello points out, is shored up despite our shrinking status because of our participation in common external and security policy, would quickly diminish. As Linda McAvan describes in her chapter, the influence a progressive government could have over climate change policy – now overtly challenged by conservative forces at home and in the Union and globally – would be undermined. If economic policy in one country makes little sense, how much less sense would be an environmental policy pursued by Britain in isolation?

Two further points; in looking back on the Blair/Brown years from 1997 to 2010, it would be difficult to single out one progressive measure which the government wanted but which was thwarted by Brussels institutions or Treaty obligations. On the other hand, some of the more crude ambitions of the Tories in dismantling labour rights, health and safety standards and the rest fall foul of protections and standards applying directly to the UK because of EU legislation. It is that constraint against a return to the laws of the economic jungle that has given extra stimulus to anti- Europeanism on the hard, ideological right of the Tory Party. Surely no one on the left believes Cameron and his eurosceptics want to repatriate social legislation for some abstruse constitutional principle, or that they want to strengthen protection for British workers. Their agenda is the removal of any impediment to the dismantling of social rights won over the last hundred and fifty years.

Any discussion in the Labour Party about Britain and Europe needs to start with the clear assertion that success for our historic goals can only be achieved by their active promotion locally, regionally, nationally and in Europe. It's a hard slog, but the alternative, to retreat, get out of the EU and build a progressive new Jerusalem in Great Britain – or, more likely, just in England because the Scots and Welsh seem in no way disposed to follow lemmings over cliff – is a symptom of ideological nostalgia on the part of armchair politicians who would like simply to get off the world, which would have to be stopped for their convenience.

MORE EUROPE NOW?

Just as UKIP will try to turn the European elections into an attack on the Union's very existence, there will be some, including European Greens and Liberals, who would like to use the occasion as a kind of referendum on 'more Europe'. Whatever sympathy the authors might have with aspirations for a stronger Europe, it is our analysis that both stances miss the essential purpose of the elections, which is to elect a Parliament with a specific job to do, and indirectly to choose a Commission president; and that the job of the Parliament is to legislate, decide on the budget, hold decision-makers in the Commission and elsewhere to account, and reflect the concerns of Europe's citizens on all questions which fall within its competence.

So debates in the election campaign – on austerity versus growth; on fair trade; on more ambitious climate change action; on job-creation; on strengthening foreign and defence policies; and on immigration, rights and freedoms – are relevant because the way people vote will affect outcomes: and the questions are there, on the table, now. But voting in the elections on constitutional questions; more Europe, less Europe, no Europe, is to all intents and purposes beside the point.

The question the left has to face now is not: is institutional reform desirable in the long-term? It is: do we need constitutional amendments to Treaties now to make the changes in policy we seek? And would those constitutional changes be possible in the foreseeable future? Whatever our longer term aspirations might be, our answer to both questions, in the short term, is no.

A change in the balance of power in the European Parliament in 2014 would reshape the Commission, the Union's executive, which would have to propose means to give effect to the policy commitments in the left's manifesto – on corporate and financial regulation, on environmental targets, on consumer rights. The new Commission, reflecting the new political balance in the European Parliament, would be constrained to shift away from imposing austerity by fiat and towards supporting growth policies. The left in Parliament could also promote coalitions with left-of-centre majorities in some national parliaments to hold their ministers in Council, particularly on economic and financial questions, in a kind of pro-growth alliance of parliamentarians. A reinvigorated left could subject the President of the European Central Bank to much greater scrutiny, and achieve a degree of accountability for a body which has to date been allowed to go far beyond its remit in terms of the legitimate operational autonomy that a central bank should be permitted.

The left and its allies should organise a regulatory offensive, ensuring that the Commission propose measures to protect consumers from the abusive use of quasi-monopoly power by large corporations and privatised utilities; or introduces stringent Europe-wide measures against tax havens and tax shopping by Amazon, Starbucks and Google. A new parliamentary majority could stop the slide to authoritarianism in a Member State even if the government concerned had political allies on the European right. These are examples of how a simple change in the political balance within the EU institutions can bring big political gains. None of this requires Treaty change.

In any case, significant Treaty amendments are, in the short term, almost beyond the realms of the possible, and are thus a distraction from the key business in hand.

Whenever significant constitutional changes were made in the past, they were only attempted when there was broad consensus among most Member States. No such consensus exists today, and even Germany, initially the keenest to effect Treaty changes, seems now to have cold feet about grand designs and a new institutional architecture – although Berlin still appears to hanker after some limited changes on questions linked to banking union, for domestic constitutional reasons. François Hollande's recent statements about possible constitutional change being required reflect more than anything his frustration at his inability to change minds in Berlin, and seem to underestimate the mountain he would have to climb to win public support for even modest Treaty modifications.

This absence of consensus is due to two factors. There are genuine concerns that any Treaty change designed to meet the challenges of the euro crisis might result in an unacceptable degree of centralised control of national finances without adequate democratic safeguards. And there is the growing certainty that just by launching the process, a eurosceptic British government would seek to mount a hijack, using the occasion either to advocate a dismantling of all progressive European instruments to safeguard social and environmental standards, or, when that was deemed unacceptable, to present a long list of opt-outs, the acceptance of which would create a dangerous precedent for others, and could start the unravelling of the single market.

There is a further danger on the institutional front. Cameron's gratuitous veto of the Fiscal Pact at the end of 2011, which had no practical benefit (except to purchase a little more time before the right-wing political vultures in Britain swooped on him) created the precedent of Member States proceeding with new treaties while bypassing the existing rule book. The left should beware that what seemed at first glance merely a technical sleight of hand was in reality a dangerous innovation. With the creation of separate and parallel structures, executive accountability to established democratic authority was threatened. And for the citizens, any further complication of the EU's institutional organisation could only exacerbate the current deep alienation.

The final reason why the momentum has gone out of Treaty change is quite simply that significant institutional reform, even if agreed by governments, would not be ratified. The thrills and spills of the ratifications of Maastricht, Amsterdam, the draft Constitution and the Lisbon texts are sufficiently fresh in the memory for even the most audacious institutional ayatollahs to hesitate before returning to the constitutional Long March. Last time, it took ten years to move from a consensus on the scope of a Treaty reached at a European summit in Laeken in 1999 to its ratification in 2009. And in the current state of opinion, with the backdrop of the worst economic and financial crisis in more than sixty years, voters would resoundingly reject almost any proposal made by their unpopular governments, particularly if it were seen to strengthen the EU institutions that have attracted such blame for their management of the crisis.

Institutional change is not going to happen in the next five years and progressives should not waste time and credibility in supporting it.

THE UK DEBATE IN PERSPECTIVE

It is in on the basis of this observation that the whole question of British membership of the Union has to be seen. For the left, one of the many nightmares associated with Cameron winning a majority at the next election would be the rolling out of his European agenda. This involves: a 'renegotiation', with at best some limited repatriation of powers to the UK (probably by specific legislative derogation rather than through Treaty change given the growing reluctance of the UK's partners to go down the constitutional route); a 'negotiating triumph' for the prime minister that fools no-one in his own party – not to mention UKIP, which will see this for the mediocre smoke-and-mirrors act it is; the collateral damage of the exercise, which will be some dilution of social, consumer and environmental policies, at least for the UK, thereby peeling off further layers of support from trade unions and the progressives for the whole European project (understandably); and then a referendum that will present a divisive quandary for the left, create huge economic uncertainty, distract the whole Union from getting on with the core business of kick-starting the European economy, and present the risk of 'exit by accident'. There is at least a possibility of such a combination of negatives producing a cataclysmic scenario, potentially leading to the consequent break-up of Britain, as first Scotland, in a second referendum, opts for independence within the European Union, and then Wales – leaving England adrift with just Northern Ireland for company in the life-boat.

And catastrophic it would be. There are some on the right who believe that the laws of geography, history and economy can be repealed, that going it alone is the route for salvation and revival. This is the dream of a kind of capitalist North Korea – but where the media is not state-controlled but state-controlling. It would be a future where myths would be spun; of past glories, and gleaming futures. The reality would be different; manufacturing already decimated; the financial sector cut down to size by its own hubris and the gradual relocation of key players to other financial centres inside the EU or beyond; the drying up of inward investment; the sidelining of the UK during the key trade negotiations with the United States and Japan which will be the main event in global commercial policy for the next decade; and the continuation of any British participation in the internal market being made subject to accepting the entire corpus of EU legislation, current and future, but without any say in its elaboration or extension. And, as with 'the Norway solution', with continued payments into the EU budget.

The rejoinder that Britain is not Norway (which is true in that Norway starts from a basis of stronger competitiveness, domestic industry and levels of natural resources than Britain), and that the UK would get a better deal because it would be in the interests of our European trading partners with their trade surplus with us to sustain presupposes an amicability in the divorce that seems implausible, given that our erstwhile partners might justifiably fear that in order to maintain competitiveness Britain would follow the 'social dumping' route of slash and burn for its welfare state, alongside aggressive devaluations.

The transatlantic trade area – a bilateral between NAFTA (the US, Canada and Mexico) and the UK – has been publicly ruled out by the Americans, who are far more interested in the multilateral trade negotiations about to start with Brussels – which, as David Martin points out, we would exclude ourselves at our peril.

Anti-Europeans argue that we could compensate for our decline in trade with the EU through a rising share in commerce with the BRICS and other eternal partners. It is indeed true that we start from such a low level of trade with such countries that the only way forward is up – but Germany, France and others are already penetrating these markets more successfully than are we; and, again, these countries are seeking multilateral trade agreements with the wider European area, rather than bilateral ones with its island offshoot.

To assert all this could be seen as defeatist, had the authors of this volume not already spelled out the alternative of intense cooperation with progressives throughout Europe to build not destroy, and to reshape a Europe with a vision that competes and contrasts with, and eventually supplants, the current conservative orthodoxy.

But there is something that would be historically even more extraordinary than the UK Conservative Party deliberately jeopardising the nation's future through its European policy – which has for a long time been a sorry parade of concessions to its Thatcherite right and to the populists even further to the right, in an attempt to appease those who are congenitally incapable of being appeased. At least were the outcome to be Britain out of Europe there would have been an element of design and deliberation in the delirium.

What would be the acme of paradox would be a Labour government saddled with an ill-thought out referendum commitment, wrung from it in opposition after some passing panic about UKIP, having to organise British exit. This could happen if Labour had to hold a referendum in, for example, the year after taking office, following a victory achieved by a psephological windfall, and facing a Tory-bequeathed economic wasteland that necessitated drastic and unpopular measures; by this time whatever sheen there might have originally been would be fast evaporating, and the government would not even have the narrative available to Cameron that 'we have made a new settlement' – because what Labour seeks is new policies for Europe not legal prestidigitations. What's more, Labour might not even be able to rely on the support in the referendum of that shrinking band – 'moderate' conservatives.

It is not unusual for a Labour government coming to office having to face economic jitters in the business and financial communities – there is nothing unhealthy about that. But a Labour government having to organise a referendum which might decide to pull us out of

Europe could well lead to a meltdown in economic activity, or capital flight. And if its view were to be defeated in the referendum, the government would either face resignation in ignominy, or would be hobbled all the way to resounding defeat at the subsequent early election.

A few party members say that the democratic argument trumps all this; that somehow a referendum is necessary because opinion polls say people want it, and that the last referendum was nearly forty years ago. The counterview is that the left should always be wary of referendums and other forms of direct democracy, which have historically been the instruments of reaction. Little of the social advance of the last hundred years would have seen the light of day if major decisions were subjected to referendums, with all the scope for manipulation in the media age that this implies. Abolish hanging? We'd have brought back drawing and quartering.

Yet at least hanging is a straightforward question, where everybody has a view. A referendum on Europe would take place against a backdrop of chronic lack of awareness and knowledge. According to a Eurobarometer poll in 2012, 80 per cent of the British people say they have little or no knowledge of the EU. Sixty per cent could not identify a single EU institution. Only 7 per cent had any idea when the next European Parliament elections would take place. This general state of blissful ignorance could be attributed to poor communication by the EU itself; or blamed on the deliberate retention of information by successive national governments; or on inertia by the pro-Europeans; or on the wilful misrepresentation of anything and everything to do with the EU by the media and energetic eurosceptics. Whatever the causes, whoever is to blame, the result makes a popular referendum on Britain's European future not the instrument for democratic choice but to a large extent its negation.

The parliamentary road for progress remains not the certain way, but the best way. It is also, ultimate paradox, singularly the British way.

ARTICULATING ANGER, OFFERING HOPE

The very last point to be made about the left in Europe and in Britain returns to the need to address the deeply felt anger and frustration felt by many at the sharp end of austerity-driven recession, which is creating the dangerous anti-politics mood almost everywhere, with all the alarming consequences that are highlighted in chapter eight.

The trouble with so many of our social democratic parties is that we have yet to strike a tone which convinces the growing numbers of disaffected people who are facing hardship in their daily lives, which for most is a new experience in the post-war era. The language we use and the means by which we express our ideas are so reasonable, so moderate, so cautious, that it all sounds to many like apologetics for the existing economic and financial order, enunciated by politicians who may not be managerially more incompetent than their conservative opponents – and faring worse would be difficult – but are devoid of passion, intensity, urgency and ultimately commitment.

The left in Europe must win back the ear of electorates with the ferocity of its attack on the incumbency of the right, and its onslaught on corporate abuse, irresponsibility and exploitation. It must, in other words, start flinging the furniture around the room.

And then it must draw on its traditional principles enunciated at the outset of this chapter, and translate them into a programme of action for the next five years, through European and national elections which can really change the decor in Europe, reconcile citizens with the political system by demonstrating that change can be delivered through it, and open up a different way of doing things in the Union, and ultimately beyond: in other words, our Europe, not theirs.